Also available at all good book stores

9781801500630

9781801501248

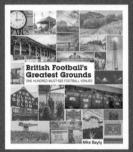
9781785316470

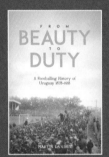
9781801501491

9781801501552

9781801503709

9781801503723

9781801501682

9781801501668

CITY OF STARS

13/5/23

CITY OF STARS
Tom Scholes

**The Controversial Story of
Paris Saint-Germain**

First published by Pitch Publishing, 2022

Pitch Publishing
9 Donnington Park,
85 Birdham Road,
Chichester,
West Sussex,
PO20 7AJ
www.pitchpublishing.co.uk
info@pitchpublishing.co.uk

ISBN 978 1 80150 153 8

Typesetting and origination by Pitch Publishing
Printed and bound in India by Replika Press Pvt. Ltd.

Contents

To my mum and dad,
without whom this book
would not have been
possible to make.

Acknowledgements

THANK YOU to my family and my friends for their support throughout this process. Thank you to my colleagues at talkSPORT who've been incredibly supportive with this project. And finally, thank you to Paris Saint-Germain FC for being so chaotic throughout your history. Without you, this book quite literally would never have been written. Allez.

Introduction

MODERN FOOTBALL is rubbish. At least, that's the opinion of the majority of football fans today. Football isn't as good as it was in the *good old days* (no one can ever specify when the *good old days* officially began, but it suspiciously always starts when the person uttering the phrase was young). Only now is money ruining football. It's killing the game. The main culprits when discussing what's 'wrong' with modern football are always the same two clubs: Manchester City and Paris Saint-Germain. Both state-owned (one by Abu Dhabi and the other by Qatar) and both have areas where they should be criticised, mainly where the money comes from, how the regimes in charge of the clubs operate in their own country, their abhorrent human rights records and their treatment of females plus the LGBTQ community.

But as fans of both clubs will tell you, those regimes and ownerships do not define their club and who they are. True, the ownership have done a very good job of shaping both clubs into a marketable image, but there was life before state ownership. Manchester City existed before Abu Dhabi and PSG certainly existed before Qatar, but the Parisian story is often dismissed as nouveau riche, a

Fabergé egg of a football club. That, to put it bluntly, is a load of old rubbish. Football in Paris existed before Qatar arrived, no matter how hard the cynics have tried to make you think otherwise.

Throughout the next 100,000 words or so, you'll be taken from the very beginning of Paris Saint-Germain's existence right up until a post-COVID-19 world. It's the story of Europe's youngest superpower and a story that may surprise you. You never know, you may grow fond of pre-Qatar PSG.

1

Pre-1970

PARIS, TO put it simply, is wonderful. It is diverse. It is culturally intriguing and important. It looks beautiful both during a summer's day and a winter's night. The architecture – such as the Eiffel Tower, the Arc de Triomphe and the Grand Palais – is superb, the art is beautiful and the historical significance of the city cannot be underestimated, both in French and global history. If you walk down the River Seine on a bright, quiet, sunny day, you will find it difficult to find an individual who doesn't find it either peaceful or enjoyable.

You can look throughout history to see France and Paris involved, including the Storming of the Bastille as part of the French Revolution, homing some of the art world's most famous and influential artists such as Pablo Picasso and Henri Matisse, while after World War One more creative brains moved in such as Ernest Hemingway, Salvador Dali and James Joyce. Perhaps the most famous, and arguably most significant, historical moment that took place in Paris was in 1940 when the German army marched through Paris after it had been declared as an 'open city' (meaning, in wartime, that the city has essentially surrendered in order to avoid all-out destruction of the infrastructure). The French Resistance during World War Two was based in Paris, and following the Treaty of Versailles, which was signed just outside of Paris in 1919, Paris and France had two massive hands in the bid to defeat Germany.

If you walk down any street in Paris, you will feel the history coming out of the walls or even the ground that you stroll upon, such is its significance in the world. But notice how I've nearly gone 300 words talking about just a handful of things that are historic and important about Paris without even mentioning sport, let alone football. That isn't to say that football isn't important in Paris – because it is – but it's something that hasn't really been a Parisian staple until the last 50 or so years. At least, for the majority of fans across the world, that is the case.

The fact of the matter is Parisian football clubs seem to have fallen by the wayside with two in particular slipping away with barely any mention, or any sort of acknowledgement for their part in the popularity of the sport in France's capital city. In fact, it's not even well known that the first recorded football club in Paris was formed by English and Scottish expats.

The two oldest clubs in the city were Racing Club de France Football – or Racing Paris – and Red Star Paris. Racing were formed in 1882 as a multidiscipline club for football and athletics with their previous home, the Croix-Catelan Stadium, hosting athletics events for the 1900 Olympic Games. Due to their status as a multi-discipline sports club, many won't recognise Racing as one of France's earliest football clubs, despite the fact that they were a founding member of Ligue 1, and because people must just assume that they are an amateur outfit, even with players such as David Ginola and Pierre Littbarski on their books over the years. They have had a grand total of ten different names, including four name changes in the 21st century alone.

The second-oldest in the city is Red Star Paris, a team with much more noted history behind them and one that is still alive and kicking as of 2022 and still manages to bring a good crowd to their games, with a tonne of history to look back on. Officially recognised as France's second-oldest football club behind Le Havre, as they were on the record as being formed in 1897 (remember, Racing wasn't solely a football club when they formed in 1882), the story goes that Red Star were formed in a Paris cafe by future FIFA president Jules Rimet and Ernest Weber, alongside Rimet's brother Modeste. The name supposedly derives out of inspiration from a woman called Miss Jenny, Rimet's English governess (private tutor), who suggested the club be named after the Red Star Line, a historic shipping line with ships built in Birkenhead on The Wirral in the UK that serviced the United States, Belgium and France, with Miss Jenny coming over from England to France on this line. Therefore, the name was Red Star, the club was formed and the club was placed into the third tier of French football. And just like that, by the turn of the 20th century, Paris had two football teams.

So why is it that these teams are hardly even mentioned in conversations about Paris and football? Red Star won five Coupe de France trophies before 1943 while Racing also won five before 1950 and went one better by actually winning Division 1 (as the top division was known then, not becoming Ligue 1 until 2002) in 1936, only the fourth club to win the title, and they even did it one season before Marseille. So it wasn't like there wasn't any success to write home about because, clearly, the two Paris clubs brought home silverware. In fact, the Coupe de France finals of 1918, 1919, 1920, 1921, 1922 and 1923 were all won by Parisian teams (Olympique de Paris won in 1918 although they merged with Red Star in 1926; CASG Paris won in 1919 although they were a team set up by the bank Société Générale and remain the only corporate team to have ever won the cup; Red Star managed a hat-trick of Coupe de France triumphs, winning from 1921 to 1923).

These six finals all took place in Paris, but it's quite incredible to think that only one venue, the stadium that hosted the 1919 final, is either still in use for football or in existence: the Parc des Princes. The Parc des Princes is situated in the 16th arrondissement (the name of a particular district or borough in the city) which is a beautiful area indeed, one fitting of a venue that was originally used for day trips, hunting and forest walks for the French royal family. Originally, le Parc was a multi-sport venue hosting athletics, football and cycling, which was mainly due to the fact that the director of the stadium was a man named Henri Desgrange, a former elite cyclist and founder of the magazine *L'Auto*, which played an important role in the inception of the Tour de France, with the final lap of honour being taken at the Parc des Princes in honour of Desgrange. The first football match for the French national team was held there (a 1-0 win over Switzerland). During the early part of the 1930s, Desgrange and his business partner Victor

Goddet worked on the reconstruction of le Parc and in 1932 opened up the newly improved stadium with a capacity of 45,000 (although that was later reduced down to 38,000). The Parc des Princes hosted the opening game of the 1938 World Cup, but the final was played in the Stade Olympique Yves-du-Manoir, the main stadium for the 1924 Olympics.

As a result of hosting no events during the 1924 Olympics, Paris City Council gave Desgrange the keys to the stadium and that's what prompted the upgrade and refurbishment. As time went on, le Parc was becoming more and more integral in the sporting landscape. Away from football, the 1954 Rugby World Cup Final was hosted there while the first European Cup Final was hosted in the stadium, in 1956, as Real Madrid beat Reims 4-3 in a game that had two of the world's greatest players involved with Alfredo Di Stéfano for Real Madrid and French maestro Raymond Kopa representing Reims.

Of course, various Coupe de France finals were played at le Parc but that was it in terms of domestic football, with the stadium being used mainly for France international football and rugby games, the occasional European Cup final and various athletics events. Racing used the Stade Olympique Yves-du-Manoir as their main stadium as it was in the Colombes area, still on the banks of the River Seine, while Red Star had a strange time of finding a home that wasn't the Parc des Princes. They were originally based in an area called Meudon, a suburb build overlooking the Seine and nicknamed 'Bellevue'. It was a beautiful area but in 1907, when Red Star had one of their many name changes and went with Red Star Amical Club, the team moved from Meudon to Grenelle in the

15th arrondissement. Three years into their Grenelle adventure, Red Star moved yet again, this time to Saint-Ouen in Seine-Saint-Denis to play in the Stade de Paris, or, to give it its current name, Stade Bauer.

But despite problems with stadia and the constant chopping and changing of Parisian clubs' homes, they carried on playing and carried on representing the capital. In 1930, the French Football Federation voted in favour of professionalism in football in France and thus Division 1 was created, with Red Star in particular being a strong advocate for professionalism and listed as one of the founding members of the new competition. In typical Red Star fashion, however, they were relegated from Division 1 and played in the inaugural Division 2 season, creating history by playing in two inaugural seasons of two different leagues, although it's doubtful that was the kind of history the club wanted to make. Fellow Parisians Club Français were also relegated in the same season but due to the financial pressure of now being a professional club the team dissolved in 1935.

Racing, on the other hand, seemed to fair a bit better than their Parisian counterparts. Finishing third in Group A in the first season of Division 1, they floated between 11th and third before finishing first in the 1935/1936 season, capturing their first Coupe de France led by goals from René Couard, and Englishman Fred Kennedy, a striker from Bury, Lancashire, who started his career with local side Rossendale United before moving to Manchester United and then Everton. Kennedy played for Racing in 1932/1933 before returning to England to play with Blackburn Rovers, then once again returning to Racing for four years and later ending his career with Stockport County.

But the fortunes of both Red Star and Racing fluctuated, with Red Star being relegated in 1938, Racing winning their last Coupe de France, all happening before the outbreak of World War Two. One week they would be fine, the next they would be battered by FC Sète, the club who eventually won the Division 1 title in that final season, four points ahead of Racing. This headline of a match report in the newspaper *L'Ouest-Éclair* from May of 1939 said all that needed to be said on the game that clinched the Division 1 for Sète: 'F.C. Sète literally choked Racing and were 4-0 ahead at half-time.'

If you look through the league tables of Division 1 after World War Two, you'll notice a trend. Very rarely are Red Star and Racing involved in anything positive with the odd exception in cup competitions. In 1948 Red Star finished rock bottom of the league on just 16 points, while Racing won the Coupe de France the following season despite being closer to the bottom of the table than Stade de Reims, who won the title with a young Raymond Kopa slowly making his way on to the footballing scene.

In the 1952/1953 season, it became official. After years of stagnation, Racing were relegated on goal difference meaning that Paris was represented in the top division by only one team: Stade Français. Stade are perhaps more well known now for their rugby team, which plays across the road from the Parc des Princes in the Stade Jean-Bouin, although they officially became a professional club in France in 1942 and have a history of merging with clubs within Paris, such as between 1942 and 1944 when they merged with Cercle Athlétique de Paris and then with Red Star for a two-year stretch from 1948. While the club's rugby department may be one of the best in the world, there is no doubting that the main reason why – if there even is a reason – fans would be aware of their footballing heritage would be because of an ex-player who then became the manager of the club before embarking on one of the most successful and influential managerial careers that the sport has ever seen.

Born in Argentina to Spanish parents before moving to Morocco at a young age, there wasn't anything overtly special about the playing career of defender Helenio Herrera. He was secure and solid as a defender but lacked anything special that made him stand out from the rest. He performed well in France with spells at various clubs including Red Star and Stade Français but a knee injury curtailed his career by the time he reached his mid-20s and forced Herrera, known by his initials H.H. by those who knew him best, to retire. Herrera was so underpaid at Stade Français – as was seemingly every other player in France at the time – that he would find different ways to earn a living. He went door to door in Paris selling brass polish to housewives and he would sneakily jam his foot in the door to prevent his prospective buyer from shutting the door on him. Due to his upbringing in Morocco – which at the time was still a French-occupied country – he was able to be called up but managed to avoid army duty due to the fact he was now a specialist in fibreglass, a material that was key in warfare, and classified as a key worker in France. Herrera's time on the sidelines gave him the ability to watch games and even allowed him to implement new ways to defend when he did eventually get back on to the field of play. It was his spell playing at Stade Français in 1942 that set him on his path to greatness, with Herrera starting to play in a style that was known in

Italian as *il béton* (translated to cement). That style would come to be known as *catenaccio* which is what Herrera's legacy is built on in the modern day.

It was also at Stade Français where he realised his true calling in life: teaching football. Herrera would teach PE during the latter days of his playing career and eventually moved on to teach physiotherapy work, gaining a first-class diploma as a masseuse, thinking it would be easier to get a job as coach–masseuse than just as a regular, run-of-the-mill coach. There was a close call in Lorient in 1945 – Herrera went to sign a contract with the club but left a day earlier than planned based on a premonition, only for the town to be the victim of an aerial bombardment the next day. At least, his own website claims he had a sudden and unknown premonition; the book *Steel Boats, Iron Hearts* by Hans Goebeler claims that the citizens of Lorient did in fact receive prior warning to the bombings and were told to flee immediately.

Herrera would soon join Stade Français where he was told by the club chairman to spend more time looking at new signings to help bolster the squad. During his spell from 1945 to 1948, Français managed to finish fifth twice, tenth and managed to reach the semi-finals of the Coupe de France before Herrera left France to go and coach Atlético Madrid in 1948, a year before the decline of Français started to take place. The year after Herrera's departure, Français finished 16th and one place above relegation before eventually returning to Division 2 the following season, finishing bottom with just 21 points. Français had the occasional flirtation with a return back to Division 1, winning Division 2 in 1952 before being relegated straight back the following season. Bar a few years in the mid-1960s, Français were destined to be a second-tier club.

That time under Herrera, while only a fleeting memory in what turned out to be an incredible career, proved to be the 'glory years' of Français, but Parisian football itself could not claim to be doing much better. Racing came agonisingly close to winning Division 1, finishing second behind Monaco by a point in 1961 and then managed to outdo themselves by finishing second the following season behind Reims, despite being level on points and level on goal difference. With Just Fontaine and Raymond Kopa, two legends of the French game, playing for Reims during that season, it does actually make Racing's achievement of finishing so close to Reims somewhat impressive even if they did end the season empty-handed. However, as so often happens with football, society dictates the feeling around the game. If people are happy, the football is usually great but if people aren't happy, the football usually suffers. France in the 1960s was going through a cultural change that affected everything, both culturally and financially and football wasn't hidden from that. If anything, it was one of the outlets that was most affected, as the book *France and the 1998 World Cup: The National Impact of a World Sporting Event* says:

'France became an urban society and this urbanisation went against the football culture that had grown up. One can explain the crisis which afflicted French football in the 1960s as a consequence of the scale of the urban change which then took place. Between 1960 and 1968 some of the most prestigious French clubs disappeared or dropped into the second division never to come back up, for example, Sète, Red Star, Le Havre, Ales, the CAP, the

CORT and they did so amidst an almost total indifference on the part of the local public.

'The cost of running a professional football club cannot be covered by gate receipts, its only source of income other than municipal funding. The small and mid-sized towns which lost their economic vitality could not sustain a professional club and those two which were expanding were peopled by families who were preoccupied by the business of making a living in a new locality, or who were more interested in new forms of leisure. This phenomenon was replicated in all European countries, where there has been a marked drop in attendances at games, but was more dramatic in France no doubt because of this great geographic and cultural upheaval.'

French football needed to change because France had changed. As the *New York Times* headlined an article in 1968, it was the 'Month of Revolution that Pushed France into the Modern World', and it did, but it was also a period in time that pushed French football forward too. Players wanted fair living wages and wanted to be treated with respect, fans didn't always want to go to the football so decided to spend their money on other activities, and the game itself was not in a great place. Parisian football was not in a healthy state on the field or off it.

On the field, the teams weren't performing admirably. In 1960, Racing were one point away from Monaco in top spot. By the end of the decade they weren't even in the second division. Red Star's last season in the top flight was in 1975 so at least they remained there for a little while longer, but to no major effect. It wasn't just failure on the pitch that was the problem, however, as Lindsay Sarah Krasnoff points out in her book *The Making of Les*

Bleus: Sport in France, 1958-2010, 'Labour issues within the professional game also contributed to football's crisis. Professional football players long complained of unfair labour limitations enforced by their contracts. The inability to be transferred and play for another team curbed a player's capacity to earn a living. While in the 1960s football players were greatly admired by most young boys, the players "are all under contract for life" in what was considered a harsh labour system. Despite attracting great attention to labour complaints of players, progress was not evident in 1968.'

And 1968 would be the turning point for culture in France and for the lives of millions. The year saw an uprising among students in France, in particular Paris, that changed how France lived and acted, and changed the entire culture in ways that can only be described by those who lived through it. Newspaper *Le Monde* described the French public at this time as being 'bored' because they had nothing to do. Everyone had their own reasons as to why they protested or stood for what they believed in. It wasn't a political uprising – or at least it didn't intend to be – but it certainly was a cultural uprising. France was at a crossroads and, quite frankly, no one really knew what was going on, and football was at the back of everyone's minds.

But, as is always the case when things go wrong in society, football ended up being used for good and the events of 1968 ended up benefitting football, in turn eventually ending up benefitting Paris too. Many people believed that getting the youth into organised sports would prevent them from misbehaving and keep them occupied. In the earlier part of the 1900s, the common consensus was that sports could only be good for creating physical strength but by the time the '60s rolled along, that viewpoint had changed. Sport was seen as not only a good way to keep an eye on the youth but by playing games that had strict rules and you had to 'obey' authority, then it was also a great way to teach the youth how to act and how to respect those in authoritative positions. More youth offender centres bought sports equipment to attempt to rehabilitate their youths, with everyone using sports as an opportunity to try and restore some form of balance – whatever balance may be – post the events of 1968.

So by the time 1970 came, the footballing landscape in Paris had changed an awful lot. It went from a position where Parisian teams won the Coupe de France on an almost automatic basis to having just one team in Division 1 at the end of the 1969/1970 campaign. A future great of football management basically started his fledgling career at a Paris club and started to introduce what would go on to be known by the wider world as his own form of *catenaccio*. While it may just be seen as an insignificant step in his career by the majority of those who glance at the CV of Helenio Herrera, to those in Paris it wasn't. Such was his popularity, he became friends with movie stars and stars of the entertainment industry. Herrera did in fact claim to have invented the system solely on his own, without knowledge of the work of Swiss manager Karl Rappan, saying he had invented and executed the system 'around 1945'. This would mean that, provided Herrera wasn't bending the truth a bit, the sweeper system that he used to dominate Italian and subsequently European football was born and developed in Paris.

Despite this, Paris seemed to have stagnated in the world of French football. In the amateur era (1893–1929), the city's teams either won the league or finished second (11 times), but since the league turned professional in 1932 only Racing managed to win the title. Racing were also the only Parisian team to finish second; meanwhile Nice and the Raymond Kopa/Just Fontaine-led Reims teams both had periods where they looked like world-beaters, demonstrated by the fact Reims were the first – and only until 1976 – French team to reach the European Cup Final. The same went for the Coupe de France, a cup that could legitimately be seen as 'Paris' Cup'. It last had a Parisian winner in 1949, which was Racing. Racing ended up being the premier Parisian team but that wasn't going to be the case for long. Because while Paris and the whole of France was changing, there was work going on in the background to add another team to the French footballing pyramid that belonged to Paris, perhaps to try and revitalise the football scene in the capital. The move to merge two clubs together had been done before but perhaps not to this level and certainly, if we look deep into the future, not with this much impact on the game.

2

La formation du Paris Saint-Germain – The formation of Paris Saint-Germain

AT THE end of the 1969/1970 Division 1 season, Red Star Paris were the sole Parisian club left to fly the flag for the capital in the top flight, despite their glory days being way behind them. They finished 26 points off of first-placed Saint-Étienne and just four points from what would have been the usual relegation places, but thanks to the expansion of the league they needn't have worried about that threat.

There was little to nothing to shout about if you were a football fan in Paris at the time. It turned out that it was quite difficult to build a strong fanbase for Parisian clubs because there were so many different kinds of people in Paris. Citizens from Breton weren't Paris fans, they were Brest fans. There were more Saint-Étienne fans and Lille fans than Paris fans because of the amount of people from those cities and towns who had relocated. The problem, however, was the fact that if you went across every major city and capital in major European countries, Paris seemed to be the odd one out.

Take a look across the continent in 1970. Arsenal had won Division 1 in England seven times before 1970 (they won their eighth title in 1970/71) while both Tottenham Hotspur and Chelsea had three league titles between them. Eleven FA Cups were won by London teams alongside two UEFA Cup Winners' Cups. Liverpool and Manchester had 37 trophies come out of their four clubs, while Bayern Munich had seven trophies, Juventus had 17, Inter Milan had 15 and AC Milan had 14. Racing Paris had six trophies, Red Star had five (looking at major honours, not Division 2 titles or Trophée des Champions honours). Paris had 11 major trophies across two teams, four fewer than Inter and three behind Milan. Ajax had 19, if you want to go further afield, and neither they nor Bayern Munich were about to enter their dominant phases. Even if you want to keep it domestic and look only at French clubs, Marseille had ten, Reims had 13 and Saint-Étienne had nine to their name.

Clearly Paris had a problem within its own league, city and country when it came to bona fide, sustained footballing success. It had to conquer its own problems before looking at anyone else in Division 1, let alone any other club in Europe. Something had to change and it had to change immediately. London and Manchester dominated England – Glasgow was the epicentre of success in Scotland, with Celtic winning 25 leagues, 20 Scottish Cups, seven Scottish League Cups and one very famous European Cup and Rangers winning 34 league titles, 19 Scottish Cups, six Scottish League Cups – while Milan,

Turin, Munich and Amsterdam were the city strongholds across Europe alongside the kings of the continent, Real Madrid, with 14 La Liga titles, 11 Copa del Rey and six European Cups. In terms of major European cities in football, Paris wasn't even on the map. Fashion? Top of the list. History, architecture? Absolutely. Paris was at the forefront of everyone's minds, except in football. Professional football in the city needed to return and on 1 August it did just that.

The final year of the Swinging Sixties was, to say the least, culturally massive: the Moon landing, Woodstock, the final Beatles performance and the release of *Abbey Road*, Charles de Gaulle stood down as French president and was replaced by Georges Pompidou, which in turn helped push forward the modernisation of Paris. It was also the year Paris FC was formed, a club based on one objective: to give Paris a new Division 1 team. Slightly less significant than some of the other events mentioned, but significant for our story.

Paris FC's only goal was to bring Division 1 football back to the capital and to create an elite football team for an elite city. The French Football Federation (FFF) formed a commission to help push through the new club and try to figure out what model they wanted Paris FC to try and take inspiration from. The three main protagonists of this commission were Fernand Sastre, the secretary general of the FFF at the time; Guy Crescent, president of Geodis Calberson, the company that would later become SNCF trains; and Henri Patrelle, the man who helped break the segregation of amateur and pro footballers in France and someone who was influential in the running of a club called Stade Saint-Germain.

Stade Saint-Germain was an amateur club in Paris that had no major standing and never pulled up any trees until 1970, when the commission sought them out for a potential merger. Stade Saint-Germain were still in Division 3 while Racing had gone out of business and Red Star had merged with Toulouse FC in 1967 which meant that CS Sedan Ardennes was the only club that Paris FC could merge with to get Division 1 status and attempt to move Sedan to Paris. Sedan refused the merger, which left Paris looking elsewhere.

By July 1969 the commission weren't in a better place. They still had no players, they still had nowhere to play but they did add Racing vice-president Pierre-Étienne Guyot, who was brought in as president. Crescent, who had taken time out to visit Madrid, had a meeting with Santiago Bernabéu, arguably the most historic and important figure in the history of Real Madrid. Bernabéu had been president for nearly 17 years by the time he met with Crescent, and Crescent was eager to learn more about how Bernabéu ran Real Madrid and how he signed so many stars like Alfredo Di Stéfano, Ferenc Puskás and former Reims man Raymond Kopa. Bernabéu suggested that the new Paris team use a model called '*socios*' which translates from Spanish to mean member or partner. The method meant that fans could pay (or contribute, to use the correct PR term) a certain amount of money per year to the club to become a member and make the club fan-owned. The *socios* would pay 25 to 40 francs (four to six Euros in modern money) to join and become part-owners/ the first supporters of the new Paris club.

The FFF commission still needed to find an actual team to merge with to give these supporters a team to support. Sedan pulled out but there was another team that was on the verge of winning promotion from Division 3 into Division 2 that Henri Patrelle was very familiar with. Paris FC merged with Stade Saint-Germain and now, alongside the fees that *socios* paid (reports suggest that over 17,400 fans paid to join up), Paris Saint-Germain was officially born, with the help of a model suggested to them by the president of Real Madrid. During the meeting he had with Crescent, Bernabéu had said, 'Count on yourself and the love of Parisians. Start at the bottom, much like we did and one day, perhaps, we will meet face to face at the highest level.'

There was no debt to be paid to Santiago Bernabéu or to Real Madrid, it was just advice. Paris Saint-Germain, along with their *socios* and the financial backing from the Paris FC side of the equation, started to create different aspects of the club. Paris FC came with the financial backing while Stade Saint-Germain came with the players, the coach, the place in Division 2 and the training complex called Camp des Loges (which is still being used by PSG as late as 2022). The colours of the club were decided, with meaning behind every decision. The red and blue was to represent France and Paris, while the white was apparently chosen to represent French royalty and the nearby Saint-Germain-en-Laye, the birthplace of King Louis XIV.

Paris Saint-Germain were ready for their first season under the name in the 1970/1971 campaign and managed to improve the squad by adding France captain Jean Djorkaeff – father of future PSG player and World Cup winner Youri – to their ranks. Alongside their already well-equipped squad that had gained promotion into

Division 2 before the merger and the coach who had taken them there in the first place, Pierre Phelipon, there was optimism about the club. Another step was the mission to find a home for the new club, and the answer fell in a familiar place.

In 1967, President Charles de Gaulle and the state put the seal of approval on a restructuring of le Parc that was set to take several years to plan, construct and open for official use. The first incarnation of the Parc des Princes was drenched in history dating back to the days of the French royal family and a period of time prior to the French Revolution, alongside sporting events such as the finishing point of the Tour de France, the Coupe de France and French international rugby, which is still impressive despite it controversially being left out as a venue for the Olympic Games in 1924. The second incarnation saw European Cups won by Alfredo Di Stéfano and Ferenc Puskás, the opening game of the 1938 World Cup and a Rugby League World Cup Final when Great Britain beat France in their own backyard, but there was still work that needed to be done.

Le Parc was a historically significant stadium across many sports, but you can see in pictures that it didn't look as grand as it perhaps should have. Go back to stadia during the 1960s and compare them to the historic pictures and it is easy to see why the Parc des Princes needed a renovation. It was hard not to be impressed by the stature and size of Wembley Stadium in the late 1960s, and the same could be said about Berlin's Olympic Stadium. These venues could rightly be called 'powerhouses' of multi-sport stadia in Europe; they had size, had stature, had an aura around them that made you understand that you were walking into something that was more of a cauldron than a sporting arena. The Parc des Princes needed something that would grab your attention, to force your mind to feel and think a certain way when you looked up and saw the stadium, and the task of creating a sight like that fell on the shoulders of two men whose lives were both changed and shaped by Paris before football was even thought of and perhaps wouldn't have been building this new stadium if it wasn't for Parisian interventions earlier in their lives.

Roger Taillibert and Siavash Teimouri were the two architects placed in charge of helping plan, create and construct the new Parc des Princes and, for two men whose backgrounds lay in Paris, that seemed fitting. Taillibert was born in a town called Châtres-sur-Cher, a commune west of Paris that was unassuming and unknown to the majority of people in France. Taillibert moved to Paris to study at the National School of Fine Arts, an art school located just across the Seine from the Louvre, taking up architecture, and as the years went on he progressed more and more. He travelled across the world, mainly to Switzerland, Finland, Mexico and the United States, and it was with internships in Germany that his vision was once again shaped. From 1962 to 1966 he was in Stuttgart and took an interest in light and mobile structures, seeing what forms could be made, and started to build his own concepts, figuring out the perfect way to carve his visions. Taillibert knew what he wanted in his designs and he was travelling the world to find the most innovative way to improve his designs.

Taillibert's work within the sports and education sector of the French government helped him massively with future work, as did his work on sports facilities in Deauville and at Font-Romeu in the Pyrenees. He was chosen as the main architect for the job of constructing the new Parisian stadium but he wasn't alone at the top of this job. He was joined by Siavash Teimouri, an Iranian-born architect who moved to Paris in 1962 when he was 25 years old. It's unclear exactly what role he played in the creation of the Parc des Princes, or if Teimouri was even involved at any point at all. A website called Contemporary Architecture of Iran lists who Teimouri was associated to and at what point in time. It points out that he and Taillibert's partnership together started in 1965 and ended just a year later, with Teimouri holding the role of architect instructor at the University of Tehran in 1969, implying that Teimouri wasn't involved in the five years it took to complete the upgraded Parc des Princes and his involvement in the project was at the very beginning, with his partnership with Taillibert ending a full year before Taillibert was even selected for the job.

For one last time, the Tour de France's final stage rolled around le Parc and, as luck would have it, a Frenchman by the name of Raymond Poulidor rode his bike into the Parc des Princes as the Tour waved au revoir to le Parc after 54 years. As the Tour rode off and as the demolition of the second incarnation of the stadium was under way, Taillibert was already planning what to do next. He chose to build the stadium out of concrete rather than steel or stone with the concrete going through a special process to ensure its strength while having its weight reduced. Two tiers were planned with 23,000 fans able to access the bottom tier and 27,000 in the upper tier, with a roof covering them but leaving the pitch to battle with rain, sun, snow or whatever may fall from the heavens. Floodlights were integrated in what was, at the time, an innovative technique used to avoid having floodlight stands across the stadium as seen in a traditional British ground, while TV cameras had their own platforms on which to film matches and events on and specific commentary booths were built, again another innovation that nowhere else in France had.

France, and the rest of Europe, hardly had many 'modern' stadia and Taillibert's vision of the new Parc des Princes placed it at the forefront of modern venues in Europe; strong enough to hold plenty of fans and robust enough to contain whatever noise those fans made.

Without a doubt, the project suffered setbacks and problems. Torrential rain? That caused delays. The 1968 protests in Paris? That caused delays. Financial issues? You better believe that caused delays. By the time the stadium and the project had been completed, it cost around 87m francs, which is a lot of money on its own but when you consider that the original estimate for the project was 45.5m francs, then a lot of money becomes a lot of lots of money.

Nevertheless, after five years of hard work and construction, the third incarnation of the Parc des Princes was unveiled and it was seen in a favourable light. It was seen as not only a great sporting stadium but also a new mark in a new era of modern Paris and modern France. Sports newspaper *L'Equipe* said, 'It is undoubtedly the most modern, the most handsome and the most comfortable stadium in Europe,' while *Le Figaro* said that it was a 'well-turned-out urban stadium'. It became clear that the media were impressed not only by the look and feel of the

Parc des Princes but also the attention to detail that was paid to the press in terms of the press box, the radio and television commentary positions and the camera areas too.

Every seat was the exact same dimension and had an unobstructed view of the pitch; it was transformative in the urbanisation of a Paris that had just gone through a cultural revolution. The Parc des Princes, finally, was ready to host professional sports and be the home of a new and impressive-looking Parisian side. Georges Pompidou opened up the stadium with the 1972 Coupe de France Final as 44,069 fans packed into le Parc to watch Marseille beat Bastia 2-1 (legendary Marseille striker Josip Skoblar scored the winner, for those who were wondering) and thus the Parc des Princes was officially opened.

It was open for business, with cup finals and international matches to be based at the Parc des Princes, the Wembley of France for that period of time. But what of Paris Saint-Germain? Paris had this brand-new, stunning stadium that Europe wanted to be a part of and wanted to see, but where was PSG in all of this? In 1970, the inaugural year of PSG, the club would split their games up between the Stade Jean-Bouin, the Stade Municipal Georges Lefèvre and occasionally the Saint-Germain-en-Laye area, but the issues of location – Saint-Germain-en-Laye is located in north-central Paris, essentially on the outskirts of the city and the mayor refused to support a club that wasn't in Paris – didn't deter the team on the field. The main goal of the first season was to be competitive in Division 2 and establish themselves as a good, solid team and club.

In terms of major signings, they brought in striker Jean-Claude Bras, midfielder Jacques Rémond, who would only have a short career, starting in 1967 at Monaco and retiring in 1973 at Avignon, Jean-Pierre Destrumelle, an experienced midfielder who made over 100 appearances for Marseille prior to his move to Paris, and Frenchman of Polish descent Roland Mitoraj from Division 1 club Saint-Étienne, but the jewel in the crown of the club and the star signing among all the big moves was Jean Djorkaeff.

By the 21st century the name Djorkaeff would be known more prominently for Jean's son and World Cup-winner Youri but, during the 1960s, Jean was a star in his own right. Making nearly 300 appearances for Lyon and Marseille from 1958 to 1970 along with 48 caps for France and an appearance at the 1966 World Cup, Jean was brought in to confirm the legitimacy of Paris Saint-Germain. He was signed as a 30-year-old to not only lead the young club and to give the playing squad a leader both on and off the pitch – Jean was captain of France at the time – but, as he later said in interviews about his time at a young PSG, 'My signing at Paris Saint-Germain was a source of great pride. When it is created, a young club can find it tough. But our goal was to achieve beautiful things. We started in National, which is the equivalent of the second division today, and we managed to climb up the first year. But it took courage and determination to get there. At the start, I was a captain because I had more experience and therefore patience. It is a great responsibility to have played this role.'

And because of this responsibility and this level of class that he poured out into the club and on to the pitch, PSG won promotion in their first season and were already making the jump into Division 1. The second division was split into three groups: North, Central and South. Paris Saint-Germain were in the Central section and the top three teams from each would move into a three-team play-off. PSG were up against South winners Monaco and North champions Lille to see who would be crowned champions of Division 2 (all three teams gained promotion regardless). The three sides would each play against each other, with PSG finishing top of the group on three points after their 4-2 win against Lille. Michel Prost, the scorer of the final PSG goal that day, said in an interview that his best sporting memory was the promotion into Division 1 with Paris.

A lot of the squad had been recruited from amateur French football or were Division 2 journeymen or even just steady hands at bigger clubs in Division 1 who simply wanted to play more football and Paris gave them that opportunity. Take a look through the squad and you'll see that this is the case. Goalkeeper Camille Choquier played lower down the leagues with SC Abbeville and SAS Épinal before arriving at Stade Saint-Germain in 1961 (he followed over from the merger), defender Jean-Claude Fitte-Duval was another who was a Stade Saint-Germain original, alongside Pierre Phelipon – who would also double up as manager of the side. Fernando Cruz joined from Benfica following 447 appearances and five European Cup finals in Portugal, Jean-Pierre Destrumelle joined from Marseille while Živko Lukić joined from Partizan Belgrade. Well, he didn't exactly 'join' from Partizan. In fact, he didn't join from anyone. Živko Lukić has one of the most extraordinary stories you'll ever read about in football.

Lukić, according to every available squad list for the PSG team in their first season, signed from Partizan

Belgrade when, in reality, he was only a part of the youth team and failed to stand out from the generation that would be known as 'Partizan babies', the name given to a select group of youngsters who would usher in a great period of success for the club in Yugoslavia. When Lukić was cut from the team, he dropped out of football altogether. He didn't find a new club like you see with a lot of players who get released at youth level; he quit the game and started to train to become a dentist. However, no one in France knew this. All they knew was players from Yugoslavia at the time tended to share the same qualities: very good at adapting to new surroundings and situations, very skilful and technically very good and relatively cheap in transfer fees.

When Paris Saint-Germain had an offer for a player who was related to the Rennes striker Ilija Lukić, they jumped at the opportunity. They didn't check up to see that he wasn't actually related to Ilija Lukić, they didn't check his background to see that he had been a dentist instead of a footballer. Živko even got a welcome from *French Football* magazine prior to his PSG debut. Živko didn't raise any alarm bells. At no point did anyone think that this guy wasn't who he said he was. Until, that is, the first game he played. Guy Crescent wrote in his autobiography a great little passage about Živko and the first time he saw him play, 'We signed a poor Yugoslavian named Lukić whose record in his country seemed fabulous. Not knowing what to do, because we were lacking players due to injuries, we gave it a shot. His mission was to neutralise our opponent's key player, Horlaville, whom we feared the most. And Lukić ... he clung to him like an octopus to a rock! But Horlaville would quickly dribble past him once, then again, then make a pass, while my unfortunate Lukić would inevitably end up on his behind!'

That was the only game that Živko played for PSG.

The opening game of the Division 2 season and the very first game that PSG played away from home was against Stade Poitiers in front of just over 4,000 spectators. Poitiers had beaten Stade Saint-Germain the previous season in the Coupe de France so it seemed rather fitting that the new club would be able to exact their revenge in their first competitive fixture. By all accounts of the game, PSG were better technically but had expected teething problems as a cohesive unit and as a team. Poitiers took the lead after the half-hour mark through Pedini before the very first goal in the new history of PSG, scored by Bernard Guignedoux. PSG held on for a draw, largely down to goalkeeper Camille Choquier who saved twice late on and kept the score down. It was a difficult game for PSG, who still needed time to train together and to work together, but Henri Patrelle knew what would await them every week as he said, 'We are now the team to beat. We will meet teams like Poitiers every Sunday and they'll be ready to play the game of their lives. Our task will be tough.'

There's nothing to suggest that Patrelle was wrong, because everyone would want to get one over the new Paris club. They followed up this draw with a win over Quevilly at home but not in Saint-Germain-en-Laye as their debut at their official home would have to wait a few weeks. This game took place at the Stade Jean-Bouin in Paris. The Živko Lukić incident was within these two fixtures and while PSG had already played Quevilly in a pre-season game – this was the first fixture that they ever played, although it wasn't officially registered, probably for good reason since they lost 3-1 – they met again following the Poitiers result. PSG won 3-2, but Živko took the headlines, being roundly made the figure of embarrassment as he was 'humiliated' by Quevilly's Daniel Horlaville.

It became clear that Živko would never play for PSG again after this performance and he was immediately dropped for Michel Prost as PSG struggled to put together a strong, consistent run of wins. Victories against Valenciennes, Caen and Brest followed the Quevilly game, sandwiched between draws with Le Havre, Lorient, Bourges and Le Mans, with their first Division 2 loss coming after the last three draws as Châteauroux won 2-0 at the Stade Georges Lefèvre in Saint-Germain-en-Laye. Reports at the time said that PSG looked 'tired and lacked an edge' while Châteauroux, who had put four goals past Brest the week prior, looked comfortable. But to use a cliché, it was almost like PSG *needed* to lose this game.

It reminded them of their weaknesses and kept them on their toes, prompting them to go back on to the training ground, improve and come back the following game refreshed, more of a team and just better in every department. Did it work? Was this defeat against Châteauroux the catalyst for a hit of the refresh button? Well, in Division 2 PSG would only lose one more game (they lost in the Coupe de France to Cuiseaux-Louhans, too), 2-1 away at Montluçon. Henri Patrelle was not too fussed by the sounds of it, saying, 'As for the result, we consider it an accident.'

PSG finished top of Division 2, five points clear of nearest side Rouen and nine clear of third-placed Limoges. It was a convincing and impressive performance from the Paris club, who took the league by storm. They had arrived in style into Division 1 and had reached their goal already.

When the club was founded, the likes of Henri Patrelle and Guy Crescent just wanted to be competitive in Division 2. Would that mean gaining promotion at the first attempt? That may have been a dream at the back of their minds but they said that they wanted to be competitive. Did they expect what actually happened? Again, that may have been a thought but it wasn't the outright goal despite the attention that was pushed on them, being a new club and a Paris club at that. Was it safe to call this inaugural season an 'overachievement', despite the reputation heading into the season? Probably not, but it was still impressive how well the club took to life in Division 2.

Yes, PSG may have been a new club but with all the players who had followed from Stade Saint-Germain, this was their second consecutive promotion and they had gone from Division 3 to Division 1 in only a few years. That's impressive regardless of what club you play for. It also meant that a lot of the club mentality had to change as well. In Division 3, it was about promotion. In Division 2, it was about stabilisation then promotion, but now in Division 1, it was about survival, stabilisation, winning the league and so on. With PSG now in the top division and the Parc des Princes close to completion, it looked as if Paris was ready to make a big push to be a new super city in football across Europe.

They had their state-of-the-art stadium – which was already being earmarked as a potential home for PSG in the future – but did they have their state-of-the-art team? Not quite, and as the next few years and seasons would show, they were far from that status. Other teams across France had better players, better coaches and much richer history, but PSG had the name and fresh new look about them and were an exciting prospect. Sure, you can be a star at Rennes or Reims, but imagine what it would be like to be *the* star for Paris Saint-Germain? That was quite possibly the thought of a lot of players of a certain level, and it's what Paris looked for. But, they still had to navigate the stormy waters of Division 1 and – perhaps most importantly and disruptive – politics in football.

3

L'histoire de deux clubs et d'une ville –
The tale of two clubs and one city

THE SECOND act is always the hardest, in any walk of life. Paris Saint-Germain were worried about exactly this. They had finished their debut season as winners of Division 2 and gained promotion to the top flight at the first attempt and now had to figure out how to play with the bigger clubs against better players but with a target remaining on their back. Everyone, yet again, wanted to get one over on the Parisians. Clubs like Marseille who came from more working-class backgrounds were simply better than the cosmopolitan Parisian club and they wanted to show it every time they faced off against one another.

A lot of eyes were on PSG for obvious reasons, and expectations were raised. Gone were the likes of Živko Lukić (who was officially released) and Fernando Cruz (who retired after just one year at the club) and in came new signings Jean-Louis Leonetti, a utility journeyman who had played for eight clubs – including Marseille – prior to joining PSG at the age of 33. Defender Daniel

Solas also joined and set the template of a modern defender by mixing up his duties in the back line. For the first ten games of the Division 1 season, Solas started as a *libero* (sweeper) and occasionally moved into the left-back spot when needed but also filled in when needed as a defensive midfielder, making him a valued part of the line-up.

Joel Camargo, another defender, started what would be a strong and important legacy at Paris Saint-Germain by becoming the first Brazilian player to ever play for the club. While Camargo's legacy at PSG is one of kick-starting a long and fruitful relationship with Brazilian players, his time there didn't last very long. He would only play two games in the course of a few months before being moved back to Brazil due to an inability to adapt to new surroundings which, in turn, affected his performance.

And one signing from Division 2 already had some history with PSG. What alerted people to how bad Živko Lukić was the schooling he received from Quevilly's Daniel Horlaville. The forward-thinking midfielder had claimed that PSG had been chasing his signature for quite some time, as had Marseille, Nantes and some foreign clubs, but after a serious knee injury Paris were the only ones who remained interested in his services. Horlaville needed to make the big step up from Division 2 to Division 1 quite quickly. The questions remained not about his talent because, by all accounts, he had that in abundance, but it was a case of whether his body could hold up after his knee injury.

With their red home shirt and blue shorts (and an away strip consisting of a blue shirt, white shorts and blue socks), PSG were ready to take on Division 1. Their debut came on 11 August 1971 and it was one to forget. Away at

Angers, a team who had finished in a mediocre position of 12th, just four points away from the relegation zone, Paris struggled to make their chances count. They fell to a 2-0 loss and, according to the match report in *France Football* magazine, Angers scored two goals in the first half, in the ninth minute then the 27th, with what proved to be their first two serious chances of the game.

It wasn't the start they had hoped for, but things did get slightly better with a 0-0 draw against a talented Bordeaux side. The draw was preserved by the excellence of PSG goalkeeper Guy Delhumeau, who had saved five clear-cut Bordeaux chances and stopped it from being a rout. By no means was it an exciting game, but a draw against a Bordeaux team that had assembled itself to challenge for the title was still impressive. One loss and one draw was how PSG's season in the top flight started so it only made logical sense that the next fixture, away at Nancy, would go in one direction.

PSG travelled to Nancy hoping for a win, feeling relatively confident against a side that was, just like Angers, relatively average. Around 1,500 PSG fans travelled up to Nancy to support the team and were reasonably excited when the Parisians took a 2-0 lead into the half-time break. They were in control and looking like they were on track to get their first win in Division 1 before Nancy pulled one back just after half-time. Jean-Claude Bras, who scored PSG's first goal, turned in his second and his team's third after Michel Prost had doubled their lead before the break. Patrice Vicq got one back for Nancy in the 80th minute. Game on. Nancy gave everything they had to find that equaliser and in the last minute of the game, they thought they had. PSG thought they had failed to win yet another game but the linesman had his flag up and the goal was ruled out for offside. The PSG players drew a sigh of relief; Nancy a sigh of exasperation.

There was uproar in the stands as Nancy fans were disgusted at the offside ruling, with 15 fans being injured in commotions among the 13,000 crowd. Police had to intervene to prevent the referee and players from being injured. It was quite heavy for a first Paris Saint-Germain win, but it wasn't a result that they would have forgotten anytime soon. By all accounts the travelling Paris fans were not involved, but ugly scenes in the stands and Paris Saint-Germain is something to keep at the back of your mind as we slowly progress through their history.

That win against Nancy put PSG on a little bit of a streak, beating Lille 4-1 at home before being brought stumbling back down to earth by a rampant Nantes side, who crushed the Parisians 6-1. The legendary Henri Michel got on the scoresheet, scoring the sixth and final blow for the Canaries, who gave PSG a not-so-subtle reminder of where they were. It was all well and good stringing wins together against the likes of Nancy and Lille, two average, run-of-the-mill teams, but PSG still had a long, long way to go if they wanted to compete with the likes of Nantes, Marseille and Saint-Étienne. This heavy reverse was their first real test against one of French football's big clubs, and a few weeks later they got the chance to test themselves again. This time the Parisians travelled to Saint-Étienne to face Les Verts ('The Greens') and it promised to be a massively important game for the club.

Something wasn't quite right with Saint-Étienne, the locals believed. They weren't as sharp, they were second to every ball and PSG just looked quicker. The only exception was the tricky forward Georges Bereta. His twists and turns had Paris chasing shadows for a large portion of the game and Jean Djorkaeff was given the task of marking him. Djorkaeff tried to keep up but couldn't handle or contain Bereta. The fans felt that if anyone was going to drag a limp and lifeless-looking Saint-Étienne over the line, it would indeed be Bereta, but while Djorkaeff was up against his man, Saint-Étienne let their guard down at the other end of the field. Bernard Guignedoux took aim from outside the box, he swung his right foot towards the ball and watched as the ball flew in off the post. It caught Saint-Étienne off guard, not least the goalkeeper, but the sheer determination of Michel Prost to keep poking and prodding before eventually knocking the ball to Guignedoux was what made the goal.

It took advantage of the fears that Saint-Étienne fans had of their team being second best to every ball, not running hard enough and not being able to keep up with a determined Paris Saint-Germain. Every fear and every flaw that those fans were worried about was exposed in this effort. Guignedoux's goal was the only one of the match and PSG had made it three wins out of seven games. The result against Saint-Étienne showed the disciplined side of Paris Saint-Germain, the one that could go head-to-head with the giants of French football and hold their own, even beating them, and the club won a fair few admirers that day, at least according to *France Football* who reported on the game, noting that the team wouldn't need to change much in order to aim higher and to rise up the Division 1 table.

The only problem that the team had was consistency. A 3-1 home win against an impressive Bastia side saw them in third place while they followed up the Bastia win with a disappointing 4-1 defeat against Nîmes at the Stade Jean-Bouin (not the one in Paris, but in Nîmes; there were multiple stadia with the same name) before another convincing win, this time at home in a Paris derby against Red Star.

That victory over Red Star left PSG in ninth place but only four points off of Marseille at the top of the table, and it was also quite a symbolic result, at least in Paris football terms. Here was Paris Saint-Germain, a new club who held high ambitions, going up against the oldest club in Paris when in the top flight for the very first time, with the former sweeping the latter away like they weren't even there. PSG were taking to life quite well in Division 1, but things were about to change on the field as results soon started to go against PSG. After that Red Star triumph, PSG would only win one more game before the turn of the year, a 1-0 home win against Sochaux with the *France Football* match report largely focusing on the fact Sochaux had an awful record in Paris and this quote from their manager, 'You haven't seen the great Sochaux and I'm sorry about that. If we had always played like this, you would have guessed that we would never have been able to take the lead, at least for a while.'

The match focused on how Sochaux couldn't get the job done against a PSG side that were now faltering. Before the next league win, Paris lost five and drew two, even being eliminated from the Coupe de France by Valenciennes in a game that they really should have won. Valenciennes were also a Division 1 side but struggled for the duration of the season, eventually being relegated. PSG travelled to Valenciennes as favourites and most would have backed them to win comfortably and reach the next round of the Coupe de France, but it didn't happen. Armed with nothing but amateur players, hope and a will to win, Valenciennes dumped PSG out of the cup with a goal in the 82nd minute. The club may have equalled their finish from the season prior, but context allows you to see how disappointing the two differing campaigns were. The previous season, PSG reached the last 64 before being beaten by Louhans-Cuiseaux FC, but PSG had to play two preliminary games before reaching the actual rounds of the Coupe de France, which was far more impressive than the 1971/72 season where they were knocked out at the same stage but played just one game. The team bounced back with a well-deserved 3-1 win at Lille, but all was not well within the club.

The PSG fans, apparently around 1,200, travelled to Lille and unveiled a banner saying 'PSG salut Lille! Vive le football et que le meilleur gagne' meaning 'Hello Lille! Long live football and may the best win!' On the day, the best did win. But there was something else lurking in the rumour mill in reports around this match, and it wasn't anything to do with football on the pitch. There was reference to a potential merger between Paris Saint-Germain and Valenciennes, with talks apparently being held after the Coupe de France game. As the reports said, there was precedent for this that was set by Paris themselves, but this seemed completely out of the question. It was unlikely to begin with and swiftly spoken down not long after and, eventually, the whole rumour was forgotten about.

That win against Lille was their only success for 14 games, ranging from 17 November, when they lost at home to Lyon despite taking the lead just before half-time, up until 29 March when they hosted Angoulême and ran out 3-0 winners after largely dominating a game that Henri Patrelle said afterwards 'must free the team'.

And Patrelle couldn't have been more accurate. An incredible game away at Reims followed up the Angoulême win, with Paris going 2-0 up only for Reims to pull it back to 2-2 before the half-hour mark and then going 3-2 ahead, then PSG snatching a point in the 73rd minute. Both teams were struggling for form in Division 1, both flirting with relegation, the thought of which was killing the Paris Saint-Germain board and forcing them to consider a merge – just like the Valenciennes one – in order to assure their top-flight status. Reims hadn't won a game in Division 1 since 16 January, 2-1 at home to Saint-Étienne, and were hovering above the drop zone, so a point was no good for either side but if one club had to take positives from it, it would probably have been Reims. The point ended their shocking run and saw them jump above Monaco in the table, leaving them just two points behind PSG.

But the next two games for Paris would prove to be vital, and when you look back at the table and see how close the points were at the end, it is very safe to say that these games saved their season, eventually keeping them in Division 1. With Red Star, Reims, Monaco and even Lille – who were five points off of them after 30 games – breathing down their neck, Paris knew that any slip-up would have been costly. It wasn't a do-or-die situation yet, but if they didn't start picking up points soon it would be. And they knew it. The coach, Pierre Phelipon, knew it. The players, who were playing for status as top-flight footballers, knew it. The fans, who travelled every week to watch the team play, knew it. And, perhaps most importantly, the board, who had formed this club with the intention of building it to challenge with elite clubs and to major Parisian football on the European and world maps, knew it.

Up first was a home game against Metz, one that they couldn't afford to drop points in. Both teams were aware of what was at stake. Metz were floating around mid-table but knew that, because of how tight the relegation battle was, they weren't out of trouble yet. A win for them would have almost secured safety while, for PSG, victory was imperative given the situation. The feeling surrounding the game would have been tense and with 6,722 fans reportedly packed into the Stade de Paris – just under 2,000 more than the last home game against Angoulême – it was bound to be a big game.

The team needed something to settle their nerves, so an early goal would do the trick. Two early goals would be just as welcome. The first big moment went to Djorkaeff, who failed to hit the target, but 11 minutes in the breakthrough came. Michel Prost hit the opener before doubling the lead and his own tally less than a minute later. For Paris, it was dreamland. They had the two early goals to settle the nerves and they started to play their own way; composed and controlled. It was everything you would want from a game of such magnitude, but Metz weren't going to go out without a fight and pulled one back after 19 minutes. Jacky Rémond scored the third for PSG and tied it all up with his third goal in as many games and a welcome return back to the starting line-up. The attacking midfielder was out injured for a period of time during the bad run of form mentioned earlier, but there was no surprise that his return coincided with the upturn in results for PSG, scoring the goals that sealed the wins against Metz and Angoulême while getting the second goal in the draw last time out against Reims. Important players pop up with important goals, and Rémond was the man for PSG on this occasion.

PSG had won the first of their two vital games and were now four points clear of 18th-placed Monaco. It wasn't a lot but it was breathing space, and with only a few games left it was a gap that any team in that fight would have taken. The task for the next of these two huge matches was simple: win. A draw wouldn't be the end of the world, but a win would make the situation a lot better. Away from the comforts of Paris, PSG travelled to Sochaux confident and assured of their job. Their good run of form had given them enough confidence to head into this game, against a side that was third in the table and only five points away from leaders Marseille, to get a win from it. Sochaux hadn't lost in their last five matches, winning each one and conceding just four goals, yet PSG still had belief.

Despite rumours about the future of the team with Paris City Council hovering around the situation, the players were focused and ready to carry on their good form against a very good, very strong and very confident Sochaux side. PSG were the team controlling most of the early stages of the game, even if the main chance fell to Sochaux after 20 minutes. It wasn't anything major, by all means, but it gave PSG a bit of a wake-up call. They had to create something or else a team like Sochaux, with the quality they had, would just find a way to carve you open.

PSG found their momentum, regained their control and prevented Sochaux creating anything else in the first 45 minutes but had to wait until just after the hour when Gérard Hallet bundled in the ball after Rémond had his shot parried. It was simple yet effective. PSG were controlling the tempo of the game against the joint second-best team in the country. The off-field situation didn't hamper them at this point, and they didn't look like losing any control of the game either. Rémond, at the heart of anything positive for Paris Saint-Germain, managed to play the ball up to Jean Djorkaeff who wrapped up the win with a delicate lob. Another huge win for Paris, and it was a vital one. They had, once again, come up with the goods when it mattered and the victory saw them move six points clear of Monaco with six games left, one of which was against Monaco at home. It was only their tenth win of the season, but arguably their best and certainly their most important. Coach Phelipon even said after the game, 'It is a timely victory, at a time when the future of the club is at stake. This success proves that the players have moral resources despite the recent events which could have traumatised them.' He understood just how big this result was.

To go away to a side challenging for the title and to play with such confidence given the precarious situation facing the very future of the club was nothing short of admirable. The players delivered when they needed to, but could they keep the run going? Could they carry on performing in the final six games to assure safety and maybe push up into mid-table and use that as the perfect springboard into the next season whatever happened to the club off the field?

The following game was away at fifth-placed Lyon, who won 3-1, with legendary striker Bernard Lacombe scoring a brace. PSG were 2-0 down within 15 minutes. They were suffocated by the sheer pace of a Lyon side who outfought them, outran them and bullied them without PSG offering anything in return. They were weak and unable to stop Lecombe's ability in front of goal and the sheer brilliance of Fleury Di Nallo, known as 'Le petit prince de Gerland' or 'The little prince of Gerland', after he dominated games at the Stade Gerland, the home of Lyon until the late 2010s. Both he and Lecombe got on the scoresheet and PSG, despite scoring a goal, looked way off the pace. They looked like they had used up all their energy in the Sochaux match and simply could not muster up anything against stronger opposition again or they looked like the mental strain of not knowing what was happening to the club at the end of the season was finally weighing them down. PSG just didn't turn up for one reason or another and a very good, well-organised and entertaining Lyon should have won by a lot larger margin. Nevertheless, the Paris players promised their own hierarchy that whoever they played next would pay for the Lyon loss. All the negativity of the loss plus the off-field distractions would be taken out on their next opponent. Who were their next opponents? Relegation rivals Monaco.

The results around Paris after the Lyon loss meant that they retained their six-point gap between themselves and the relegation zone, so they had effectively saved their season, although it wasn't rubber-stamped heading into this Monaco game. This was back in the era where a win was only two points so looking back at the table following the PSG loss to Lyon, victory for Monaco against Paris would have closed the gap down to four points. It was certainly still all to play for regardless of how unlikely it was that either Monaco or fellow strugglers Lille would suddenly go on a winning run of form, or Red Star and Reims, to condemn Paris, but the possibility was still there – as it had been for the majority of the season.

But PSG didn't play like their safety was at stake. Nor did they play with any real urgency, rather opting for a relaxed approach to the game. Monaco created their chances and failed to take them while PSG just ambled towards the final whistle, knowing that they would be OK in the end. The gap between them and Monaco was still six points, so what was there to worry about? The following week, the gap was cut down to four points. Monaco had gone to mid-table Rennes and won 3-1, while PSG were beaten 3-0 at Ajaccio despite giving quite a good account of themselves. Despite the rather large gap in the score, the gap in quality wasn't equal to the scoreline, certainly not according to the *France Football* report that suggested that PSG and Ajaccio played similar styles and with similar tempo, but the Parisians just couldn't finish whatever chances they created while Ajaccio just outclassed them in the final third. No lucky deflections, no missed fouls or offside calls, just three very well-worked and entirely deserved goals. So would this slip-up awaken PSG and give them a kick up the rear to spring them into a flurry over the final few games to fully ensure their safety?

Yes, Monaco may have won, but realistically were they likely to win their next three games to overturn this points differential? As Paris welcomed league leaders and champions-elect Marseille, the wet and soggy Parisians' grass wasn't of any help to the hosts, who literally let Marseille slip into the lead two minutes after kick-off when Édouard Kula, a former Racing Club player, intercepted a rogue pass to get Marseille going. By half-time it was 2-0 to Marseille and despite a goal at the hour mark from Jean-Claude Bras for the Parisians, the game was over.

The players agreed with club officials that none of the playing staff would speak to the press openly about the delicate off-field situation that PSG found itself in, with Paris City Council becoming even more involved in the club's affairs and a potential name change being rumoured, but nothing official would happen until the end of the season. And while it was agreed to not be publicly spoken about, it would have been hard to keep focused in a relegation fight with noise in the background that could potentially threaten your livelihood. But, given results elsewhere, Paris headed into their game the following week away at Rennes knowing a point would be enough to ensure their survival and keep them in Division 1. Monaco lost at home to Lyon while Lille drew 3-3 with basement club Angoulême; PSG could ease up.

Their game against Rennes would be moot if Monaco and Lille both failed to win and PSG picked up their point, and given the return of Daniel Horlaville, the creative playmaker who was brought in to be a difference-maker but only managed to make seven appearances up until this Rennes game due to constant injury issues, it seemed a foregone conclusion that PSG, at the end of the 37th round of French Division 1 fixtures, would assure their top-flight status for the 1972/73 season. With Monaco losing at Marseille and Lille only drawing at home to Reims, all that was left was for PSG to pick up their point, which they duly did without any hassle. Having taken the lead just after half-time, letting it slip just before the hour didn't seem to bother anyone and neither did the loss on the final day of the season at home to Angers because all that mattered – at the time – was that Paris Saint-Germain were safe. Despite only winning ten games, despite having the fourth-worst defence in the league and being just four points off of relegation, the players on the field had done their jobs, but the main question surrounding the conclusion of the 1971/72 season was not where the club finished in the league table, nor was it who the main transfer of the summer was going to be. It was far bigger than that.

With the rumours of a club merger or some form of change within the club itself never going away, it left many wondering what team would show up in the following campaign. Which players would be there? Who would be the coach? Would there be new owners, a new stadium, a new name? There were so many questions that needed to be answered but to fully understand the predicament that PSG found themselves in at the end of the 1971/72 season, you have to trace the steps back a bit to see where the commotion started from and why it had reached its boiling point at the end of their debut season in Division 1.

Paris Saint-Germain is a rather good name for a Parisian-based club with roots in the Saint-Germain-en-Laye region of the city – such was the thinking of everyone involved in the decision-making. It correctly identifies the two key places in the club's short history, but for some it wasn't good enough. It simply wasn't 'Parisian' enough. It was an issue that had been brewing since before the 1971/72 season had even started, and a full year later, 20 June to be precise, Paris Saint-Germain was no longer the same club. It had broken up into two separate clubs: Paris Saint-Germain and Paris FC. But how did this happen? It would be understandable if the club merged with another outfit but to disband altogether?

Well, it wasn't entirely their own decision and for the entire backstory, you have to go back to July of 1971. Paris City Council had offered the club some financial aid during their infant years to help them grow and to help them move into European football's elite, thus helping the city in the process. However, the financial 'gift' came with one request: change the name back to Paris Football Club. The board of Paris Saint-Germain thought nothing of this and carried on planning for the 1971/72 season under the PSG name, but the fight had already begun between the club and the City of Paris, who wanted a more 'Parisian' name, but Guy Crescent and Henri Patrelle, who were completely and utterly horrified by these actions, ignored the request and ignored the financial offering of 850,000 francs. They felt that, while the money would have offered a boost to the club, it wasn't worth the name change and bowing to political pressure, which could have – and most likely would have – opened the door for the government and other political bodies to worm their way into the business of the club.

Two representatives of the Parisian municipality joined the Paris Saint-Germain board in a bid to try and find a solution to the ongoing problem, something that Crescent was furious about. Crescent left the presidency solely to Patrelle and exited the club altogether. To put this entire situation into perspective, this was a club that at the start of the 1971/72 season had sent Crescent to Brazil to meet representatives of Santos in a bid to bring Pelé to Paris. In the words of Crescent, the club wanted to 'bring another Eiffel Tower to Paris' and there wasn't anybody bigger in the world of football at the time than Pelé himself. According to the reports in *L'Equipe* at the time, officials flew to Brazil and offered Pelé the chance to join at the start of the 1972/73 season, with the idea of opening the new Parc des Princes stadium with the superstar as the main attraction.

Santos were struggling financially at the time so while they almost certainly did not want to lose Pelé on the cheap, PSG knew that they could at least try to sign him on a lower price than perhaps ever before. The deal said that Pelé had to play 60 games, 40 of which being at le Parc, and Pelé and Santos would get 40 per cent of the gate receipts; a true case of football fans literally paying a player's wages with their ticket money. It appealed to Pelé, it appealed to Santos, it appealed to Paris Saint-Germain, and TV cameras caught Crescent after one of his trips to Brazil and the man looked happy. He looked like a man who had just signed the best player in the world for his club. So what happened? Well, Santos got a better financial offer elsewhere; not from a club but from the USA. Santos were offered a lucrative friendly tour of the US with Pelé as the main attraction, with the money received helping any financial woes the club had. Pelé initially claimed that he didn't move to Paris due to family reasons but in late 1971, he had a different answer when questioned about why the transfer had fallen through, 'I was invited to come to Paris, to play here. Unfortunately I had an appointment with Santos, my contract had not been terminated. And I intend to end my career with Santos, the only club I have played for.'

Pelé would eventually leave Santos to join New York Cosmos in 1975 and be the star of the brand-new North American Soccer League, with Paris Saint-Germain wary of Warner Communications, the main owners and funders of the Cosmos, and claiming that Warner had been trying to get Pelé into the United States since 1971. Many people expected that if Pelé was ever going to leave Santos, it would be for a club like Juventus or Real Madrid or even to make history and leave his legacy at a club that needed a historic figure to build around, such as Paris Saint-Germain. Pelé did leave his legacy with a club that needed a historic figure to build around, albeit in the United States and not in Europe, but that is a transfer that almost epitomises PSG in this era. They made all the right moves and impressed all the right people but eventually the light at the end of the tunnel was shut away from them because of financial reasons.

With Crescent now gone and the legal battle between the club and the City of Paris ongoing, the players visited the Parc des Princes for the very first time, despite not knowing if they were even going to be playing in the stadium at all for the club. They visited the stadium in February 1972, halfway through the season. Even at this point those players were not sure exactly how this was going to end for them or their club. Yet they managed to put it to one side and find a way to – eventually – pick up the results that helped them avoid the relegation places. The supporters were split on this ordeal, too. Some wanted to remain how they were, no name change or anything like that. Others, who wanted to just have a club in Paris whatever the cost, weren't fussed about the semantics. They simply just wanted to have a Parisian club so badly that they didn't seem to care how they got it or how they kept hold of it.

Paris Saint-Germain, Paris Football Club, it didn't matter to the latter set of fans, all they were interested in was a successful Paris club. The situation had become one that could not be repaired. The board of PSG did not want to change the name, while the City of Paris did not want to financially help a club that wasn't strictly 'Parisian', and thus wanted them to change their name to represent their city. In hindsight, the moment that PSG's board refused to comply and change their name, it was game over from that point on.

In April, the City of Paris made it very, very clear: no name change, no money. It really was as simple and as cut-throat as that, but PSG did not budge. 'If by any chance the members of your association refuse the appellation to change the name to Paris Football Club, or if the parent organisations oppose to this amendment, or even if your club does not maintain D1 status after this season, the repayment of the instalments financed by our subsidy will be made with your club,' was the actual line from the City of Paris, and while it was declared as a statement it was more of a threat, but the issue had become so heated and toxic that it was put to a vote.

If you thought that after one vote the issue would be sorted, think again. There was one vote, the first vote, that had to be cancelled because there was a miscount. Finally the situation was resolved; 1,191 voters were registered, 939 votes were actually cast with just 316 in favour of keeping the Saint-Germain name and 623 in favour of the conditions set by the City. For now, PSG had been saved. They had survived the name change but it also meant they lost their subsidised money from the City and, as the City had threatened once things got very heated, they lost the right to open up the Parc des Princes.

But that wasn't the end of it. The City didn't give up after that vote, they kept going and kept trying to have a Paris team that they wanted. The Paris FC side of the club, which had originally merged with Stade Saint-Germain to form Paris Saint-Germain, decided that it was to split away from PSG – with a nudge in this direction from the pressure from Parisian political figures – and reformed solely as Paris Football Club, exactly what the city had wanted from the start. The bitter split was finally settled in June of 1972 with the conditions that Paris Saint-Germain were given 800,000 francs over two seasons but would forfeit their squad, the right to play at the new Parc des Princes and, perhaps most surprising of all, would be relegated into Division 3 and given amateur status in place of CA Montreuil, the club that Paris FC merged with and was used as a reserve side. Paris FC, on the other hand, were given both PSG's professional players and the top-flight status, plus the exclusive right to play at le Parc in Division 1.

The finalised agreement was signed by Henri Patrelle, Guy Crescent and Pierre-Étienne Guyot, three men who had been integral to the initial formation of Paris Saint-Germain, but it was the former who signed as 'President of Paris Saint-Germain FC' while Crescent and Guyot signed as 'President and Vice-President of Paris Football Club'. Perhaps the most damning part of this saga wasn't the voting battles or the heated debates in the Paris general assembly or the clear political influence in the re-formation of Paris Football Club, but this from the Paris Saint-Germain club captain, Jean Djorkaeff, who said about the split, 'It was good in Saint-Germain. We felt at home. When we became Paris Football Club, we felt like lost, little children.'

While Guyot and Crescent claimed 'Paris FC will be a great club for the capital,' the new Paris Saint-Germain – what is known as PSG 72 – had to find a way back to the top of French football after being sent down three leagues having retained their top-flight status just mere months before. They had to find a way to rebuild, reform and regain the respect that they were earning from other clubs during the 1971/72 season, but with only an amateur status that was going to take a lot of time and a lot of resources. The majority of *socios* decided to stay within the Parisian parameters and supported Paris FC in Division 1, so add the fans to the list of things lost by Paris Saint-Germain in this saga. PSG had built themselves up in a short space of time to be a Division 1 team but now they had plummeted back down the leagues into amateur status and had to rebuild all over again.

Seventeen first-team players departed, 12 of whom went to Paris FC. Even the manager Pierre Phelipon left to take over at Bordeaux, eventually helping them to mid-table mediocrity, but he was already within the confines of the club. In hindsight, the logic was understandable. With 17 first-team players leaving and the youth players being pushed into the first team out of need more than necessity, who else would be better suited to this particular job than the club's youth coach, Robert Vicot? He had worked extensively with the very same players who were having to make the step up into the first team and he knew how he wanted to play: fast, exciting and high-pressing football, epitomised in a wonderful 7-0 home win against Concarneau. They followed that up with a 6-1 victory away at Rouen B, giving the impression that PSG were set to steamroller their way through Division 3, but it wouldn't exactly work out that way. Seven losses in the season meant that they only finished second in the table, behind Quevilly, a team who managed to beat PSG both home and away in this season by an aggregate score of 5-1. The northern club finished top of the division by six points and defensively were outstanding, conceding just 12 goals all campaign, yet their luck was about to completely turn upside down, with PSG proving to be the main benefactor. Quevilly were suffering from major financial issues, which wasn't uncommon for teams at that level, and couldn't afford to upgrade their stadium to the required standards of Division 2, meaning they had to announce that they had to cancel their own promotion.

As a result, Paris Saint-Germain were promoted in their place. It was the lifeline that PSG needed. They were expected to run roughshod over the league and to gain promotion in style and with very little trouble, but while they had style and were an entertaining side they lost out to Quevilly before the reversal of the promotion. Had PSG not been promoted via default, how much of the future would have been changed? They needed to get promoted and they found themselves in the same position they had a few seasons previously: planning for a new season in Division 2 with the main goal of reaching Division 1, preferably at the first attempt. But there was something different about the following season that could easily be pointed towards being the exact moment that PSG became PSG. They had young and talented players coached by a very intelligent man in Robert Vicot and a president who knew what he wanted from his football club, but they didn't have the same swagger or presence of a Parisian club. The 1973/74 season can be seen as the one when Paris Saint-Germain changed their identity to what we know it as today, and it all changed thanks to someone famed for his work within the fashion world. What could be more Parisian than that?

The 1973 Paris Cup Final was a day that should be remembered as one of the most important days in the history of Paris Saint-Germain. Yes, the club won the regional tournament 1-0 against Poissy thanks to another goal from that season's top scorer, Christian André, his 27th in all competitions, but it was more than just a cup win and a triumph to celebrate alongside their promotion. It was the day that the club moved into a new realm. As the players and coach Vicot were celebrating in the dressing room, a group of six suave and confident-looking men strode into what can only be presumed as a happy yet hygienically terrible room. Jean-Paul Belmondo, Francis Borelli, Charles Talar and Bernard Brochand entered before the two other men followed – the fashion designer Daniel Hechter and France footballing god Just Fontaine. The players, still experiencing the high of winning the Paris Cup, were taken aback. They all looked at the star with awe, respect and admiration, but they still didn't know why Fontaine, or any of the other men, were in their dressing room. Was it to congratulate them? No. The group were there to take over. Hechter, born and raised in Paris, was desperate to force his way into the football scene in France and had been trying to seek out a team to invest in and control for a while. He tried Red Star and Sedan, but to no avail.

He tried Paris FC as well, but felt that Paris Saint-Germain would be the easiest option because of their position and situation they had just moved away from. Hechter had financially invested in the club in May 1973, hence the visit into the winning dressing room, but he would later go on to become the president of the management committee (containing Belmondo, Borelli, Talar and Brochand) while Henri Patrelle retained his title as president. To avoid another potential lawsuit with Paris FC, the club name of Paris Saint-Germain and the club colours of red, white and blue (les Rouge et Bleu being PSG's nickname) were now protected by contract, putting the club in a much more secure and stable position going forward. The colours were symbolic even in themselves. The red and blue symbolised Paris and nods towards French Revolution figures Lafayette and Jean Sylvain Bailly while the white symbolised French royalty and the region of Saint-Germain-en-Laye.

The next changes were the badge and the kits. The colour of the kits – red, white and blue – remained the same but the design changed thanks to the work of Hechter. Hechter designed a blue shirt with a red bar running down the middle of the shirt, framed and flanked by white lines, giving the club the same kind of shirt that they wear today, with every design from then on more or less following the same style. The location of the red bar may change, but the design and colours of the home shirt remain the same. Depending on what you read and who you believe, the inspiration for the shirt varies. Some say that Hechter was inspired by the design of the kits of Dutch side Ajax, who were just becoming dominant in the European Cup around this time, but instead of red and white Hechter changed it to match up with the colours of the French flag. However, Hechter himself provided a different explanation:

'In the street, I saw a Ford Mustang with its central strip on the hood which extends on the roof and I transposed that. I started to draw and I found this central band on the jersey when, at the time, the bands were horizontal. Only Ajax Amsterdam had a central strip; some even believed that I was inspired by it, which was not the case. I presented my sketches to the club committee, everyone found the jersey superb. Two years later, an Italian magazine estimated that the PSG outfit was the most beautiful in Europe.'

Having the style of your iconic kits inspired by a Ford Mustang might be the most 1970s reason ever, but it might also be the coolest, so you can either believe the rumours about the Ajax inspiration or the Ford Mustang inspiration from Hechter himself.

Next, the club crest was to be changed, and this would end up being one of the more symbolic and important alterations in the history of the club. The original crest was simply a blue ball with a red ship inside of one of the hexagons because, in the Paris coat of arms, a white vessel is in the centre and it was the club's way of showing their

Parisian roots, but the Hechter era crest was completely different. A blue circle with a red Eiffel Tower had a white cradle underneath the base of the tower with the fleur-de-lis on it. The fleur-de-lis was used by French royalty to represent nobility while the cradle was in reference to the birth of King Louis XIV, who was born in Saint-Germain-en-Laye.

While Patrelle was still technically president, the day-to-day running of the club was more down to Hechter and his entourage who made up the management committee with Patrelle essentially acting as an adviser and making sure Hechter didn't run the club into the ground. However, the first decision that Hechter made concerning actual sporting matters was one that shocked France and made waves across the nation, exactly what he had intended to do. Just Fontaine was appointed as co-manager alongside Vicot. Why keep Vicot? Fontaine was a big name and the idea was that he would inspire his players, but Vicot knew the club and knew the players, so it only made sense to keep him on even if it was in a diminished role or as an assistant manager.

A new wave of players were signed, including Brazilian Armando Monteiro, an imposing striker who was more adept at scoring with his head than perhaps any other part of his anatomy. Following Monteiro was François M'Pelé, not quite the Pelé the club had been trying to sign a season ago but still a very talented one nonetheless, as his time at PSG showed. Hailing from the Congo and only joining in December of the 1973/74 season, he still had a huge effect on PSG.

The reign of Fontaine opened up in typical goalscoring fashion that was befitting of the great man himself.

'Irresistible' was how they were described by the press who kept a close eye on proceedings, with PSG being faster, quicker, smarter and better all round than Béziers in beating them 4-1, even if Just Fontaine himself was trying to keep the plaudits to a minimum, saying, 'Let's not get carried away, I said it already: this season should be a transition season.' And he was right. Due to the lack of supreme financial support – despite the money Hechter had invested into the club – Fontaine felt that he couldn't spend a lot, saying in an interview many years later, 'For the price of a fingernail of a player today, I had to make a team.' But that was exactly why Vicot was kept on: to improve the players that the club already had.

Hechter invested into the playing squad but not to a level that filled Fontaine with immediate hopes of another promotion. But while Fontaine was trying not to get too carried away, the players had other ideas, albeit for a brief period of time at the start of the season. The win against Béziers was followed up by defeating Toulouse with another stunning and breathtaking attacking display then taking care of Toulon 1-0 and Angoulême 3-2, finishing this run of games at the top of Division 2. Their opening four games resulted in four wins, but between the Angoulême victory and Christmas, PSG would only win five more times. They lost seven, including a fixture against Sète that Paris Saint-Germain had actually won but had the win taken from them due to an issue surrounding the registration of a player who didn't even play in the match himself. The rule in France at the time was clubs had to have one player under the age of 21 on their team sheet. They didn't have to play him or sub him on; they just had to have him with the squad and have him registered as a substitute. Fontaine and Vicot named a young 18-year-old by the name of Christian Quéré on the squad with, a defender who was known for being quiet and reserved, eventually making only eight appearances for the club. But he never arrived. As the story goes, the young man missed the flight that the team took to Sète and therefore wasn't able to be on the bench, despite being registered as part of the matchday squad. PSG won the game 2-0 but the record books will show that Sète were awarded the 3-0 victory.

In the midst of that indifferent and inconsistent run of form and results, a big day happened for Paris Saint-Germain that went exactly to plan. One of their five wins prior to Christmas was in a Paris derby against Red Star, but it wasn't a usual city encounter that PSG had come to expect. It was a momentous one and took place in the brand-new arena built in the Porte de Saint-Cloud region. It was the first game that Paris Saint-Germain had played at the Parc des Princes.

While the game between PSG and Red Star took place as the opening act for Paris FC's Division 1 clash against Sochaux, that didn't seem to bother the players or the fans. Red Star came into the game as the unbeaten league leaders but found that they were no match for a Parisian side well and truly buoyed by the 33,872 fans in attendance. PSG won 3-1, and the fans in le Parc that day were suitably pleased. Reports suggested that following the Paris FC game, fans were pleased with the fact that Paris had produced two teams capable of playing exciting, entertaining football. But it was PSG who set the tone for history, starting off the tradition of warming up prior to kick-off in front of the Boulogne end of the stadium.

The game at the Parc des Princes seemed to be a welcome sign for PSG, who needed a boost at that particular time in the league. It was sandwiched between the infamous loss against Sète and another disappointing 2-1 defeat against Mantes and leaving them in a tough position with their fixtures. Such was the inconsistency of the team, they hadn't won two games in a row since September and hadn't even managed to draw a game since October. Their next draw wouldn't be until mid-January, but, after that, PSG's form started to turn positively.

Châteauroux and Red Star were the only two teams to hand out defeats to les Rouge et Bleu between January to the end of the regular season in May, with PSG winning ten games. At the start of the run, a home game against Ajaccio, who were fourth in the table. By the time they squared off against Vittel on 15 May they had already wrapped up second place behind Red Star, who finished just four points clear. They beat Vittel with a convincing 2-0 win which, despite a relatively close scoreline, wasn't in doubt.

The fact that PSG had sealed up second place meant that they secured a place in a play-off with Valenciennes to see who would go up into Division 1. The play-off structure worked differently in 1973/74 to how it does now, with no relegation play-off needed. In modern Ligue 1 seasons, the team that finished third bottom of Ligue 1 played against the team that finished third in Ligue 2 and the winner would either stay in Ligue 1 or earn promotion to the top flight. In 1973/74, however, Division 2 was split up into two tables, Group A and Group B. Lille finished top of Group A and earned themselves a tie against Red

Star, who finished top of Group B, while Valenciennes and Paris Saint-Germain went head-to-head in a battle of the runners-up. It was a huge game for PSG, who were already exceeding everyone's expectations including their own manager who said at the start of the season that it was just a 'transition season'. Lille eventually ended up coasting through their tie against Red Star, losing the first leg 2-0 at the Stade de Paris but trouncing their opponents 5-0 on home soil, leaving it up to the runners-up to fight it out for that final place.

Valenciennes, who had knocked Paris Saint-Germain out of the Coupe de France a few seasons ago in embarrassing fashion, had found themselves relegated from Division 1 and rebuilding in the second tier, led by their coach and former Paris Saint-Germain midfielder Jean-Pierre Destrumelle. Destrumelle was previously the reserve team manager at PSG before their split and left the club instead of following Paris FC to take over Valenciennes, getting them to within touching distance of a return to Division 1. All that stood between him, his club and a top-flight return was his former employers, who were also looking for a return to Division 1 in much more sensational fashion. Back-to-back promotions is hard enough to do when you have a fully functioning club behind you, let alone when you have a rookie manager rebuilding after relegation into the amateur divisions, trying to work the club's way back into relevancy while the club that had taken its place was revelling in what Division 1 had to offer.

And, rather predictably, as tends to be the case with high-stake games, the first half of the first leg was quite tense in the opening exchanges and from PSG's point of view, that was understandable. Reports were suggesting that, at the start of the season, Daniel Hechter had essentially managed to get a sponsorship deal with Radio RTL for the following season under one condition: that PSG were playing in Division 1. It was a move that would help the club financially if it came off but also produced a lot of unwanted pressure throughout the campaign – despite Fontaine saying it was a transition season. If PSG won promotion, 1.2m francs would be coming their way but if they lost, it may have spelt another barren spell for the club when they looked certain to be getting themselves back on track.

But while the game and the atmosphere was tense, the match itself was quite open with PSG attacking with free will. Most people, reporters and fans mainly, had expected the Parisians to keep the score to a minimum for the second leg, where they would be expected to win the tie overall. That was the general thought and consensus on how PSG's game plan would play out, but when they opened the scoring after 22 minutes through François M'Pelé it surprised a few. When they kept creating chance after chance, it felt like the Parisians were going to be heading back to the capital with a good win under their belts, even if the half-time scoreline of 1-0 should have and could have been a lot more convincing. At 1-0 the game is well and truly in the balance but at 2-0 or 3-0, as PSG should have been leading, it would have more or less been lights out for Valenciennes. But this is football, it is never simple. Just when you think you have all the answers, the beautiful game comes and changes the questions.

It was at the hour mark when the game turned on its head after the hosts came out of the half-time break with more verve, more passion and a bit more fight as Patrick Jeskowiak, one of the attacking threats in the Valenciennes team, levelled before the Polish striker Erwin Wilczek scored a penalty that created an uproar on the field. PSG's Jean-Louis Leonetti eventually said, 'The referee directed the life of the two clubs this evening, he could have been more serene and not be caught in such childishness on the penalty,' and judging by this reaction, it was a controversial decision to say the least. Valenciennes had pulled ahead and eventually ran out 2-1 winners, leaving PSG having to go home, set up camp at the Parc des Princes and overturn a deficit that, as Hechter's deal with RTL made clear, could either make or break the club all over again.

Hechter sat on the touchline among the substitutes and his coaches Robert Vicot and Just Fontaine, puffing on his cigar, as a ball of many emotions. Nervousness. Anxiousness. Excitement. Hechter felt it. You could see it in his face just before kick-off. He understood just how important this game was to the club. To Paris. To his own reputation. To help guide a team into Division 1 is an incredible accomplishment, and Hechter wanted to feel the happiness and jubilation of adding another Parisian club to the top flight. You could see in his eyes how nervous he was but the rest of the team, as they emerged from the tunnel, looked focused. They looked like they knew exactly what they had to do: win by two clear goals. Le Parc, with just under 20,000 fans in the stands, was ready for what could have either been an incredible promotion party or the second funeral for the Parisian club in three years, but no one was expecting that.

Hechter, still smoking his cigar on the bench, let out a sigh. The referee blew his whistle and the game was under way. PSG started on the front foot, pushing their agenda and looking to strike as early as they could. It was a surprisingly fast-paced affair with both teams taking as few touches on the ball as possible in order to keep play moving, something that worked to perfection when François M'Pelé took a touch on the edge of the 18-yard box, did a half turn with his body to create a better angle for the shot and fired the ball into the back of the net. PSG had got one goal and were halfway to reaching their objective. One more goal and they would be promoted.

But while the focus remained on Paris Saint-Germain, with their star head coach and famous president on the sidelines, Valenciennes had completely taken a back seat in this affair. They were the ones with the advantage, leading on aggregate after their 2-1 win in the first leg. They held the keys to PSG's destiny, and equalised four minutes after M'Pelé opened the scoring. A complete mess at the back from PSG after failing to clear a poor corner resulted in Pierre Neubert, who was unmarked at the back post, nodding the ball into an empty net. It wasn't the end of the world but it made PSG's job a lot harder. Half-time came and the bench was not feeling any better. The nerves were still written all over the face of Hechter, while Fontaine continued to bark orders at his troops who themselves were on the brink of losing their composure.

They were shouting at and questioning each other following the Valenciennes equaliser and looking like the pressure was getting to them. In the dressing room the players looked exhausted, perhaps not just physically, but more mentally than anything else. They had a look of 'what more do we have to do' but Fontaine could only encourage them to keep going. A handful of goals in the next 45 minutes, then they could complete their mission. Valenciennes came out after the break pushing harder, looking to hit PSG on the break and catch them when their guard was down. PSG themselves had a couple of efforts, tame ones, but Valenciennes hit a potentially fatal blow after 48 minutes. Erwin Wilczek was left all alone in the box without a defender around him and slid the ball underneath Jacky Planchard, the PSG goalkeeper. At 1-1, the game was salvageable but at 2-1 to Valenciennes, it represented more of an uphill task than anything PSG had faced in their history up until this point. They needed to pick themselves up off the floor and find a way to get back into the game. They kept creating chances, but they kept failing to put them away, until M'Pelé played a pass into the path of the onrushing Jean-Pierre Dogliani who managed to stretch his big toe out far enough to beat the ball past the Valenciennes goalkeeper, and now the game was back level.

'Paris, Paris, Paris' sang the home fans as they willed their side on, knowing that the situation now reverted back to the original task at hand. Two more Paris goals and PSG would be back in the top flight. Just after the hour PSG pulled ahead and, once again, it was a little slipped finish under the goalkeeper's body, with the shot leaving the foot of Michel Marella, a man who wasn't even signed to a professional contract and used to work in a children's clothing store. One goal. One more goal. One more goal separated Paris Saint-Germain and top-flight French football, and they had plenty of time to get it.

It simply wouldn't be PSG if a vital match was settled without any drama and no contentious decisions at all, and that wouldn't change in this one either. The ball was lofted over the Valenciennes back line, who played an offside trap to perfection. Each man stepped up on time, with the line keeping shape throughout the move. Dogliani raced on to the ball and was open in the box. There wasn't anyone separating Dogliani and goalkeeper Escale, with the back line all stepping up with their arms raised, appealing to the linesman for an offside call. Surely the official would raise his flag, play would stop and Valenciennes would take any momentum and sting out of the game?

Dogliani wasn't deterred by their protests as he bore down on goal knowing he would have to do something spectacular to beat Escale from there. His body swerved to the left, the goalkeeper followed, but the ball stayed still. Dogliani's deft feint had tricked Escale and the move had left the forward with an empty net to tap the ball into. It's the type of move that, if performed in a European Cup Final or at a World Cup, would be remembered by millions across the world and replicated on playgrounds, school fields and by every opponent in Europe, but while Dogliani and his team-mates ran into the left-hand corner flag to celebrate what could be the most important goal in the young, infant years of the club, Valenciennes were seething. Escale sprinted to the touchline as if he was competing in a 100m race at the Olympics but, instead of the prize of a gold medal, his reward was the opportunity to roar in the face of the officials.

Dogliani's feint and finish is a joy to watch in slow motion, but so are the protestations after the goal. Escale running like a tiger finding its prey, referee Wurtz literally leaping out of the grasp of one of the Valenciennes players who will undoubtedly claim he was just looking for a simple explanation. To add insult to injury for Escale, the ref's leap of faith took him to the touchline where he was booked for his protests. The goal seemed to seal the match there and then. PSG were on cloud nine and felt that nothing could stop the inevitable – the inevitable being promotion – while the visitors felt so hard done by that they couldn't muster up the strength to fight back. So when the final whistle went, it was officially confirmed. Paris Saint-Germain had found their way back into Division 1, the top flight of French football. After essentially being kicked out of professional football by the City of Paris, the team that Henri Patrelle had stuck by had finally returned to where Patrelle and the club felt that they belonged.

Just like before kick-off, the fans in the Parc des Princes were chanting 'Paris, Paris, Paris' over and over again. For a city that was hungry for a successful football team, this was about as close to success as you could get outside of Division 1, and with Paris FC not having a night like this in their short history, it proved to be a huge night for PSG. Not only had they won, but they overcame any odds that were stacked against them, and the fans in the stadium, whether they were original PSG supporters or Parisians thirsting for a football fix, had been treated to an outstanding game.

The Paris Saint-Germain bench erupted at the final whistle, with Hechter, Vicot and Fontaine embracing, and running on to the pitch at the same time, mobbed by cameras and reporters wanting to capture the exact moment of jubilation from three architects of this triumph. Escale was still raving at the referee, demanding an answer as to why Dogliani wasn't flagged as offside – perhaps the fact he got sold so easily on a dummy added to the fact he was probably trying to place the blame elsewhere – but no one in red and blue cared. Such was the intensity of the celebrations, Fontaine suffered a heart attack but thankfully survived and carried on in his post as co-manager.

The celebrations from the players, who continued with their laps of honour around the Parc des Princes pitch, carried on way into the night but others at the club knew that, while PSG had won the battle in Division 2, they had to win the war in Division 1 and immediately went about planning how they would attack French football's elite once again. Who would they sign? Who would they sell? Where would they play? Who would be manager? There wasn't a single easy answer to any of those questions and the likes of Patrelle, Hechter, Vicot and the recovering Fontaine knew this. While the players basked in the glowing light of their incredible comeback win over Valenciennes, the powers that be set about trying to plan far ahead.

4

La Renaissance – The return

'PARIS IN the promised land but after a massive struggle' read the headline of the following day's *L'Equipe*. It had been a struggle for PSG, both on and off the pitch. Their first game in Division 1 was back in August of 1971, but between then and the heroic and triumphant promotion play-off victory against Valenciennes the club had changed drastically in such a short space of time. In June, Henri Patrelle departed as president and was named as honorary president, but the falling out between he and Hechter wasn't pleasant at all.

Patrelle was looking to help and support Paris FC, the club that was formed following the original battle with the City of Paris a few years ago and had just been relegated to Division 2 the same season that PSG had earned promotion to Division 1, but Hechter refused to provide any sort of help. Hechter was still bitter and angry at Paris FC for not helping his club when PSG needed it the most and flat out refused to do anything to assist PFC. The involvement of Patrelle in wanting to help Paris FC was linked to his ties to the French Football Federation

(FFF), but Hechter's refusal to lend a helping hand to the cash-stricken Paris FC meant two things: Paris FC lost their status as a professional club and lost the use of the Parc des Princes (moving to Porte de Montreuil, not too far from the site of the old Bastille prison), and the departure of Patrelle from the club in an official capacity.

With his kit in place and his personnel more heavily involved both on and off the pitch, Hechter was slowly making the club his own with the assistance of his 'gang' – as *France Football* called them – in particular Francis Borelli who had stepped up significantly in the first few years of the Hechter era and was helping to shape their image as the premier Parisian club. His appointment, Just Fontaine, had managed to stay on despite his scare at the end of the Valenciennes thriller and the acquisition of Algerian superstar Mustapha Dahleb managed to be the statement signing of this season that Hechter wanted to make. Hechter wanted to make the other clubs feel like Paris Saint-Germain had arrived in Division 1, not just to make up the numbers, not just to compete, but to take over.

A fee of 1.35m francs was, in 1974, a French record. At the time it was a massive move to make, especially for a player like Dahleb. But while it was a lot of money, it was a price that was clearly worth paying considering how good Dahleb was. Future France manager Raymond Domenech – who would spend a brief time at PSG later on in his career – was playing for Lyon at the time of Dahleb's arrival and was clearly a big fan, 'I have a soft spot for Mustapha Dahleb, who marked his era. He had an exceptional talent, he is a creator who has the profile of the players we are talking about today like Messi. Dahleb had genius above all, he was capable of anything. He's the best player in PSG history.' Bear in mind that Domenech was speaking in the mid-2010s, so PSG had some pretty sizeable stars by that time, yet he remained insistent on his love of Dahleb.

Dahleb was the youngest player in France to get a pro trainee contract (at the age of 14) and became professional at 17, despite having to convince his own father that football was the career path for him. Eventually having to return to Algeria for his military service in 1971, Dahleb was back at Sedan two years later a completely different being. His 17 goals in 27 games for Sedan weren't enough to save them from relegation but were enough for Dahleb to earn himself a move to newly promoted PSG, who were looking for a major signing to confirm their re-entry into the French top flight, beating Reims, Belgian club Anderlecht and Real Madrid to his signature. Hechter had gotten his star signing, PSG had the focal point of their team and they felt ready to take on Division 1. Dahleb was perhaps the first star player of Paris Saint-Germain, the first player that the club had signed who made people look in their direction in an envious way, the first player who neutrals would pay hard-earned money just to watch his wizardry on the ball.

With the signing of Dahleb, PSG felt like they were making the right moves forward. They weren't in a position to challenge for the league title straight away but the capture of Dahleb signalled two things: they were able to attract star names and they were now the premier Parisian club. With Paris FC now dwindling in Division 2, the name and look of Paris Saint-Germain allowed them to stand out among the other Parisian clubs, and the newly reformed competition called the Tournoi de Paris was the perfect opportunity for PSG (and mainly Hechter) to flex their muscles in front of a wider audience.

The Tournoi de Paris was a pre-season friendly tournament that held the template for future competitions like the Intercontinental Cup and the FIFA Club World Cup where the best teams from across the globe would turn out and play each other and be unofficially announced as the 'best team in the world'. Founded in 1957 by Racing Paris to celebrate their 25th birthday, Racing invited Real Madrid, Brazilian club Vasco da Gama and Rot-Weiss Essen from Germany to compete, with Vasco beating Racing and Alfredo Di Stéfano's Madrid to be crowned winners. A few years later, with the aid of inspiration from the Tournoi de Paris, the Intercontinental Cup was created and that competition alongside the Tournoi de Paris allowed teams from South America to pit themselves, albeit unofficially, against top European sides.

But while the Tournoi had influenced other nations and confederations, it had a stop-start life. Running from 1957 to 1966, it was then halted until 1973 when Paris FC brought the competition back, finishing third behind Feyenoord and Bayern Munich but ahead of Marseille. There was no Tournoi in 1974 but Hechter wanted to bring it back in 1975 perhaps for no other reason than because he could. Valencia and Sporting Lisbon flew in from Spain and Portugal respectively while Brazilians Fluminense also made the trek to play the Parisians in the Parc des Princes. But while this particular edition of the Tournoi is rather insignificant, it did manage to birth one of the greatest myths in the history of Paris Saint-Germain and it all centred around a man who appeared for PSG in this Tournoi de Paris, but never actually played for the club at any stage in his career.

Adidas parties, much like any other party held by a global fashion and sporting corporation, are the same thing. There is food, there is drink, there are many famous faces who know each other well enough to have a small conversation but perhaps not well enough to know exactly what they do or even what their name is. But in 1975, at a party hosted by Adidas, everyone knew Daniel Hechter. His fashion was everywhere and anybody who was anybody owned something made from the Hechter brand, while some even wore the clothes themselves.

One of those Hechter wearers was none other than Johan Cruyff. A year removed from his incredible performance with the Total Football brand of Dutch football at the 1974 World Cup in West Germany, Cruyff was recovering from his first full season at Barcelona and had just been named European Footballer of the Year months prior. There was no one better in the world of football in the summer of 1975 than Johan Cruyff. Cruyff enjoyed the work of Hechter in the fashion world and when the two met at one of the Adidas parties, they struck up a friendship. Cruyff was a fan of Hechter and his fashion; Hechter was a fan of Cruyff and his football. It was a match made in heaven. So when the two started to chat a bit more, the topic of playing for Paris Saint-Germain came up, but not on a permanent basis.

As Hechter said many years afterwards, 'When I asked him to come and strengthen Paris Saint-Germain for the tournament, he said yes immediately.' Cruyff had agreed to play for PSG in the Tournoi de Paris, not for money, not to swap a life in Catalonia for one in Paris, but to help his friend out and to simply play football. There was no money exchanged, but a range of Hechter's fashion designs were given to Cruyff as a 'thank you' from the president. Manager Just Fontaine was taken aback by the situation and when Hechter asked whether he wanted to manage Cruyff, Fontaine replied by saying 'obviously'.

Naturally the rumour mill started to churn and Cruyff to PSG was formulated. Cruyff wasn't planning on leaving Barcelona and PSG couldn't afford his fee or his wages, so that transfer was dead in the water immediately, but you can't blame the Paris fans and media for wanting to believe it to be true. Who wouldn't want the European Footballer of the Year at their club? But they had to make do with Cruyff playing for PSG in the Tournoi alongside another guest in the shape of Yugoslavia captain and Red Star Belgrade superstar Dragan Džajić, who had just recently signed for Bastia and was once described by Pelé as a 'Balkan miracle – a real wizard. I'm just sorry he's not Brazilian because I've never seen such a natural footballer.' Of course, it's a very Pelé thing to do to lavish praise on someone he probably never saw play, but the point that Džajić was a top player was there to be seen by all and while he certainly wasn't as big a name as Cruyff was, the PSG players certainly didn't treat the duo any differently once they arrived in Paris.

'When you find yourself next to these guys, you shouldn't pour into fanaticism. I avoided asking for an autograph or a photo,' said defender Jean-Marc Pilorget, who was only 17 years old at the time. François Brisson, the striker who was also 17 but younger than Pilorget by four whole days, said, 'I was young! I went directly to Cruyff to ask him for an autograph.' In fact, Éric Renaut says he still has his photo up in his home of himself with Cruyff and Džajić, proudly displayed for all to see. And this just shows what PSG was like as a club at the time. It was still young and still learning, experiencing what it was like to be in the company of elite players, while the players themselves were going through the same experiences too. The players were excited to share a dressing room alongside one of the all-time greats in Johan Cruyff and naturally wanted a souvenir to remember the occasion by. It was a friendly tournament and he wasn't even technically their own player, so they were allowed to let their hair down.

Cruyff looked genuinely happy to be involved. His big, beaming smile was noticeable straight away, regardless of who he was standing next to, and by all accounts his style of play mirrored his emotions as well. Most players would run, sprint, jog or walk around the pitch, especially in a friendly tournament such as the Tournoi, but Cruyff floated, according to those involved. The sheer elegance of the man was enough to impress his new and temporary team-mates, with Fontaine saying to him, 'Play as you want, wherever you want,' and Cruyff did.

Perched in his favourite position of being just behind the main striker, the Dutch maestro inspired Paris to a 3-1 victory over Sporting Lisbon and set up a clash against Valencia in front of around 40,000 fans in le Parc on Thursday, 19 June. But those 40,000 fans, for whatever reason, weren't happy with Cruyff. Every time he touched the ball it was greeted with a thunderous chorus of boos and whistles, with the locals perhaps upset that the great man wasn't joining permanently and rather just playing in this tournament. Did the boos and whistles get to Cruyff? Maybe so, as Valencia won the final 1-0 and were crowned champions of the Tournoi de Paris 1975, but the focus was still on Cruyff – as it always was – and he even gave a short explanation and apology to the Parisian players. 'I'm sorry, I'm tired because I had a difficult season. A month ago, I even had to go to bed. I didn't have enough training and I only played one game,' and just like that, both Cruyff and Džajić rode off into the sunset, never to actually sign for PSG, almost like a summer romance that leads to nowhere but eventually spirals off into its own tale. The summer of 1975 will be remembered by PSG fans as the one where Cruyff nearly joined despite never looking to permanently sign for the club, but why debunk a myth that's harmless and people find fun? It probably didn't actually serve PSG any good during their return season back in Division 1 because they had spent a few games playing with a team built and thriving off of a man who wasn't going to be there when the competitive games eventually did kick off.

With the Tournoi successfully over and Cruyff back in Barcelona, Division 1 was around the corner and the opening match saw PSG travel to Montbéliard to play Sochaux, which they won 1-0 thanks to Christian André's goal and the heroics of goalkeeper Ilija Pantelić, who joined in the summer from Bastia. It was exactly the kind of start that PSG had hoped for and, although the performance itself may not have been exceptional, the final result certainly was.

But despite that opening-day win, PSG were brought thundering back down to earth the following week by a humbling and humiliating 6-1 defeat away at Reims, with all six goals scored by a 24-year-old striker from Buenos Aires by the name of Carlos Bianchi, who could only be described as a complete and utter goal machine and who would play a huge part in the history of Paris Saint-Germain further down the line. In the 1974/75 season he was just the scourge of the club and the scorer of plenty of goals. What made the 6-1 loss even worse was that François M'Pelé had given PSG the lead after 16 minutes and Bianchi levelled things up eight minutes later. By the 69th minute the destruction was complete and PSG were left to travel all the way back to Paris bruised – both mentally and physically – embarrassed and with a stark warning from Division 1 mainstays and veterans. This wasn't a league where you could take games off, and PSG knew that.

It's more than likely that the adjustment time from being the team to beat in Division 2 to becoming an underdog almost every week was getting to them, as their next two results showed. A home draw against Metz wasn't the end of the world, on the face of it, but when you look at how the game panned out you realise it was a missed opportunity that they couldn't afford so early on in the season. The complexion could have been so much different if they had just held on to their two-goal lead but by the 50th minute the score was level and PSG were chasing a result rather than securing one.

Two wins out of their first three games would have been admirable and very, very promising. But one win, one draw and a terribly humiliating loss was what it read in the record books. Could they make something out of their next away game, a trip up north to Lille and to the estimated 10,000 fans crammed into the Stade Henri-Jooris? After ten minutes the likelihood of PSG grabbing a win looked slim, and after 23 minutes the situation looked even bleaker when they trailed 2-0. It wasn't a disaster, but it wasn't what was needed. Fontaine and Vicot had lined the team up in a defensive mindset, looking to nullify Lille and essentially dominate the game by doing nothing. Lille restricted Paris to long-range efforts that troubled no one other than the spectators multiple rows back behind the goal, and the hosts played with more flair, more style and more attacking intent, which eventually came to fruition in a dazzling three-minute spell which saw them score three goals amid a complete capitulation from the visitors. Stanislav Karasi, a Yugoslavian striker who signed for Lille after many strong years at Red Star Belgrade, opened the flurry before doubling his tally three minutes later just after René Riefa had made it 4-0. The game finished 5-0 and another away-day humiliation for PSG. Fontaine leapt to the defence of his back line, saying, 'We must not criticise the defence. We dominated the ball for 30 minutes and if we had scored, the match could have been completely different.'

We will never know whether that may have been the case but for PSG, it was two losses out of four to start their return back to Division 1 and they were giving fans plenty of reasons as to why they shouldn't be there. A lack of service to the forwards didn't help and setting up to sit back and control a game and soak up pressure defensively is useless if your defenders struggle to contain teams that have dynamic, exciting and pacy players. There wasn't much to inspire hope either. PSG had the chance to redeem themselves at the Parc des Princes with the visit of Angers, but two minutes into the game Angers had already taken the lead. A shaky defence had been made even more nervous by the tension in the stands at the recent performances (3,000 fans decided not to return from the 2-2 draw with Metz, deciding it would serve them better to stay away than watch the team), which in turn led to even more nerves among the players which was firmly exposed with the ease at which Angers opened the scoring. Luckily for PSG, they had François M'Pelé, who fired back immediately. Three minutes in, two goals, one for each side and Just Fontaine was pulling his hair out on the sidelines. The equaliser woke Paris up.

Mustapha Dahleb decided to take the game by the scruff of the neck and controlled the first half, wasting a good chance as it became evidently clear that the next goal would go in favour of the hosts. Chance after chance was created and subsequently missed, so the feeling of that second Paris goal became more inevitable as the clock ticked. Alas, that wasn't the case, for that would simply be too easy and predictable for this Paris Saint-Germain side. Make your domination count and go into the half-time break with a well-earned and fully deserved lead? Not on your life! The Paris defence tried to play offside, albeit unsuccessfully, allowing Angers' Boško Antić to sneak in and give his side the lead. Somehow, PSG had managed to dominate a game yet go behind twice. If it wasn't a concern before, it was certainly a concern now.

The second half started with PSG pressing hard to get back into the game, but yet again failing to take whatever chances they created. Then it was the turn of Angers to control the ball and fail to take advantage. Regardless of the score, the crowd at le Parc was thoroughly entertained by the game, with its fast-flowing football and seemingly endless attacking play.

Eventually, on 70 minutes, M'Pelé equalised. He could have chosen to pass to Dahleb but didn't. He could have chosen to pass to Dogliani, who had hit the post minutes beforehand, but didn't. He went it alone, capitalised on the mistakes made by the Angers defence and brought PSG level. M'Pelé did it again ten minutes later, grabbing the win and completing his hat-trick. To say it was a boring match would be a lie. To say it was a complete, composed and all-round excellent display from Paris Saint-Germain would also be a lie. Regardless, it got the job done. It brought two valuable points (this was still the era of two points for a win and the era of bonus points, which would be eliminated in the 1976/77 campaign while three points for a win was introduced in 1988/89) and helped PSG start to move forward and form a semi-decent and competitive side. They had seven players out injured for this game while Pantelić was nursing a shoulder injury, yet was one of the most important players on the pitch that night against Angers. Fontaine himself said after the game, 'It is a victory of will and courage. Thank you to the public who encouraged us despite the difficulties.'

The win saw PSG into 14th place, about right for an inconsistent side although if you want to spin that into a positive light, they were only two points off of Reims, Marseille and Nîmes, who occupied first, second and third. Of course, this says more about the tightness of Division 1 than anything else, but it was an encouraging sign. However, in rather predictable fashion, PSG lost their next game 4-2 to Nice before bouncing back with a win at the Parc des Princes against Rennes, leaving them in 12th place but unable to string together a run of positive results.

At the turn of September they had already conceded 20 goals – the worst record in the league, ahead of Monaco who were on 18 goals – and had scored just 11. It wasn't good enough even if the performances weren't as bad as the results suggested at times. Just Fontaine was furious after the Nice loss and claimed that his side had deserved a draw but the constant theme throughout the return to Division 1 was blatantly obvious. PSG could play some wonderful and exciting attacking football, but couldn't defend and batten down the hatches when needed, hence their terrible defensive record. In 38 Division 1 games PSG only won consecutively twice, 3-1 at home to Lens in October and by the same scoreline at Troyes, while the second lot of back-to-back wins came in December against Reims and Metz. After the winter break, they only picked up 13 points compared to the 23 they won in the first half of the campaign. Seventeen goals were scored after Christmas but 40 beforehand.

PSG were 12th in the final round of Division 1 games of 1974, three points of a spot for the qualifying rounds of the UEFA Cup. They weren't favourites to jump into those places and steal a place from the teams around them, but it showed that if they could just manage to string together a good run of form and some decent consistency as the season went on then anything was possible. The three games that stand out when you go back and look at the results from the first half of the campaign were against rivals or the big teams in the league and where the measure of PSG's mental toughness and talent could be measured against the competition and teams that they wanted to compete with in the future.

First, a thrilling game against Lyon followed the 2-1 win against Rennes at the Stade Gerland and it was a chance for PSG to make a big step forward. Not only would a win have meant their first back-to-back victories since promotion, but it would have been a scalp of a traditional top side and sent a message out to those around them that they shouldn't be taken lightly. Their big threats came from sheer pace and skill of Dahleb and Louis Floch – a summer signing who was once described by an unnamed manager as 'worth nothing', with the same individual going on to add, 'If the gates of the Parc des Princes were wide open, Floch would miss them and end up in Boulogne-Billancourt.' Despite this damning assessment, Daniel Hechter bought him anyway and he helped to bamboozle the Lyon back line with Raymond and Albert Domenech being put into work and put into action immediately. Albert put the ball into his own net trying to clear a cross.

Lyon were shaky initially and the pace of PSG didn't help them to settle down. Floch should have scored a gilt-edged chance when he failed to convert a cross from Dahleb, and PSG were looking more and more unlikely to take advantage of their dominance, but with the help of another fine performance from Pantelić they were able to dodge Lyon bullets from every angle. Floch and Dahleb combined again to double PSG's lead with Dahleb making it three goals in two games (his brace against Rennes sealed the two points last time out) and PSG looked not only impressive but dominant too.

As the report in *L'Equipe* suggested, Fontaine wanted his players to go into 'overdrive' to get more goals instead of maintaining the lead that they already had. Perhaps he was fearful that against a team like Lyon, a two-goal advantage with his defence wouldn't be enough. On the other hand, it may just have been a case of Fontaine not knowing when to calm things down and the relative managerial experience started to seep its way through. Only time would tell, but when Jacky Novi scored a third, Fontaine looked vindicated. Such was the brilliance of Novi's goal, the home fans applauded a goal that they probably felt was the icing on the cake for PSG, who completely blew Lyon away. Disorganised defensively and unable to connect in attack, Lyon were shocking and weren't able to contribute to the game at all. On the flip side, PSG put in about as close to a perfect performance as you're likely to see.

Trailing 3-0 in front of their own fans looking like more goals were on the horizon, it's easy to see why the game looked out of sight for Lyon. The home supporters booed but their players reacted in the second half. They started stronger after the half-time interval, looking more compact and composed in the right areas, but still couldn't stop PSG adding a fourth just after the hour. Dogliani, who ran the show and moved the PSG players like they were his own personal chess pieces on a Stade Gerland-shaped chessboard, found M'Pelé and surely it was game over. Well, you would have thought so, but not quite. Bernard Lacombe, the legend of Lyon, pulled one back, just three minutes later, that seemed to galvanise the team and some of the fans who remained hopeful and faithful. Four minutes later Yves Mariot got another to bring it back to 4-2, and the momentum that the Parisians had was now lost.

The crowd was getting louder every touch of the ball and Lyon felt the game changing. PSG could too, but they were powerless to stop it. It was almost like they were stuck in time while being fully conscious of what was happening around them. They knew Lyon were coming at them with pace and force, but couldn't tackle, couldn't intercept, couldn't save, couldn't pass, couldn't do anything to prevent the inevitable. Making up for the mistake his brother made in the third minute, which now felt like a lifetime ago for Fontaine, Vicot, Hechter and PSG, Raymond Domenech got a third before Lacombe equalised at 4-4 in the 79th minute. PSG were stunned. With 23 minutes left of the game they had been cruising and were winning 4-0 but with 11 minutes left they were now all at sea and were drawing 4-4. No one could quite believe how that had happened.

Lyon were stunned at how they managed to pull off a four-goal comeback while PSG were qually as estunned as to how they managed to let their lead slip away like water running through their fingertips. One minute it was in their grasp and the very next it was completely gone. But it completely summed up exactly what this PSG side was: exciting, fast, entertaining and occasionally a deadly mix of being lethal in front of goal and efficient, while also having the defensive fragility to throw away a 4-0 lead away from home. Before the first whistle, PSG probably would have been OK with a point. But after a near-perfect first half and a collapse of Parisian-sized proportions they felt like they had been robbed out of a win. They only had themselves to blame.

After a 1-1 draw at home to Bastia and a 3-2 home loss to Nantes, PSG made the trip down south to face Marseille, who were aiming to challenge for the title and looking towards the likes of Saint-Étienne rather than Paris Saint-Germain. While there has always been animosity between those in the south and those in the capital, the rivalry wasn't quite what it is today and this being the first meeting since PSG returned to Division 1, it was always going to be an exciting fixture. And when Dahleb opened the scoring after 11 minutes it looked like the game was about to explode into life, but when legendary striker Josip Skoblar levelled a minute later, it opened up Marseille to flood PSG with attack after attack. Georges Eo put Marseille ahead before a second from Skoblar before half-time, with Albert Emon scoring the fourth and Dogliani grabbing a consolation for PSG a minute after Emon's goal. Just like the very first meeting between these two clubs, it ended 4-2 and PSG looked lost with even coach Fontaine saying after the game, 'We have given too many gifts to our opponents. I think we fought with ourselves and this is a problem that we all have to solve together.'

Fontaine himself reportedly requested total and unlimited access to his squad or else he would resign from his post as manager, and that seemed to work with the two back-to-back wins over Lens and Troyes coming in this period before a loss against Monaco at home that was only settled by an own goal from Jacky Novi. The third of the three tasty games was coming up, an away trip to the formidable Saint-Étienne, and PSG travelled in inconsistent form. Following the loss against Monaco, the Parisians bounced back with a win away at Bordeaux but, unsurprisingly, drew the follow-up at home to Nîmes. Would the Saint-Étienne game be a make or break moment? They had put in a fantastic showing for the first hour or so against Lyon and the Marseille game was one in which they shot themselves in the foot, so could they bring back a Lyon-style performance without the capitulation that was seen in both the Lyon and Marseille matches?

Well, it wasn't quite as disappointing as the Marseille performance nor was it a complete capitulation akin to what was seen against Lyon, but PSG did let a two-goal lead slip in the dying seconds of the game. François M'Pelé had given PSG the lead in the first quarter of the first half and they held on to that until the 73rd minute. The wildly popular (at least among Saint-Étienne fans) Argentinian defender Osvaldo Piazza levelled things up before the tide of the game turned yet again. Dahleb put PSG ahead with only nine minutes left, despite claims of him being offside, but reports suggest that he was right on the very edge of onside. This should have been enough for the win for PSG, but that would be far too simple for them. Hervé Revelli, one of seven players to have won Division 1 a joint-record seven times, popped up in the 89th minute with an equaliser to send the home fans wild.

But that wasn't the end of it. Just as the home fans had started to calm down and just as PSG were resigning themselves to just a point, when they had two in their hands, once again, they let victory slip away from their grasp. The Saint-Étienne scorer, Dominique Bathenay, would eventually go on to play for Paris Saint-Germain a few years later and would be a mainstay at the club for several years. But on 20 November 1974 he was no friend of PSG. Paris were furious. Not with themselves, but with the match officials. Reports of the game say that fights broke out at the full-time whistle and that there were allegations of the stoppage-time goals being over the time limit. PSG, leading up until stoppage time, threw the game away and weren't helped by what they claimed to be shoddy officiating.

It was the same old story for PSG against bigger teams from further up the table. They performed admirably and showed spectators that when all the wheels turned in the right direction, they could be an entertaining and threatening side. But they also showed that while they had fun and exciting attacking players, their defensive core let them down late on in games and from positions that you shouldn't drop points in. A good run of form of three wins, one draw and one loss before the winter break helped PSG's league position but they knew that they could have been higher up if they hadn't dropped points along the way. A hard-fought victory over Paris rivals Red Star in front of just under 30,000 fans at the Parc des Princes kicked off this mini run, but once they got back from the winter break – in 12th place in the table and seven points away from the relegation zone – their season was about to change. Their second half of this campaign was littered with disappointing results, but why was that? There's a good reason for the dip in form. It coincided with an outstanding run in the Coupe de France.

The Coupe de France and Paris Saint-Germain, up until February of 1975, was an almost non-existent relationship. In the 1973/74 season, the Parisians reached the quarter-finals where they would eventually lose 7-2 to Reims on aggregate (they lost the home tie 5-0 with Carlos Bianchi scoring a hat-trick, typically) but with the race for promotion on their mind at the time you could forgive PSG for not exactly taking the Coupe de France as seriously as they possibly could have because of other, far more pressing issues. In 1975, however, that wasn't the case.

PSG weren't exactly clear of relegation trouble by the time the Coupe de France last 64 rolled around in February, but a mid-table position gave them a little bit more licence to try and go far into the tournament, one that opened up with a potential banana skin (or une peau de banane potentielle, if you're looking for a literal translation). SR Saint-Dié, an amateur side, were the opponents. Saint-Dié were perhaps more well known for the bottled water that is bottled and sold in the town of Vittel than anything else, so to get PSG to come to the Stade Jean Bouloumié was a big deal for them and the town.

Fontaine had to leave out Dahleb and Ilija Pantelić due to injuries but started Louis Floch and François M'Pelé in case of emergency and it was the decision to start those two that eventually ended up saving PSG. Bernard Monnin opened the scoring for Saint-Dié after just 14 minutes and the Division 3 club managed to take the lead into the half-time interval. A 1-0 lead at home to Paris Saint-Germain seemed like a dream for Saint-Dié but it was nothing short of a nightmare for Fontaine and his charges, with the former furious at his side on the touchline. The duo of Floch and M'Pelé managed to give PSG the lead by the 70th minute but Christian Mayet equalised after stand-in goalkeeper Jacky Blanchard gave away a needless penalty. The score finished 2-2 and a replay back in Paris was needed, but Fontaine was less than happy with his team's performance, saying, 'We must forget this day. My players were very weak. They missed everything they wanted and even everything they didn't want!'

By all accounts, this seemed like a rather lacklustre PSG performance, one that on another day could have resulted in them being knocked out and made the laughing stock of French football. The replay, not held in Paris but at the Stade Marcel Picot in Nancy, was much more straightforward. M'Pelé grabbed a double while captain Dogliani opened the scoring and Othniel Dossevi got in on the act late on to wrap up the tie and to send PSG through to the last 32 to face second division side Sète. This match proved to be a relative walk in the park for Paris Saint-Germain but also a showcase in dazzling ability for Mustapha Dahleb. A hat-trick from the Algerian set PSG on their way to a 4-2 victory before taking Sète back to Paris (again, not at the Parc des Princes but at the Stade de Paris, which was at least closer to home) to defeat them with a comfortable 4-0 victory.

Fontaine had said after the first leg, 'We must not underestimate the Sétois, who are always comfortable outside,' but he needn't have worried. PSG were comfortable winners and set themselves up perfectly for their next match, which was back in Division 1 with Marseille travelling north to Paris and being held to a 0-0 draw. The report in *France Football* was surprised at the sloppiness of PSG's play but in front of 3,593 fans (PSG's lowest in any game that season, with their lowest at the Parc des Princes being 5,187 in the penultimate Division 1 clash against Strasbourg), they had no issues in the grand scheme of things. The 4-0 win was deserved and while they weren't at the top of their game, the first-leg result allowed them to take their foot off the accelerator for 90 minutes.

By the time the round of 16 against Sochaux came around, PSG were confident of their safety. The 1-0 win over Bordeaux had put a seven-point gap between themselves and Sochaux in 18th, with PSG being closer to third in the league than their cup opponents. By no means were they out of the woods just yet, but there was enough distance between them and relegation to focus on the Coupe de France (funnily enough, Sochaux actually beat PSG on the final day of the Division 1 season to stay up by a point, sending Rennes down in the process). PSG were favourites for the tie and the first leg showed why. The match report ended with this quote, 'Avec un tel résultat obtenu à l'extérieur, il faudrait une catastrophe pour que le PSG ne passent pas en quart de finale,' which translates to, 'With such a result gained away from home, it would be a disaster for PSG not to reach the quarter-finals.' With the game over by the 52nd minute thanks to goals from Dahleb, M'Pelé and Louis Floch, PSG went into the second leg 3-0 up and firmly in the driver's seat. A second-minute penalty from M'Pelé opened up an early lead in the return fixture at home and killed the tie off if it hadn't been already. Dahleb would make it 2-0 with his sixth goal of the Coupe de France and PSG had avoided the disaster that the report of the first leg had predicted and reached the quarter-final stage with relative ease. They looked assured defensively – an improvement on what was seen throughout their Division 1 fixtures – and going forward they had their usual style and confidence. But while the Coupe de France run was a positive to keep ahold of, life for Paris Saint-Germain at this time wasn't great.

In Division 1, it was almost like no matter how hard they tried, PSG couldn't hit a good run of form. Three wins after the winter break saw the Parc des Princes hold under 10,000 fans in four out of the six PSG games it hosted – the only two that reached over 10,000 were against title-chasing duo Marseille and Saint-Étienne, with Marseille drawing 42,247 fans while Saint-Étienne drew 38,600 spectators. As a result of the poor results in the league, fans stayed away from le Parc. They wanted no part of a team that didn't win, and the club were losing more money than expected as a result. They lost money in almost every game they played at the Parc des Princes and were seriously considering leaving the stadium in order to keep the club afloat.

Paris City Council, which was still in favour of a merger between Paris Saint-Germain, Paris FC and Racing Paris as late as December 1974, would eventually give PSG a subsidy equivalent to €850,000 in order to keep them going and eventually saving them from either suffering from severe financial difficulty or going out of business completely, much like the previous season's play-off final had posed a similar threat. There was a tension between Just Fontaine, who wanted more control regarding signings, and the board, who saw Fontaine and Robert Vicot – who was still technically joint manager at this point – as strictly coaches, but the tension would simmer under the Coupe de France run for a while, proving not to be a massive distraction. In fact, the only thing that seemed to distract PSG was their own domestic league form.

The progress in the Coupe de France, however, was potentially about to reach boiling point. PSG were up against Marseille and while it isn't the derby that we know it as today, it was still heated. Some 30,000 rabid fans packed into the Stade Vélodrome to watch Marseille host PSG. Marseille, the bigger club with much more history and trophies in their locker than Paris Saint-Germain, were favourites. PSG, on the other hand, were seen as the inferior team and that had some merit to it. They weren't consistently stronger than Marseille and up until this first leg, they hadn't even managed to beat them. The closest they got was a 1-1 draw back in March of the 1974/75 season, so you would be forgiven for thinking that PSG weren't exactly hotly tipped heading into this one. And after a first half that produced no goals, the second 45 minutes exploded into action both on and off the pitch. Georges Bereta had put Marseille ahead on 54 minutes before legendary Brazilian winger Jairzinho, in his sole season at Marseille, doubled the lead six minutes later. The fans in attendance were going wild. The north vs south element of this derby was something that has never been lost on those in the stands or those watching and listening from home or elsewhere.

The atmosphere in the Stade Vélodrome that night has been described as 'heavy' by reports in France, but in the space of 14 minutes the mood completely changed. PSG were awarded a penalty on the hour so M'Pelé dutifully took the ball, placed it on to the spot and halved the deficit, but he wasn't done with just that and ten minutes later he equalised. Marseille fans, reacting to the fact their side had just blown a two-goal lead, were furious. The awarding of the penalty that allowed PSG back into the game sent the crowd apoplectic, but letting the lead slip in a way that was probably more associated with their opponents at the time, rather than the mighty Marseille, was perhaps a reason why the crowd and the fans were so incensed because it was so unlike their team. Regardless, PSG took advantage and went into the second leg four days later level on aggregate and looking to prove a point that they could match Marseille and, when it really mattered, they could actually beat them. However, at the full-time whistle that return leg seemed very, very far away. The immediate danger and attention for PSG wasn't how they were going to win the quarter-final, but instead a case of how they were going to escape the Vélodrome unscathed.

At full time, a riot broke out. Compagnies Républicaines de Sécurité (CRS), who were specialists in dealing with big crowds and large-scale riots, were called in to help ease the pressure. Charles Tahar, a leader within the boardroom at PSG, lay prone on the floor of the team bus before the rest of the squad and Daniel Hechter joined him. Hechter himself was advised to use the back exits of the Vélodrome to avoid confrontation and to leave safely. The players' team bus was pelted from all corners, with CRS unable to prevent Molotov cocktails, stones and other objects flying over them and towards the vehicle. The driver couldn't move from his position so the fans targeted him and threw stuff in his direction. This perhaps served as the main motivation for PSG in the second leg. Not only did they have the chance to reach the Coupe de France semi-finals, not only did they have the chance to get one over one of the predominant 'big boys' in French football, but they could also stick their fingers up at the fans who targeted them following the first leg. But Fontaine had words of wisdom once the dust had settled, saying, 'Be careful, it's far from being in the palm of your hands. We will have to fight from the first to the last second, but I am hopeful. We are going to play our season in one game. With this null result, we are, morally speaking, slightly advantaged.' PSG knew their task at hand, but did they have the confidence and ability to pull it off in front of a reported crowd of over 46,000 fans?

With le Parc packed, the fans were at top voice. 'Paris, Paris, Paris' said the Parisians who, perhaps for the first time, were out in large numbers to back PSG and PSG only, not attending the game as neutral supporters but to support their club. Hechter, who was in attendance as per usual, was amazed by the noise and atmosphere. Fontaine said of the crowd, 'It's incredible. It's the first time they've been like this with us.'

The game itself started with a bit of back-and-forth action with the two teams trading chances early on. Louis Floch opened the scoring and sent Hechter leaping into the air, Fontaine following him. Marseille wanted a penalty just before half-time but the referee waved away their protests, angering their players. At this point the Marseille team were at boiling point themselves, much like their fans after the first leg. They felt that decisions weren't going their way and frustration eventually would turn into anger.

Jacques Laposte added a second for PSG late on just as two incidents overshadowed the action on the pitch. Both Jairzinho and Paulo Cézar reacted towards the match officials with the latter of the two Brazilians spitting at the referee. Cézar would only be suspended for four games while Jairzinho was banned from playing in France for an entire year, prompting his departure from Marseille at the end of the season. At full time, emotions were high. Fontaine disappeared out of sight to hide his own feelings while the players and fans rejoiced at their first victory over Marseille in a competitive fixture and also booking their place in the Coupe de France semi-finals, their best performance in the competition at that point in time. With Fontaine nowhere to be seen, Roberto Vicot took on the media duties and said, 'Since the start of our cup journey, we have had an indisputable chance. Everything succeeds us, it is our strength and that does not detract from the indisputable value of our team.'

The result had the potential to be a huge turning point for Paris Saint-Germain and could have kick-started the new wave of success for the club but that would be thinking far too distant into the future. They first had to secure their safety in the French Division 1 – which they did – and they had to prepare themselves mentally for the Coupe de France semi-final, a one-legged tie against Lens who had a reputation for not only being an inconsistent side but one that could score goals at the drop of a hat while opening up their defence to allow you a goal in return. The two teams would only finish seven points apart in the Division 1 table and by the time that the semi-final rolled around, the league was over. PSG had stayed up and both teams had only one focus: the Coupe de France.

The build-up to the semi-final, at least for Paris Saint-Germain, was like that of a final. The fans were singing and preparing their celebrations like they were about to lift the cup at the end of the 90 minutes. But while that would probably be frowned upon in modern football (fans celebrating reaching a semi-final would probably be described in such glowing terms as 'tinpot'), just to reach the Coupe de France Final in this season would mean so much more than receiving a medal as either winners or runners-up. Given that Saint-Étienne had won their semi-final against Corsican club SC Bastia and were also champions of Division 1, that meant that whoever faced Les Verts would earn themselves a spot in the following season's UEFA Cup Winners' Cup. With Saint-Étienne being French champions, they were already due to play in the European Cup and therefore couldn't enter the Cup Winners' Cup, so whoever finished runners-up in the Coupe de France would take their place.

The semi-final had gone from a single game to reach a domestic cup final to being a qualifier to reach a major European competition for the first time in PSG's history. To reach the Cup Winners' Cup would have been a monumental achievement for a club as young as PSG and could have been the platform to take them to another level. To be a Parisian club is one thing but to be a Parisian club in a European competition was other-worldly, at this point in time. But PSG knew that while it was healthy to dream and to speculate about the future that may be ahead of them, they still had to win their semi-final.

Of the 16,000 fans allowed into the Stade Auguste-Delaune, 4,000 of them were Parisians who made the journey east to support their team, but their team was in disarray and their preparation was not up to scratch. Boss Fontaine was still not 100 per cent and had another heart attack scare while Jacky Bade was absent due to a family issue. To make matters worse for PSG they were also without the supreme talents of Guy Nosibor, a reliable striker who provided a decent threat off the bench, Jean-Pierre Dogliani, and, perhaps most crucially, Mustapha Dahleb. Eric Renaut replaced the unavailable Bade and 18 minutes into the game he grabbed the spotlight, but for the wrong reasons. The defender conceded a penalty which was converted by Polish striker Eugeniusz Faber to make it 1-0 to Lens. Disaster, but not the end of the world. As PSG had shown during their run in the Coupe de France, nothing seemed to faze them. They had gone behind before, in tougher atmospheres and to better opposition, so they backed their own ability in this kind of situation.

Just after the half-hour mark, they equalised. François M'Pelé's shot was just too much for the palms of the Lens goalkeeper Lannoy to handle and PSG were back on level terms and had the momentum on their side. The second half started with both teams trading chances like two heavyweight boxers throwing blows at one another, constantly trying to get the upper hand while conscious that one hit to their own body could result in the end of the bout. Neither side budged. The clock kept ticking down, minute by minute, and extra time loomed as both teams looked to land the final blow to send them into Europe and the Coupe de France Final. With just eight minutes of normal time left on the referee's watch, PSG got into a good position. Denis Bauda floated a ball into the box, just begging to be headed goalwards. Jacques Laposte, the midfielder who had only scored one goal in the entire season up until this game, was the one who rose highest in the box. He nodded it in for 2-1 to PSG in the dying embers of the game.

But Lens wouldn't lay down without a fight or without a response. They had conceded late on but eight minutes was still enough time to grab an equaliser and send the game into extra time. Faber was played through on goal after some shoddy defensive work and some good perseverance to make it 2-2, punishing PSG for not seeing the game out. There was now an extra 30 minutes to play as a result of that equaliser and Lens had the momentum. Their equaliser was like a dagger into the heart of a PSG side who were stunned at how easily they had allowed Lens to draw level.

As the night got darker and the game got longer, Lens grew in confidence and PSG faded out, and were caught out by a quickly taken free kick around 25 yards from goal. Lens were still setting up to take the set piece while Casimir Juraszek drifted out to a wider position, to the right-hand corner of the 18-yard box. PSG were still setting up their wall and were just getting into position when the ball was stabbed smartly into the path of Juraszek, who was left one on one with Pantelić. With the angle closing down, Juraszek slotted home and Lens would go on to hold on to their 3-2 lead, moving on to not only the Coupe de France Final but also that much-coveted Cup Winners' Cup place.

The Parisians were heartbroken at full time. In the stands, the travelling fans could not believe that they had, once again (and certainly not for the last time), seen PSG throw away a lead in the latter stages of an important game, and on the pitch the players were inconsolable. The questionable looks on the faces of the players ask the same question that everyone else was asking, 'How has that happened?' PSG were 2-1 up with six minutes plus added time left in the game, but eventually lost in extra time to a team that they had already beaten that season in Division 1. Goalscorer Jacques Laposte said after the game, 'We again give a goal away to our opponent. It is like our team is the Santa Claus of French football,' but he had every right to be upset and annoyed, because they had successfully snatched defeat from the jaws of victory, and in turn ruined their chance for a European adventure the following season.

Despite the disappointment in the Coupe de France and the lacklustre season in their return back to Division 1, Fontaine and Vicot held on to their roles and progressed through to the 1975/76 season looking to at least build upon the cup run that had so nearly resulted in triumph. However, after another inconsistent campaign resulting in finishing a mediocre 14th and just four points off the relegation zone, and a quarter-final exit in the Coupe de France at the hands of Lyon (although PSG did get their revenge on Lens in the last 32), the managerial duo were sent packing. After stabilising the club and returning them to the top division, many felt that Fontaine had done as well as he possibly could. With financial issues once again (PSG were apparently running with a deficit of 7m francs at the time), Fontaine could do no more than mid-table finishes and the odd good cup run every so often, but a management committee set up to aid Paris Saint-Germain was in the mindset that Fontaine wasn't the man to take them forward. The pressure from both the new committee and fans forced Daniel Hechter's hand and while Hechter claimed he did everything to keep his friend at the club as the manager and coach, he had to say au revoir to 'Justo', as he was known by those who admired, befriended and loved him. Would it be stagnation or secure stability that the Fontaine reign would be remembered for? Either way, PSG were in a much healthier position once Fontaine at the time departed and the club owed him a good amount of respect for the French goalscoring hero returning them to Division 1 and also keeping them there.

Fontaine's replacement was Velibor Vasović, the Yugoslavian sweeper who was revered by those within the game as being tactically ahead of most other players and possessing a never-say-die attitude. Vasović was born in 1939 – the ninth child of the family – and lived through World War Two as a young child, watching on as his own father was taken prisoner by the Nazis. Having just guided Angers to Division 1, Vasović seemed like a good fit for PSG at the time. But despite Vasović being renowned as a great defender, his Angers team didn't have the same mindset. The 40 goals let in was the joint-second most conceded by a team in Group B of Division 2 but they did have the third most goals in the entire division (68) and had the services of the league's top scorer, Marc Berdoll, to thank for that stat. Was Vasović the man to sort out the defensive issues that often plagued PSG when it mattered most or was it to be another man to stabilise the club for the next year or few?

The transfers out of the club were quite significant with Jean-Pierre Dogliani, who had the captaincy taken off him the prior season by Fontaine and given to Portuguese defender Humberto Coelho – signed from Benfica off the back of being named 1974's Portuguese Player of the Year – departing, as well as Louis Floch, who moved on to Brest. Only two players joined who weren't already either part of the youth academy or out on loan at another club – Mohamed Ali Messaoud from Algeria and Philippe Redon – meaning that while Fontaine was gone, the core of the squad he had was still intact for Vasović to work with.

'I need players who are fighting. Otherwise, it's not worth entering the field,' said Vasović after PSG picked up their first win of the season, at home to Nancy, following two losses in a row, first at home to Lyon then a poor 1-0 defeat at Nice. In fact, that victory against Nancy would be the only one PSG picked up in their first five Division 1 games under the stewardship of Vasović, and it wasn't looking good for the new boss. After defeats against Laval and Nîmes, PSG were rock bottom of Division 1 with just two points. It was early in the season and one win could change anything but the early signs weren't good despite Vasović saying after the Nîmes loss, 'Don't panic, let's wait a month before making a first assessment.'

It was completely reasonable for him to call for calm because he was right. This would take time. But whatever Vasović said to his players after that loss against Nîmes must have worked, because it sparked a miraculous upturn in form. Eight games unbeaten, spanning from the middle of September to 20 November, was enough to parachute the Parisians from rock bottom to seventh in the Division 1 standings. In the middle of that run was a big victory over Saint-Étienne at the Parc des Princes. It wasn't big in the sense of 4-0, 5-0 or 6-0 but in that it proved PSG were capable of handling themselves against the traditionally stronger teams in France. The progression throughout the years from PSG in these kinds of games were evident for all to see and the performance itself was one to be impressed by.

Although Saint-Étienne were absolutely livid at the decision to rule their goal out for offside – the camera angle made it more or less impossible to see but the sheer anger and rage on the faces of the Saint-Étienne squad on the footage probably tells you all you need to know – PSG played with pace, confidence, without fear and without any worry. M'Pelé opened up the scoring with an absolute bullet of a penalty before Dahleb sealed the win after the hour with a tap-in at the back post following outstanding work to create the chance from M'Pelé himself. Being two goals up with 30 minutes to go was something that, a few seasons previously, would have invited pressure on to PSG but their confidence in this game ruled out any kind of comeback from the visitors. The two points were staying in Paris and PSG were more than happy to give them a nice home.

In a rather ironic and completely expected turn of events, the unbeaten run was stopped in November in a rearranged fixture against Marseille. After PSG took a 1-0 lead early on in the game, Marseille fought back to win 2-1 thanks to an 89th-minute clincher. A few things may have changed at Paris Saint-Germain over the years but they never quite forgot to lose their nasty habit of throwing away leads by conceding late goals. That would stay with them for quite some time.

The remit for Vasović at the start of the season was to achieve qualification for a European competition, whether that be via Division 1 or via the Coupe de France. That was what Hechter and the board were aiming for and it felt that after a few years of stability under Just Fontaine, it was time to push on and to aim higher. But the club was having changes of its own in the stands, with spectators, who would often visit the Parc des Princes to watch the star players from opposing sides, now slowly transforming themselves into passionate and vocal Paris Saint-Germain fans. In 1975 a group called 'The Club of Friends of PSG' was formed, situating themselves in the Paris Stand with a banner that simply read 'The Spirit Club'. Most of the paying customers into le Parc at the time were either neutral fans who wanted to see the stars from the likes of Reims, Marseille and Saint-Étienne or fans of the visiting clubs, travelling to the capital to voice their displeasure at the capital team.

Much like any new club, it took time for PSG to grow their own organic fans and to entice people to come and pay to watch them rather than the opposition and despite the odd occasion when fans were excited by what PSG produced, such as the Division 2 play-off against Valenciennes, they still weren't securing the right amount of fans into the stands. In 1976, the first fan-dedicated section was introduced into the Parc des Princes. Young PSG supporters were located in the K section of the ground, later renamed Kop K (named after the Kop at Anfield) and it worked. By the early months of 1977, around 3,000 fans were official subscribers to the Young PSG Supporters' Club and the vast amount of interest in becoming a member forced the club into allowing the fans to stand behind the goal at the Boulogne Stand (the south stand or, if you're watching a game on television, to the right of the camera shot), with Kop K now becoming known as the Kop of Boulogne. While the inception of fans groups started during the transition from Kop K to the Kop of Boulogne, it's worth waiting for the stories on their impact later on, so the true meaning of the individual fan groups is not lost in the midst of everything else.

With fans slowly starting to filter back in to the stadium and the youth of Paris finally getting involved in supporting the club of their city, PSG's results didn't do much to help their situation in the league. Their form either side of the winter break wasn't too bad, losing just once in Division 1 from the middle of December up until the beginning of March, a run which saw them reach as high as fifth in the table. Vasović, like any good coach, was always on the lookout for new talent to improve his squad and what better time than when the team is on a red-hot run of form. After drawing 0-0 at home to Nîmes, PSG were fifth and just two points off a potential UEFA Cup spot. If they had beaten Nîmes they would have been joint third. That's the fine margins they were dealing with but Vasović had spotted a talented player a few weeks ago who had caught his eye. It was someone he knew that PSG not only wanted but needed to sign because this young player was set to be the future superstar of world football.

In mid-January, Paris Saint-Germain went out on to the road to face a Nancy side who weren't too far behind them in the Division 1 table and thus posed a big threat. It may not have been a fixture on the level of Marseille or Saint-Étienne, but its importance was not lost on the PSG players. They knew they had to win to not only keep the distance between themselves and Nancy but also to make those around them aware that, on any given day, PSG could beat them and beat them well. A 2-1 result gave PSG the two points on the day, but while Vasović loved the win his mind was elsewhere. Someone on that Nancy team had made an impression on him. A few weeks later, in March when PSG had dropped a few more points and were starting their descent down the table, consistently losing distance between themselves and those at the top, Vasović made a request to the board to sign one player. That player was the one he saw against Nancy, the one who stuck in his mind. That player was Michel Platini.

By the time PSG faced off against Nancy in January of 1977, Platini was already someone who had a reputation and was gaining more and more admirers by the day. One may be forgiven for only picturing the Frenchman as the UEFA president who was eventually involved in seemingly every FIFA controversy, but before his time in the boardroom Platini was a genuine footballing superstar. Joining Nancy in 1972 at the age of 17, he went on to make his debut against Nîmes in 1973 and, despite a few injuries alongside relegation into Division 2 the following season, the expectation on his young shoulders grew when Nancy went down. His role in the team – combined with his sheer talent, ability and also the fact he managed to stay fit – meant that Platini contributed more in the second tier. His 17 goals saw Nancy rocket back up into Division 1, which is where the meetings with Paris Saint-Germain began.

His first appearance against the Parisians came in November 1975 when he played as the number ten for Nancy in a 4-2 loss. Mustapha Dahleb scored a hat-trick and outshone the young Frenchman at the time, even intercepting a wayward Platini pass en route for one of his three goals. Nancy did gain their revenge later on in the season with a 4-1 win at the Parc des Princes which was not only humiliating for PSG but also caused the fans to chant for the resignation of Just Fontaine, but there was no Platini. So far, the young talent was yet to make his mark against PSG and was yet to emerge as a true star to keep an eye on, despite his Division 2 exploits. Platini, who had just turned 21 by August of 1976, laced up his boots to play PSG but his Nancy side fell to another loss, 2-0 this time at the Parc des Princes. Again, Nancy would lose to PSG later on in the Division 1 season but after this particular game Vasović took notice. The two sides faced off in January 1977 and in the following March Vasović went to Daniel Hechter and demanded the signing of Platini. 'No matter what he may cost, it will never be too expensive,' proclaimed Vasović, but his request ultimately fell on deaf ears. PSG could have stolen a march on a player the world would soon become extremely familiar with, but Platini's rise perhaps started a little bit earlier than expected.

When the final positions of the Ballon d'Or were released in December of 1977, there was somewhat of a surprise in third place. Allan Simonsen of Borussia Mönchengladbach won the award with Hamburg's Kevin Keegan making it a Bundesliga duo at the top of the standings but Michel Platini, with five first-place votes, grabbed third ahead of the likes of Roberto Bettega, Johan Cruyff and Klaus Fischer, and finishing light years ahead of the likes of Marius Trésor, Trevor Brooking, Ruud Krol and Rob Rensenbrink. It's impressive enough that Platini finished third ahead of some of these greats at the age of 22 but, without playing in the European Cup, without playing in the UEFA Cup or even the Cup Winners' Cup and with no international tournament to showcase his abilities, it was a complete shock. Borussia Mönchengladbach managed to get to the European Cup Final, which explains the win for Simonsen, while Keegan lifted the trophy with Liverpool against the Germans before his move to Hamburg, but it goes to show how special Platini was (the fact that journalists from across Europe voted for the award back in 1977 and the *France Football* magazine influence can't be ignored seeing as they would see Platini regularly and only occasionally see stars from other leagues which probably explains how Platini also finished fifth in 1976, but that's not to take away from his ability). The fact that Platini was so highly rated at this stage in his career and still PSG decided not to spend big money on him was either a show of the little funds that they had left to splash out on future stars or a severe lack of foresight from the powers that be.

The run of form after that Nancy game, however, was so bad that it forced PSG into change quite rapidly. After a run of five consecutive wins, a home draw with Nîmes left them fifth in the Division 1 table, but from that point on 20 January up until 3 May, PSG would only beat Reims and Lens. By the time they next won a game they were tenth. Their objective had to be to qualify for Europe the following season and while no one expected to be floating around in a title challenge and potentially a place in the European Cup, a UEFA Cup spot was more than realistic. But that poor run ultimately laid to rest any hope of Europe, and Vasović, who was appointed as manager for the sole reason of gaining European qualification, was already planning his departure, saying after his final game, 'PSG existed before me, it will exist after me.'

Pierre Alonzo replaced him in a caretaker role before Hechter announced that Jean-Michel Larqué, still only 29 years old and still plying his trade with Saint-Étienne, would be the manager for the next campaign. Alonzo saw out the season with an impressive run of three wins, two draws and one loss which meant PSG finished ninth in the table, five points off of Bastia who claimed the final UEFA Cup spot. It wasn't the worst season in the world but had PSG been able to gain an extra few wins

– they lost seven times by one goal – then maybe things would have been different. With Nantes finishing nine points clear of Lens in the title race, PSG winning the championship would have been nothing more than just a pipe dream but a few more victories could have easily seen them jump up to third or even second, perhaps giving more credit to the team than the final table suggested.

It was a much more impressive season than recent Division 1 campaigns, but work was still needed. The club was still growing, the players were still getting to grips with the pressure of playing for the only Paris club in the top flight and, with that added expectation on your shoulders, it was never going to be an easy task. Without money flying in to buy whoever they wished – someone like Michel Platini would have definitely made a difference in the season – then it was always going to be an uphill struggle for Paris Saint-Germain. But for Hechter, struggle wasn't something he particularly enjoyed and didn't want to see his club not try to overcome whatever struggle may come their way. While Platini was perhaps too far out of their price range, that didn't stop Hechter and PSG spending big in the summer for the 1977/78 season. But while money was spent, there was a price to pay that resulted in yet more upheaval and yet more change at the very top of the club.

5

Une nouvelle ère – A new era

'I SCORED goals all my life without ever being able to see much. I knew where the ball would go. I could smell it. It was the striker's instinct.'

Those are words that any goalscoring striker will appreciate and completely understand the meaning of, but this quote in particular is from Carlos Bianchi, the great – but often forgotten – Argentinian striker. Bianchi, perhaps better known for being one of the greatest managers in the history of Boca Juniors, is one of the first true legends of Paris Saint-Germain. Buenos Aires-born Bianchi's father worked on a newspaper kiosk as the main source of the family's income. Carlos, up until the age of 18, helped his father and looked set to be a salesman just like his old man. Once he hit 18, however, everything changed. Since the age of 11, Bianchi had been a part of the youth academy at Velez Sarsfield – the Buenos Aires club that is often overlooked in favour of the mega clubs in Boca Juniors and River Plate – and would learn what it meant to enhance your own talent and ability in a way that could aid the team.

Bianchi officially made his professional debut against Boca in a 1-1 draw and would be named in the Velez squad that won their first league title, the 1968 Campeonato Nacional, in spectacular fashion. There was a three-way tie at the top of the Nacional that season with Velez, River Plate and Racing all level on 22 points (Rosario Central and Boca Juniors were only a point behind them; it would have made things a lot more interesting had they been level too), which meant that the three teams went into a play-off. Each team played each other once, with Velez and River both finishing with two wins each and with an identical goal difference. So, what separated the two clubs? Goals scored. Velez scored five and River could only manage three. Thus Velez – and Bianchi – were champions.

By the time Bianchi was 22, he already had two golden boots to his name and had been capped by the Argentinian national team, so it was safe to say that he was someone who many in Argentina were very familiar with. But when the striker moved to Europe to join Reims, his days as Argentina's talisman were over. He wasn't capped again after 1972 and many speculated that his move to a league that was considered weaker than the rest of Europe was the reason why. It had to be, because his goalscoring record for Reims was simply sublime; 107 goals in 124 games for Reims is a stat line that wouldn't seem out of place next to names like Cristiano Ronaldo or Lionel Messi, but the short-sighted Bianchi (that's not a criticism of the man, but he was literally short-sighted in terms of his vision) was expecting to make a move elsewhere and move to bigger clubs in the future, so impressive were his stats at both Velez and Reims.

While Bianchi's Reims sides never quite managed to match his own high standards (their highest finish with Bianchi in their side was fifth), the man himself was in amazing form. Out of his four years in a Reims shirt, the Argentine won the Division 1 golden boot three times and the only year he missed out on the gong was when he broke his tibia and fibula in a friendly against Barcelona at the Parc des Princes when Reims and Paris Saint-Germain merged for a one-off encounter against the Catalan club. The player who won the golden boot in the season that Bianchi missed was Delio Onnis of Monaco, a fellow Argentine striker who Bianchi eventually managed to replace at Reims. Despite Onnis winning the award, Monaco only finished above Reims by a point and a rejuvenated Bianchi returned the following season with a hefty 34 goals to bring the boot back to his home.

In any other side, Bianchi would have been the most feared striker in Europe. His skill and deadly eye for goal would have translated in any team in any league and he wouldn't have looked out of place regardless of where he went. He had the tenacity and aggression to stamp his authority on to an English First Division game while having the knowledge to penetrate the meanest defence in Italy's Serie A. His hard work and sheer determinism – plus his poacher style – would have gone down a treat in Germany's Bundesliga while he was quick enough, both with his brain and his feet, to make the most of what La Liga had to offer in Spain.

A battle between Bianchi and Gerd Müller would have been a joy to watch while you would imagine that Bianchi's qualities would have him head and shoulders above anyone in England. Bianchi in Spain would have

seen him cross over with future 1978 World Cup hero
Mario Kempes, which could have changed the events of
that particular tournament, and in Italy he could have
broken record after record. Of course, we can sit here
and contemplate the career that Bianchi had in a parallel
universe for days on end, but the point remains that he
was deadly in front of goal but wasn't able to have a team
built around him to allow him to showcase his talents to
a wider audience who would have been wowed by what
he could do.

Bianchi was a big player in France and Reims knew it,
and when financial trouble hit and assets were needed to
be sold in order to keep the club going, Bianchi was at the
top of that list. There was interest from across the country
and that was to be expected. You don't score over 100
goals for a club in just four years and be forgotten about
but for Bianchi his interest was raised in a particular club
in the south of France, in the coastal town of Saint-Tropez
located between Nice and Marseille, when the owner met
him face to face and pleaded with him to join.

Daniel Hechter knew a good deal when he saw one.
He may have been a fashion designer running a football
club in Paris but that didn't mean he wasn't prudent and
it didn't mean that he couldn't recognise a good deal
when he saw one. Yes, Hechter may have passed up on
the chance to sign a young Michel Platini but that was a
decision more financially driven whereas the signing of
Carlos Bianchi came from Hechter's desire and a move
from his heart. Bianchi had impressed against PSG before
– the time he scored all six goals for Reims in their 6-1
demolition of the Parisians stood out – and Hechter
was determined to make the move a possibility. With a

little help in the fundraising department to help ease any financial burdens that may have been placed on PSG, Hechter sealed the deal for 1.5m francs. Hechter had added yet another marquee signing to his club but while Mustapha Dahleb – arguably the first major signing for Paris Saint-Germain – was a big deal and was a signing who influenced the team on the field, to sign a goalscorer as gifted and as talented as Bianchi was even bigger.

It was perhaps the first time that PSG made a signing that forced other clubs across the continent to sit up and take notice. Signing a player who was once coveted by the likes of Real Madrid and Barcelona (or so Bianchi says, claiming that the closed borders to Spain meant he wasn't able to join those clubs and by the time they did open he had already given his word to Reims) was a huge statement. But what Hechter didn't know at the time was that signing Carlos Bianchi would be his last signing for PSG.

The 1977/78 season was full of disappointment, controversy, change and for a campaign that offered a bright new future and offered hope to Paris Saint-Germain, it resulted in another year wasted on chaos. Velibor Vasović was sacked for failing to deliver European football when it looked like a strong possibility earlier in the season and was replaced by Jean-Michel Larqué, the former Saint-Étienne midfielder, appointed as player-manager. On the surface the move to hire Larqué was somewhere between being very bold and brave with their future and being risky for no real reason. Yes, Larqué had been an outstanding player for Saint-Étienne and had shown tremendous leadership skills on the pitch both for his club and France, but to translate those same skills on to the bench was a different task entirely. At the age of 29, Larqué still felt that he could combine the life of a footballer and the life of a coach into one, but as he pointed out many times, to do both and to be successful is more or less impossible. Even with the likes of Dahleb, Bianchi, François M'Pelé and new signing Jean-Pierre Adams in the squad, it was going to be a tough ask for Larqué to improve on last seasons finish. But the story of Adams is one that needs to be told, not only because it's incredibly interesting but it also gives a good account and good reasoning as to why Hechter was so keen on bringing him into the fold.

Born in Dakar, Senegal, Adams was the oldest in a large family and was sent to further his education in France at the age of nine. Growing up as a black child in a predominantly white society wasn't easy for Jean-Pierre, but his tremendous footballing skills – plus his personality and charm – gained him respect from all over, which was impressive for someone of his age. By the time he turned 19, however, life had attempted to throw various spanners into the works. A serious knee injury nearly derailed his career while he also lost team-mates from his club, Montargis, with Michel Slota being hit by a car while out riding his bike and, tragically, Alain Guerton died after contracting a virus following a trip to Asia. Even Adams himself was involved in a car accident, which left him with just a few cuts and scars, while his close friend Guy Beudot wasn't quite as fortunate, sadly passing away.

Adams would eventually be recommend to Nîmes after impressing in the French military team during his national service, signing initially as a striker but later being trained to play as a centre-back after working on various aspects of his game, with coaches seeing him as a player who had the potential to combine a perfect mix of physical quality, tactical knowledge and technical ability. It wasn't easy for Jean-Pierre but his work ethic and attitude forced him to keep on track. His form and adaptability to whatever position he played was exceptional, with former Argentina captain Angel Marcos saying, 'In the rugged defence of Nîmes, there is a pillar, a kind of force of nature, a colossus of uncommon athletic power: Jean-Pierre Adams. I rarely suffered against a direct opponent. I always dreaded the two annual confrontations [with Adams] as they were a real challenge and I tried, every time, to detach myself from my merciless "bodyguard".'

As his game developed, more clubs became interested and a move to Nice furthered not only his career but his ability as a defender who was capable of battling any striker he played against, while also being able to pick up the ball and play beautiful passes or make mazy runs. Often deployed as a defensive midfielder or as a centre-back, Adams wouldn't have been out of place as a sweeper in the sense that he could start an attack from deep and run a team if he so wished. By this time, Adams was already a France international and had formed a formidable defensive partnership with the great Marius Trésor, media dubbing the duo as the 'Garde Noire' or the 'Black Guard'. Even Franz Beckenbauer went on to say that Adams and Trésor 'have formed one of the best central defensive partnerships in all of Europe'.

Funnily enough, the partnership only came to most minds after a game against the USSR at the Parc des Princes, a stadium that had been dubbed as Adams's 'Stade du Désespoir' (Stadium of Despair) after losing two cup finals at the ground he would eventually call home. Hechter, enthused by the idea of having someone as talented as Adams in his squad, brought him to Paris and tried to drip out the last remaining years out of his peak, but unfortunately he wasn't able to give what he could for Nice anymore. At 29, his body had started to wind down which was completely understandable.

However, in the midst of a coaching course, Adams had to pull out to get a knee problem seen to by a doctor. A scan had shown muscle damage to the knee but after he had been recognised by a football-mad medic, Jean-Pierre had an operation quickly scheduled for only a few days later. 'It's all fine! I'm in great shape,' was what he told his wife before going under the needle, but the operation itself would prove to be a disaster. There was an issue with his anaesthetic, the anaesthetist who was looking after Jean-Pierre's operation also had eight other operations on the go, while his bed wasn't the right one for this particular operation and the surgery itself was overseen by a trainee doctor because the hospital that Jean-Pierre was in was on strike. One tube that was in Adams's body was actually blocking the pathway to his lungs rather than ventilating them which ultimately caused him to suffer a cardiac arrest. The trainee who oversaw the operation – which could have been delayed as it was listed as 'non-urgent' – later admitted that they weren't 'up to the task I was entrusted with'.

That operation was on Wednesday, 17 March 1982. Jean-Pierre Adams never woke up from the coma and died on 6 September 2021. For a man who was once regarded as one of the best in his trade in the continent, it was a sad way to end.

Adams was signed by PSG off the back of his impressive stint at Nice, but he was more than just a talented defender. He was a trailblazer. Without the success and story of Adams, would Lilian Thuram have become a World Cup winner for France? What about Patrick Vieira or Marcel Desailly? Adams paved a way for African-born football players to make their mark in France and did it with the same style, passion, commitment, charisma as he did everything else in his life. If anything, Adams peaked too early in his career and missed out many years in the France national team. Adams played his last game for France in 1975, three years before Marius Trésor – his former partner in crime – would captain the side at the 1978 World Cup and to a fourth-placed finish at the 1982 World Cup.

Hechter may have brought in Jean-Pierre Adams to Paris Saint-Germain at the tail end of his career but can you blame him? Having watched Adams for years in top sides in French football, Hechter thought that he had found the perfect player for the new spine of his team. It just happened to be the perfect player at the wrong time. Jean-Pierre Adams was a player known for being gifted, loved and respected and it's only fair that his influence on and off the field is remembered for what it truly was: game-changing.

While Adams and Bianchi were the two star names brought in to PSG by Hechter to aid the new boss Larqué, the squad from the previous season remained largely the same. Dahleb was now captain while Daniel Bernard was brought in to replace goalkeeper Ilija Pantelić, who had retired at the end of the previous season. For Larqué, however, it was a nightmare start despite a fairly decent pre-season. A defensive horror show allowed a Michel Platini-led Nancy to stroll to a 4-1 victory while PSG reverted to type and let a two-goal lead slip at home to Reims, with Bianchi scoring a brace against his former club before an 88th-minute equaliser from the visitors stole a point. A draw against Strasbourg was followed by losses at home to Bordeaux and away to Marseille, arguably their worst performance according to *France Football* reports.

If you were looking for positives, you could point to the fact that Bianchi had started like a house on fire and had four goals in five games with PSG managing to score in every one of them. If you were looking for negatives, then you had plenty to choose from. Despite their consistency in shape and personnel, the defence looked lost and out of place. It was unable to deal with pace and wasn't providing any support to the rest of the team. Perhaps a change in goalkeeper and the addition of Adams into the spine of the back line had an influence on this, but it wasn't good enough. PSG also returned to their habit of throwing away leads, or at least throwing away points from good positions. In the first two games against Nancy and Reims they either were ahead or level but only picked up one point. It was also noted that the early goals PSG conceded were a major issue. PSG had conceded three times in the first seven minutes in the first five matches, giving themselves an uphill battle before the players had a chance to fully work themselves into the game.

This start to the season had left PSG bottom of the table and one of only three teams without a win on the board. That would soon change with four victories in a row, against Valenciennes, Rouen, Metz and a big result away at Lyon with the help of a Carlos Bianchi brace (PSG did nearly throw it away in the final stages, with Lyon grabbing two goals in the 74th and 82nd minutes). That victory prompted a crowd of more than 40,000 to attend the next game, against Nice at the Parc des Princes, in what was a noisy and passionate showing for their club, just like Hechter had wanted for years. Sadly for those fans of a Paris persuasion, all they could do was sit back and watch helplessly as Nice tore their team apart, winning 3-0 and sending the Parisians back down to 11th in the table.

The season was tinged with inconsistency, brilliant individual performances, lacklustre team displays and false dawns, but one slither of hope was in the 8-2 demolition of Troyes at the Parc des Princes. In front of fewer than 10,000 fans, PSG put on an attacking clinic in terms of how to dismantle their opponents and showcased what their talents could do when they truly hit top form. Within eight minutes of the kick-off, PSG were 2-0 up. Bianchi opened the scoring before the club's all-time record appearance maker, Jean-Marc Pilorget, took the ball through the middle of the pitch and smacked it into the top-left corner from about 20 yards. By half-time it was 4-1 to PSG, and Bianchi, who had been targeted by fans in the Nice defeat a few weeks prior with whistles and chants, fired back in the only way that he knew how, scoring goal after goal after goal after goal. His haul of four was the first time a PSG player had done so in a Division 1 match, although it wasn't the first time in the club's history. Eric Renaut hit four in Division 3 back in 1973 while Mustapha Dahleb did so earlier in the year in the Coupe de France. Incredibly enough, Renaut,

Dahleb and Bianchi were all in the starting line-up for this Troyes game.

'It's not nice to be whistled at, because that doesn't encourage you to play better,' said Bianchi in his post-match interview, 'but you have to be patient, accept it and say to yourself that you'll get revenge sooner or later. It came today.' Bianchi knew his quality would shine through at some point and what better way to get the fans back on your side than hitting four goals in an 8-2 win. But, in typical PSG fashion, this form wouldn't carry on. The beating of Troyes and a comprehensive 4-1 victory at home against Saint-Étienne were their only two wins from October to 17 December, the final game of the first half of the season. Jean-Michel Larqué had gotten one over his former club with that 4-1 win but followed it up with a loss away at Lens, a defeat at Sochaux and four consecutive draws, with Bianchi scoring five of their six goals in this dreadful run of form.

It was becoming blatantly obvious that PSG thrived most when Bianchi was on fire but when the fire wasn't burning as bright as many would have liked, the rest of the team suffered. Of PSG's six wins heading into the middle of December, Bianchi had scored in all but two. He already had 18 goals to his name which was even more remarkable when you realise that PSG as a whole in Division 1 up until this point only had 38 goals. On the face of it, that isn't too bad. But having one striker scoring nearly half of your goals isn't a positive. It's a positive to have a prolific striker like Bianchi but it isn't healthy to rely on him as much as PSG did. Dahleb and François M'Pelé also contributed but wouldn't hit double figures in goals for the rest of the season.

PSG rounded off 1977 with a win at Bordeaux, only their third victory without Bianchi scoring. It put them in 12th place, a long way off their idealistic target of challenging for a position in the UEFA Cup, but while the club had witnessed change in the managerial front and on the pitch with the introduction of stars like Bianchi and (the now rarely used from the start of games) Jean-Pierre Adams, off the pitch and in the boardroom there was about to be a huge change that would arguably be one of the biggest and most controversial moments in the club's history.

For quite a while, Paris Saint-Germain were attracting a good amount of fans into the Parc des Princes. Attendance figures would seemingly rise continually and year after year, the club would secure more fans for their membership groups/fan clubs and rather than going to le Parc to watch the opposition – as many fans had done for years – they were going to see PSG and the stars they were bringing in. This was music to the ears of the ambitious Daniel Hechter, a president who was the embodiment of Paris. Fashionable, direct, passionate, you name it. If Hechter wanted something, he would go out of his way to at least try his hardest to get it and a good example of this is the story of how he nearly signed Franz Beckenbauer. Hechter claimed that before his move from Bayern Munich to New York Cosmos, the German was on the verge of signing for Paris Saint-Germain in 1975. Hechter wanted it and Beckenbauer seemed quite keen, but RTL, the sponsors of PSG at the time who often helped fund certain transfers – their financial involvement in the club saved them in the early stages of their life – didn't want to contribute a lot of money to sign a defender.

That's what Hechter told *Le Parisien*, so it's impossible to say how true the story is, simply because no one in their right mind would willingly turn down a player like Franz Beckenbauer, with Hechter also being quoted in *Le Journal du Dimanche* as saying, 'I went to meet him in Munich. We agreed on the salary, high but not disproportionate given his status. He was ready to but the management of RTL, our sponsor, did not want to put money for a defender. I was mad with rage. His arrival would have changed the history of PSG.'

And the thing is, Hechter was probably right. If Beckenbauer had gone to PSG the chances are that Saint-Étienne would have won the European Cup in 1975/76 instead of losing the final to Bayern Munich, PSG might have been able to attract bigger names with the spine being anchored by Der Kaiser himself, and he would have brought legitimacy along with him. In the mid-1970s he would have been huge for Paris. His profile was enough to bring attention wherever he went – as he eventually found out in New York alongside Pelé at the Cosmos – but that was the type of ambition that Hechter had for his club, and at that point in time it was *his* club. No one made any decisions without Hechter getting final say and he was the one who convinced players to join the club.

Of course, the mention of Franz Beckenbauer and Michel Platini already shows you the potential team that PSG could have had at this time – whether Hechter wanted to pin the missed opportunities of those two players on RTL and sponsorship, we are none the wiser – but for whatever reason, neither transfer came to pass. It's fun to imagine what could have happened with Beckenbauer as the sweeper, leading the back line with Platini and Dahleb feeding balls in to Bianchi up top. With a few extra pieces around them, that could have made Paris Saint-Germain title contenders. But eventually the ambition of Hechter caught up with him. He wanted the best for his club but to what lengths was he willing to go in order to bring in a few extra francs to make sure that they didn't miss out on the likes of Beckenbauer and Platini again? He didn't want to rely on the say-so of sponsors on whether the club could sign a player. If RTL hadn't said no to Beckenbauer, then the German World Cup winner would have been a Parisian. So Hechter looked for ways to make PSG more self-sustainable and financially competitive, or at least give them the financial power off the field to attract stars to make them a force on the field.

Hechter, returning to Paris from his time abroad, saw a newspaper with a headline that struck him. 'Wanted' was plastered across the top of the front page of *L'Equipe* with his face underneath the line. There were accusations being thrown at him and Paris Saint-Germain that the club had falsified tickets and that the money used from these 'double tickets' was being used to fund players and club operations. This scandal would later qualify as a breach of trust and forgery, forcing the football authorities to act. With the front page featuring Hechter and none of the players who allegedly benefited from this 'slush fund' scandal, the main focus was solely on Hechter himself, but he wasn't the only one involved.

Philippe Lacourtablaise, the administrative secretary for RTL, was the sponsor's man inside the club and worked alongside Alain Rosen. The scheme was quite simple. Money was taken from the gate receipts to help pay the players' wages and to help ease the club's financial burden. According to some versions of this event, Hechter had suspicious of Rosen since he first arrived at the club and was concerned that Rosen was taking some of the money for himself instead of putting it into the club, despite the sums of money taken from these gate receipts not being registered into the relevant accounts. Basically, PSG were paying players with money that – officially – they didn't have. Hechter and Rosen had been involved in setting up two ticket offices – one was official and another wasn't. The funds in the unofficial ticket office went to pay players and other members of staff undisclosed amounts of cash, and it completely shook PSG.

With the matter being so serious – like the courts eventually said, it was forgery and mistrust – an investigation was called to figure out exactly what was going on; whether it was an administrative error or something far more serious. But, as Hechter would try to argue, this wasn't entirely uncommon in France. The average wage for a player in France was around 12,000 francs a month – around £10,000 – but they were regularly taking home more than that due to, as they were called in various reports, bribes from their clubs. To call them bribes seems a bit harsh and immediately strikes the wrong tone and puts a negative connotation into the head of whoever reads it, but it's easy to think of it as an unofficial bonus. Players get goal bonuses and similar incentives all the time, but these weren't written into any contract, nor were they given out for goals scored or clean sheets kept; instead they were paid out to keep players happy and to try and keep them at their clubs. A bit like the drug scandal that plagued cycling not so long ago, it was a scenario where everyone was doing something wrong which meant you had to follow suit to keep up. That doesn't make it right and it doesn't justify what PSG and Hechter did with those two ticket offices, but it shows how easy it is to fall into traps set by the actions of other clubs.

As investigators tried to look into the dealings of the scandal, it became clear that Hechter was being placed front and centre of the proceedings. An example had to be made of someone in French football and that someone just happened to be Hechter. He expected to be suspended from football for six months and essentially be given a slap on the wrist and told not to do it again, but he was wrong. After eight hours of deliberation, the group that would be known as the 'committee of five' announced their verdict. Hechter would be banned from football for life. 'This is the real scandal! A masquerade of justice,' shouted Hechter as he found out the verdict. One report even published the reasons why the 'committee of five' came to this decision, 'The existence of a slush fund supplied by the decrease in receipts from friendly matches; the reduction in the income from tickets to matches and the payment to certain players or employees of the club of undeclared sums.' With Hechter now banned from football for life, Paris Saint-Germain had to deal with a whole load of questions from those outside of the game but also those from inside the club. Bianchi would later say in an interview many years later that Hechter was, 'A gentleman. The way he got kicked out of the club was not normal. This person loved football and, without him, Paris Saint-Germain would not exist,' while manager Jean-Michel Larqué described Hechter simply as 'a good chairman', but while Hechter was banned and was on his way out, he still had one more game left to oversee before handing over the reins to one of his board members, Francis Borelli.

The home match with Marseille would be the first game back from the winter break and the first fixture of 1978, yet it was the last of the new era. Hechter was well liked by players and fans alike, so to come up against Marseille at the Parc des Princes seemed to be the perfect scenario for PSG's players and fans to both give their president the send-off that they felt he deserved.

The suspension of Hechter came just two days prior to this game so while the threat of a ban loomed large over the preparation, the sheer magnitude of a lifetime ban (rather than just for six months) was huge. The players felt the punishment was a huge injustice against Hechter and reckoned that, like many others did, he was being made the scapegoat for the entire scandal. Some 33,386 fans crammed themselves into le Parc to bid farewell to their president but also to get one over the title-chasing Marseille side who had already beaten them once this season. The already excited crowd were treated to the referee blowing his whistle and pointing to the penalty spot within the first minute, giving Bianchi the chance to give PSG an early lead. He stepped up but his shot was saved by Gérard Migeon, the Marseille goalkeeper, and the score remained 0-0. But PSG weren't deterred by this and they kept pushing and probing, trying to find a way to break through. But in the midst of the Parisian pressure, Marseille were awarded a penalty of their own and Boubacar Sarr – who would later join PSG – converted from the spot for 1-0 after 12 minutes.

It was a goal against the run of play but it gifted PSG with the perfect opportunity to show their mental resilience and not bow down to the pressure of falling behind in the first half. The fans stayed by their side and kept chanting, mainly choruses of 'Hechter president, Hechter president, Hechter president'. By no means was it the fans turning their focus away from the players or the action on the field but more a reminder of why this game mattered so much. The fans wanted to show their support for the outgoing Hechter and spur the players on. And it worked. The blue and white tidal wave kept rushing towards the Marseille goal and the constant attacking pressure eventually gifted PSG a goal from François Brisson with a lovely strike to level. On the stroke of half-time, PSG got the lead they had deserved since the first minute. Dahleb followed up from a Bianchi shot that was spilled by Migeon and, despite the tight angle, managed to poke the ball home.

PSG had overcome one mental road block – the ability to come back from a goal down – and now had to overcome another one in the second half, the ability to hold on to a lead and not throw away yet another victory. But PSG didn't leave anything behind in the second half and, to put it bluntly, absolutely battered Marseille for yet another 45 minutes. An own goal from Marius Trésor – one half of the Garde Noire with Jean-Pierre Adams – made it 3-1 before François M'Pelé decided it was time he scored a few, just for good measure. His first, an emphatic penalty before 50 minutes were on the clock, all but sealed the win before rounding off the famous and historic result with the goal of the game, a 30-yard bullet that flew in off the right-hand post. A 5-1 win at the Parc des Princes; incroyable. The fans were ecstatic, the players were at the top of their game and their outgoing president was the king of the castle for one last time. As each member of the squad went to bid him farewell for one last time, the Parc des Princes fans continued to do what they had done from first whistle to last and sang 'Hechter president, Hechter president, Hechter president' over and over again.

The players carried Hechter around to allow him a lap of honour and to let him wave off his fans, with Dahleb giving the match ball to Hechter as a souvenir for the famous victory. For one last game, the Parc des Princes and Paris Saint-Germain belonged to Daniel Hechter, the man who saved PSG from extinction, who gave them their famous colour and shirt design, protected their unique name from mergers, moved them from Division 3 to Division 1 in a handful of years in a state-of-the-art stadium, gave them the Camp des Loges training ground and completely changed the club.

Without Hechter, there would be no Paris Saint-Germain. Hechter himself knew this, despite being known by his closest friends as a humble man. The fans who were chanting his name knew this. The players he signed and who were carrying him around his pitch knew this. Hechter was departing but would forever be linked to PSG and will be a celebrated part of their history. Trophies and European football may have eluded PSG during his tenure but the club grew and grew under his stewardship and, despite the dark and murky ending to his reign, his name is one that is loved by fans. However, while Hechter had laid the groundwork for a successful future for the capital club, his successor had more than enough ideas in the bank to figure out how to take PSG to the top.

As a member of the 'gang of pink shirts', the group who took over PSG in the early 1970s, Francis Borelli was a man who was as much a part of the fabric that made Paris Saint-Germain as anyone else in the world at that time. Whatever decision PSG made, Borelli had a say in it. Borelli was forever in the background but now, in incredibly difficult circumstances, he had the chance to mould the club the way he wanted to. Described as an energetic and fiery gentleman, Borelli wanted to make PSG not just a football club, but a family. It's almost definitely the same rhetoric that every new chairman or president sets out at the start of their reign but those around Borelli felt he was a kind and generous man who truly loved what the club was and what it could be.

Former colleague Charles Talar said that he 'only lived for Paris Saint-Germain'. Given the controversial and tumultuous time that PSG found themselves in upon his arrival, Borelli's optimism provided some hope to a team that, despite hammering Marseille 5-1, were still struggling for consistency. The Marseille win pushed PSG up to tenth in the Division 1 standings, but they wouldn't move higher than that for the rest of the campaign. PSG followed up their triumph over Marseille with a loss away at Valenciennes despite heading into the match as favourites, taking the lead after four minutes and facing a team forging a reputation for being average at home but strong on the road. In typical PSG fashion, however, the script was flipped almost immediately. A Carlos Bianchi hat-trick against Rouen gave PSG a win before losing once again to a Patrick Battiston-inspired Metz side. Inconsistency was king in this campaign but given the upheaval at the club, Francis Borelli and PSG just wanted to keep their heads under the radar, see out the remaining games and start again for the next campaign.

Borelli made it absolutely clear from the outset that he wanted to create a family rather than just a team so finding the right individuals for that task wasn't going to be an overnight job. Time was needed to weed out any potential problems and also to find the players and coaching staff who would fit their criteria. With the exception of maybe Bianchi, Mustapha Dahleb and Jean-Marc Pilorget, everyone was under the microscope. Even the manager wasn't entirely out of the woods yet, but was at least afforded time to try and figure out a plan.

The second half of the season was yet again riddled with inconsistency, winning six games following the Marseille thrashing in Hechter's final game but losing eight including the final three. Monaco and Michel Platini's Nancy both left the Parc des Princes with maximum points. The former's win pushed them closer towards the Division 1 title, which they won by a point, and Nancy used Paris Saint-Germain as the perfect testing ground for their Coupe de France Final against Nice a few days later. Nancy would win that final 1-0 thanks to a goal from Platini, who also scored in the semi-final and against PSG in this game. If only PSG had stumped up the money to buy him; what a difference a transfer makes.

From that Marseille win in January until the end of the season, it was a stark reminder of what PSG – and Borelli – had to do to change not only their fortunes on the pitch but their culture off it. Bianchi was top scorer in Division 1 with 37 goals, an astounding number and eight clear of Delio Onnis of Monaco in second place, but no one else in the PSG side hit double figures in goals that season. Bianchi scored 39 in all competitions while Dahleb and M'Pelé scored nine each, with M'Pelé only scoring seven in the league. Bianchi was one of two players to make an appearance in every Division 1 game, alongside Philippe Redon, so while Paris Saint-Germain were certainly not a one-man team, the stats showed that when Bianchi was on form – which was quite often – then they performed well. If Bianchi had a rare off-day then it was almost certainly lights out for the Parisians. That needed to change. It would take time to find a way to make another goalscorer work in this side alongside a deadly marksman like Bianchi, but it needed to work if PSG were to be successful.

The following season, Borelli's first full season as president of the club, proved to be another frustrating one. PSG and the rest of France could only watch on as Strasbourg came out on top of a three-way title race against Nantes and Saint-Étienne to win the title. A team containing the likes of Arsène Wenger, Raymond Domenech and former PSG man Jacky Novi were triumphant, but Paris as a whole was anything but. Larqué stepped down from his role as player-manager to focus solely on being a part of the midfield and was replaced by Pierre Alonzo as caretaker until the club found a suitable replacement.

One win in their first six games of the season left PSG in 17th place, with their 2-0 loss away at Bordeaux leading to a report in *France Football* tearing them to shreds, saying, 'Poor Paris-Saint-Germain will never have been able to put a strain on a Bordeaux team which had no difficulty in maintaining their unbeaten position. The Girondins would indeed have been very capable of winning it by more goals if Baratelli had not produced an excellent match and saved a penalty shot by Giresse. Despite the missed golden opportunity, Carniglia's men were not in the least bit discouraged and with the set going very well, they had to secure their success with one goal per half. The Parisian attack, if we speak of it, did not really worry a defense which remained the best of the Championnet, while the situation of P.-S.-G. was becoming more and more critical. Which was normal for a team without soul and without great players, albeit with names.'

A team without soul and without great players is about as damning as you could get, but it wasn't far from the truth. The results spoke louder than anything else, and it certainly seemed that the club was lacking direction. Even Bianchi said in an interview with *SoFoot* that he felt PSG were lacking 'professionalism' and 'consistency' at the time. Not exactly how you would want a legend to remember his time at your club, but it was indicative of PSG at the time. Mid-table mediocrity followed throughout the season, never going above 11th in the table and never challenging for the Coupe de France, going out in the last 32 to Monaco. For their league match against Monaco in November 1978, PSG didn't even have a manager on the bench according to match reports. Pierre Alonzo wasn't listed as head trainer while Velibor Vasović, returning to the club having not managed anywhere following his original departure from PSG in 1977, wasn't officially confirmed as boss until the following game against Strasbourg, a game in which they came from behind at home to win 2-1. Borelli wanted a man who he could trust at the helm of his club and went with Vasović, the appointment steadying the rocky ship in the second half of the season. Winless from 2 December 1978 up until 2 March 1979, PSG could only hope for a mid-table finish. Seven wins followed the winter break with just five losses, very impressive considering the first half of the season resulted in 11 defeats. Five of those reverses had come by the end of September, further highlighting the work that Vasović had done since his appointment.

A 4-3 win over Marseille and a 3-0 victory against champions Monaco – Bianchi scored in both games – were the highlights of the second half of the season and, while the form was sketchy and thoroughly inconsistent, it did at least point towards something positive for PSG. Forty-three goals were conceded before the winter break, reduced to 19 in 14 games after the break. Admittedly, there were 24 matches played prior to the break but the goals to games ratio is far better in the latter stages of the season. Defensively PSG had tightened up, but what about going forward? Rather predictably, the team still relied on Bianchi for the majority of their goals. He scored 32 in 1978/79, which was just two fewer than the rest of the team combined.

The link-up between Bianchi and Dahleb was still exceptional – Bianchi even went on to say, 'We didn't need to talk. There was no need. He knew exactly what I was going to do and I knew exactly what he was going to do.' – but it almost papered over the cracks. Carlos Bianchi scored in 12 of PSG's wins in Division 1 during that season, and only twice were they victorious without him scoring. For a side hoping to challenge for honours and take on the more established clubs in France, that, once again, shouldn't be seen as a positive. Did taking the captaincy off Dahleb and handing it over to Dominique Bathenay, signed in the summer of 1978 from Saint-Étienne, help the Algerian's form? Probably not, but that is probably something we won't ever find out unless the man himself ever speaks on the subject.

But while the season on the pitch was rather disappointing, moves were being made off it that would ultimately form a major part of Paris Saint-Germain's make-up. They weren't happening at boardroom level or among the staff at the club, but rather in the stands where Parisians were choosing to back PSG over rivals Paris FC. It mustn't be forgotten that Paris FC actually gained promotion the year prior and France was treated to a rare double Parisian derby. It was a big moment for football in Paris because if Paris FC managed to survive their first season back and give PSG a run for their money, with PSG themselves gradually making the right steps forward, then Paris would have been able to boast two top-flight teams, something that it hadn't really been able to do for a while.

For the first time since the 1974/195 season, French football had a top-flight Parisian derby, but this particular match-up hit differently to the others. The battle was now on to find out who was the 'real' Parisian team. Was it the newer, bolder Paris Saint-Germain with their star names and Parc des Princes but a distinct lack of history and success, or was it the team that effectively got chosen to be the club of the city at the expense of PSG? Only time would tell. It said a lot about PSG's rise that in such a short space of time they could more or less outgrow the club that they split from all those years ago but it also spoke volumes that in the first meeting between these two in the 1978/79 season, Paris FC were unlucky not to come away from le Parc with a win. *France Football* described the promoted side as 'a real team that moves the ball quickly and with accuracy. They feel the joy of playing football,' before describing PSG as 'fragmented, it looks like it is made up of cells that have little connection'. The same match report also said that the 2-2 draw that these two played out was a fair result, claiming, 'While PSG had the better chances, Paris FC played better and were more spectacular, which the 25,000 fans in attendance appreciated.'

Of course, playing spectacularly doesn't win you games on its own but the line about the fans at the end of the piece points more towards the real battle that these two clubs were having off the pitch. They weren't just battling for points or for places in the table, they were battling for fans and for the right to be the premium Parisian club. This draw was portrayed as PSG being able to get the result because they had the better players, who created – and ultimately scored – better chances than PFC, but PFC played better football, therefore the fans appreciated them more. That wouldn't have been the case if you were a PSG fan who didn't care much for a club that essentially took your place in Division 1 all those years ago and helped move you down to Division 3, taking a handful of players while they were at it.

Later in the season, in PSG's final Division 1 match before the winter break, the two sides could only manage a 1-1 draw, meaning that on the pitch nothing could separate them. But PSG had the advantage from the get-go in terms of drawing in more fans with the Parc des Princes while Paris FC only occasionally played at le Parc, thus giving PSG the chance to bring more fans into the stadium. Their 'ten matches for ten francs' scheme for younger fans had worked, and Kop K had been a good place for supporters to congregate and essentially start their version of a PSG 'ultras' group. The plan was put in place in 1976, but the youth seats moved in 1978, prompting the Kop to move along with it. The prices in Kop K were increasing but fans weren't exactly happy with that and looked to move around the Parc des Princes. They moved to behind the goal in the Boulogne end of the stadium, spawning something completely different to what was seen elsewhere. One supporter told the *Paris Tribune* that they were inspired by other fans who placed themselves behind goals, mainly Liverpool and their world-famous Kop (the Spion Kop, to give it the proper name) and now, in 1978, the Kop de Boulogne was officially a part of PSG's fabric.

The KdB and the many branch-off groups who would come in later years were known for far-right chants, songs, banners, with the same fan who told of the inspiration behind the KdB saying, 'We decided to go to Boulogne because there were too many blacks in Auteuil [the other end of the stadium]. And yes, already. In the team, there were a lot of blacks in the stands ... We could have landed at Auteuil if ... but no, it was Boulogne.' This tells you all you need to know about the level of decision-making behind the Kop de Boulogne at the time.

Members of the Kop were named '*kobistes*' (more or less the same as calling someone who stood on the Anfield Kop a 'Kopite') and began to recognise other fan groups as years went on, including the likes of the Boulogne Boys, who were founded as an official supporters' group in 1985 and were the first of their kind for the KdB. In a matter of years, culminating in 1978/79 when PSG needed fans on their side perhaps more than ever, the fans who flocked to the Parc des Princes went from spectators who wanted to see an entertaining game of football to those who went to see PSG win.

Despite the efforts of Paris FC, who were nicknamed 'Paris1' by PSG fans in jest at the club and French radio station Europe1, to try and overtake PSG in the popularity race, the results were there for all to see and ultimately shaped the way this race, to be Paris's top club, went. Paris FC were relegated on goal difference – a 5-0 loss away at Nice didn't help their cause and just one clean sheet in their final two wins against Sochaux and Bordeaux would have kept them up – and the average attendances between the two sides indicated that PSG, admittedly with a much larger stadium and better team, were the choice of the fans. On average, 24,322 took to the Parc des Princes to watch PSG while only 8,040 went to see Paris FC.

Paris FC haven't been back to the top flight since that season and have been overshadowed by PSG ever since. The two aren't seen as main rivals now because of the lack of matches played against one another, the lack of knowledge about another Parisian team by the wider footballing world and the fact that PSG's rivals have changed from Paris FC and Red Star to Marseille, Lyon and even the likes of Barcelona on the continent. There's always place for a good Parisian derby and French football would probably be better off for it but even as the 1970s drew to a close, PSG were the dominant capital club and were slowly making moves towards success. Francis Borelli knew he needed the right blend in his squad to balance out a fairly lopsided line-up and he needed a manager he could trust to see through the plans he wanted to lay out. Velibor Vasović was kept on as head coach, but Carlos Bianchi was out of the door and was soon followed by François M'Pelé, leaving Mustapha Dahleb to link up with the new arrival, signed from Paris FC, Jean-François Beltramini, and Marseille's Boubacar Sarr. Things were changing for PSG and they were moving out a lot of what had taken them to where they were. Little did they know, however, that PSG were about to enter their first golden era.

6

La théorie de Bianchi –
The Bianchi theory

CARLOS BIANCHI, the goal machine of Paris Saint-Germain, had moved on. In a bid to try and win some silverware with Strasbourg, Bianchi jumped ship to the eastern side of France. While Bianchi departed Paris, citing the lack of trophies and professionalism at the club and telling *SoFoot* that while he enjoyed his years at PSG he preferred his time with Reims, the club moved on and tried to build a team around a changing culture rather than around one goalscoring striker that could leave at the drop of a hat.

The Argentine striker – who somehow missed out on the 1978 Argentina World Cup squad and therefore missed out on a World Cup winners' medal – would only spend a year with Strasbourg and score just eight Division 1 goals before heading back to Velez Sarsfield for a four-year spell. How many trophies did he win with Strasbourg? The same as he did for Paris Saint-Germain: none. But the departure of Bianchi had me thinking about a theory that usually applies in American sports but is focused around a team that has one star player who is responsible for anything positive happening who leaves that team, only for them to improve and essentially get better and better without said star. See the 'Ewing Theory' as an explanation.

Patrick Ewing was *the* star of the New York Knicks basketball team in the 1990s. The team ran everything through him and it was thought that if the Knicks were to achieve anything in an era dominated by Michael Jordan and the Chicago Bulls, Ewing would have to be their beating heart. They signed players based on how Ewing could work with them and how they could complement him. In 1999, however, the Knicks lost Ewing to an injury for the series against the Indiana Pacers. Everyone wrote them off, saying that without their star man they had no chance of winning a game, let alone an entire series. Somehow the Knicks won the series and advanced to the NBA Finals. After being written off without their star man, the Knicks came back and managed to pull off an upset.

Somewhere in the US at the time, a writer named Bill Simmons (author of the wonderful *The Book of Basketball* and head honcho at US sports website The Ringer) developed an idea around these events. The theory he helped concoct was based around two rules: the team has a star player who receives a lot of attention but never wins anything; the star player leaves the team and everybody writes the team off. For the theory to work, the end result has to be that the team who was written off wins when they are least expected to because of the absence of their star. Simmons called it the Ewing Theory.

This ties in to Paris Saint-Germain. Carlos Bianchi was the star of the team, regardless of the talent levels of the players around him. We have already covered how over-reliant PSG were on Bianchi to the point where it was probably detrimental to the success of the team. But could PSG actually succeed without the man who had scored an incredible 71 goals in 80 games? By way of context, after 81 games, Lionel Messi only had 35 goals for Barcelona. It took Cristiano Ronaldo until 2007/08 to reach 71 goals in his club career, his sixth season in top-flight football. Bianchi reached that number in two seasons. It's a question that needs to be kept in the back of your mind as we move into another new era of Paris Saint-Germain and explore the idea of the 'Bianchi theory'. It's a theory that meets all the criteria for the original Ewing Theory, but this one makes so much more sense, as you'll find out.

The departure of Bianchi was the pivotal moment for this team in terms of trying to move forward on the pitch, but a key moment came off it with Francis Borelli going to the City of Paris, proclaiming PSG to be the premier Parisian club – not exactly hard when your main rivals had just been relegated the season prior – and receiving 5m francs for the club, with 2.5m francs used to wipe out any debt. That, while it may not concern the average fan, was huge for PSG. The days of relying on RTL for financial help to sign players was slowly fading away and they were being built to be self-sufficient or at least operate on a more free-flowing basis. They wanted to control their own money and this was a giant step in that direction.

Jean-François Beltramini was brought in from Paris FC alongside fellow forward Boubacar Sarr, signed from

Marseille, and had the task of contributing to a more team-friendly PSG, with Mustapha Dahleb providing more creativity. Opening the season with a 1-1 draw at the Stade Gerland against Lyon wasn't the worst way to open a season, especially when PSG were in a tough situation heading into the game. Velibor Vasović said after the game, 'After the training sessions leading up to this meeting, I could only have thirteen fully fit players and not one more. These are hardly the ideal conditions for a first league meeting, and that's how I had to field [Jean-Noël] Huck for the right-back. I therefore consider that we put in a very convincing performance, and especially encouraging for the rest of the season. The attackers should improve over the matches, starting with the one we will play against Marseille next Friday.' PSG's forwards had missed more chances than expected, and they should have come away with a win against a Lyon side who didn't really pose much danger to the Parisian back line. With one point in the bag, PSG knew where they could improve. But in their next game against Marseille it was a completely different matter.

In front of a sold-out Parc des Princes, Marseille took the lead within 11 minutes. PSG didn't have their head screwed on properly from the first whistle and allowed Didier Six to pounce through their defence and poke home under goalkeeper Dominique Baratelli. A nightmare start for PSG, but it was the perfect time to test their new strength. Could they pull together as a team and find a way back into the game? Time was on their side, so they needn't have worried about glancing up at the scoreboard to see minute after minute ticking away. Staying calm was key, as was trusting their own ability as a team.

Abel Braga, a Brazilian who was signed from Vasco da Gama that summer, was given an opportunity when PSG had a free kick towards the left-hand edge of the penalty area, the perfect angle for a right-footer to curl in to the top-left corner of the goal. Braga, with his impressive figure suitable for an Olympian – broad shoulders, slender frame but impressive height – rather than a footballer, treated the free kick like a penalty, shooting low and hard with plenty of power. He had levelled things up and flew to the touchline to celebrate with the adoring PSG fans after bringing their team back into the game.

Marseille, who by this point had essentially resigned themselves to fending off whatever PSG threw at them, had to keep sitting deep, just looking to survive rather than hit on the counter-attack. The momentum had swung into PSG's direction and they took it in their stride, looking for that winner. As the 70th minute struck, so did PSG. Dominique Bathenay, the captain who followed previous manager Jean-Michel Larqué over from Saint-Étienne, popped up with an all-important winner. PSG managed to see out the remaining 20 or so minutes and took home maximum points. With a reported 45,000 in attendance to see the result, PSG were slowly getting the better of their rivals, one by one.

A victory over Marseille has always been sweet – even if at that stage they weren't the rivals we know them as today – and the win saw PSG jump up to seventh in the table, their highest position in Division 1 at any point since February 1977. It may have only been after two games but it was a promising start. It showed that the character of this team was there when it needed to be and showed that, while it was still a huge work in progress,

PSG were looking upwards and a poor Marseille side were looking worryingly downwards.

Again, like the finances that Borelli had used to solve more problems behind the scenes, this was a step in the right direction for PSG but the question still remained as to how things would look as time went on. Would they miss Carlos Bianchi and his goals or would they be spread throughout the team and result in a more balanced side? Following up the Marseille win with a loss away at Sochaux wasn't the way that PSG saw the next fixture going but they managed to bounce back with a convincing victory at home against Laval after once again creating chance after chance. Sarr scored twice while Bernard Bureau, the forward who made his debut with PSG the previous season, added a third.

By this stage of the season PSG were sitting in a respectable eighth place, but the players knew full well that they could improve on that. They played better than eighth and just needed to start taking a few more chances but that was not news to those on the field or on the sidelines. Dahleb was creating and looking like his magical self while there were five different scorers across PSG's opening five Division 1 games, already an improvement on the previous season (although by the fifth match of 1978/79, PSG had only scored two goals in total). Yet, despite having quite a positive and prosperous start – albeit after just four games and two wins – whatever goodwill and positivity they had created for themselves went straight out of the window and that victory against Laval on 17 August was their last for eight games, a run that spanned to 19 October. They plummeted from eighth and looking like they had all the makings to push towards the UEFA Cup or even become dark horses for the title, all the way down to 15th, a familiar position over the past few years.

So, how bad was that run of form? Well, it went like this. A 2-2 draw with Monaco wasn't too bad given the talent that Monaco had in their ranks but PSG then failed the following week to break down a Brestois defence that was just waiting to be knocked down and missing chance after chance, they had to settle for a point. They then allowed themselves to fall behind 4-0 away at Nantes before staging a mini comeback to still lose 4-2, following this by being battered at Lens.

Returning to the Parc des Princes the following weekend in front of an average turnout of just 13,387, PSG lost yet again, this time to a Nancy side who were dominant for the first 45 minutes but nearly let the hosts grab something from this match. A Saint-Étienne team who weren't fully at the races still managed to beat PSG, although losing to Les Verts wasn't the end of the world, even if there was a chance for the Parisans to level multiple times. Sometimes, you just hold your hands up and say it wasn't your day. In fact, it hadn't been PSG's day for nearly two months at this point and that poor run continued in front of less than 10,000 fans at le Parc (their second-lowest attendance of the season) in an entertaining yet frustrating game as they went behind twice against Nice, yet on both occasions managed to equalise just a minute after they had conceded. Yet again, however, the story of the fixture was PSG's missed chances, even if the draw may have been a fair result.

The run continued for one more game, a poor 2-0 loss away at Nîmes. It wouldn't be Paris Saint-Germain if there wasn't some form of collapse that was nearly impossible to explain. It seemed to be something that was ingrained in the club at this point, the ability to throw away leads and to find a way to not make the most of a good thing. That was why Bianchi left and it was the mindset that Francis Borelli was trying to change. Borelli's future plans were now in need of a switch, not because of the run of results – form is temporary, as the first half of a famous cliché goes – but because the manager had just packed his bags and left PSG and France altogether. On the face of it, the decision for Velibor Vasović to go may have been down to the results but when you dig a little deeper and find out the real reason, you can't blame him.

Back in 1979, UNECATEF – the National Union of French Football Coaches and Technical Managers – had Guy Roux as their president. Roux, one of the most legendary French managers of all time, had been with Auxerre since 1961 after he became player-coach at the age of just 23. He had taken Auxerre from the fourth tier of French football to the Coupe de France Final in 1979 before finally reaching Division 1 in 1980. It was an incredible rise and, despite the fact his trophy cabinet would be fairly empty by the time he retired (the 1995/96 Division 1 title, four Coupe de France triumphs and the 1979/80 Division 2 stand out), Roux had the respect and admiration across the board when it came to managers and coaches because they could recognise just how good a job he had been doing at Auxerre.

Even in 1979 – a time when all Roux had won was the Division 4 title – he had authority and people listened to what he had to say. What Roux had to say about Vasović was why PSG lost their manager, but the reasoning

depends on where you read it. Some reports suggest that
Roux made the point that Vasović didn't have the correct
coaching badges to coach in the top flight. This is what
one study said about coaching in France, 'The French
Football Federation created, in 1942, national courses
for French coaches to improve the situation and these
became obligatory in order to coach a professional team.
Certification was obtained only after passing demanding
specific tests but, despite the knowledge acquired during
these courses, the coach still had to define, empirically and
scientifically, training fundamentals when he arrived in
his club.' Roux was apparently questioning whether or not
Vasović had the right certificates for the job, prompting
the Yugoslavian to lose his faith in UNECATEF and his
fellow coaches.

The second story is slightly different in the reasoning
but ultimately ends with the same outcome. Roux said that
he would prefer a Frenchman to be managing Paris Saint-
Germain because it would be fitting for a countryman to
be in the capital, completely offending Vasović and again
resulting in him leaving France for good after losing faith
in his union and his peers.

The first story seems to have a little bit more substance
behind it because it would make sense for the president
of UNECATEF to have a concern about who is actually
qualified to manage Division 1 clubs, but also because the
second story seems to be so ridiculous that it can't be true
and absurd to focus in solely on PSG. In October 1979,
Bordeaux had the Argentine Luis Carniglia in charge
(replaced a year later by Belgian Raymond Goethals),
Nantes had Spaniard José Arribas who had finished
second the previous year while winning the Coupe de

France and would eventually win the 1979/80 Division 1 title, so to call out PSG for having a foreign manager wouldn't give Roux the best look considering that Vasović wasn't the only non-French boss.

Either way, the fact remained that Vasović had left PSG and the Parisians were, once again, looking for another manager to lead them forward in the longer term, but initially to take a path that had at least some ray of hope and optimism rather than yet another season of dull, mundane and utterly predictable outcomes. Vasović had gone and with PSG turning to Pierre Alonzo as caretaker again, alongside former youth manager Camille Choquier as co-caretaker, the hunt for a new manager was on. The duo would take charge of the loss against Nîmes before taking PSG on a bit of a winning run, defeating Valenciennes at home in a convincing 3-0 win and hanging on to a 2-1 victory away at Angers to lift the team into 11th. It still wasn't the desired place in the standings that the club was looking for, but it was a much-improved showing and an improvement on 15th. Alonzo and Choquier would step aside following the Angers triumph as Borelli had found his man.

Known for his time primarily as a forward for Saint-Étienne during the mid to late 1950s and early 60s, Georges Peyroche had some pedigree behind him. As a player, he won Division 1 and Coupe de France with Les Verts while guiding Lille to the Division 2 crown in 1974 as a manager. Peyroche knew how to win, whether as a boss or as a player, but he had what PSG were looking for: the ability to guide this talented group towards success. They had all the tools to do it and the indifferent form during the 1979/80 season showed that perhaps all that was needed was know-how and guidance, something which Borelli felt that Peyroche offered. Many probably didn't realise the ride that Peyroche was about to send PSG on, but his reign started off in impressive fashion and, perhaps more importantly, with two massive points.

When Peyroche was officially announced, PSG were being tipped to fall into a relegation battle. Another season of disappointment was looming over the Parc des Princes heading into November, although those two wins against Valenciennes and Angers lifted spirits. Many, however, likely expected the run to end with French champions Strasbourg coming in to the city, aided by the efforts of Carlos Bianchi who started the game up front despite suffering from a severe drop in form following his departure from le Parc. But for PSG, it did seem like the odds were stacked against them somewhat. The champions heading to your home with a striker looking to not only get back into his groove of scoring goal after goal but also looking to prove a point and show why he left in the first place: to play for a team that can truly challenge.

Peyroche had also only taken charge of one training session, the day before the game, so he had minimal time to try and impose his ideas on to his new group of players, although he was able to welcome Dahleb back to the starting line-up after missing a month and a half with a thigh problem (which probably explains why, for that time, PSG were so rotten in form). It didn't look like a win was on the cards, especially when PSG had to weather an early Strasbourg storm with Bianchi and Joël Tanter trying their luck but eventually only being restricted to long-range efforts. PSG didn't have many clear-cut chances themselves, mainly down to a dominant

Strasbourg showing and the performance of their goalkeeper Dominique Dropsy, perhaps the worst name you can have as a stopper. Dropsy kept Sarr's effort out but was helpless to stop the next shot from Jean-François Beltramini, who managed to score his fourth goal in the last three home matches with an absolute belter into the top-left corner. It was a goal worthy of a victory, but PSG still had to see out the last five minutes of the half and the rest of the game. They had to switch on, focus on the task at hand and see off Strasbourg in what would, rightly, be regarded as an upset but also a huge win. Yes, they would be taking the scalp of the champions, and making it three wins in a row, which was not only a boost on the pitch but, with a new manager in place, it was a huge boost mentally for the players as well. Being able to show that they could go toe-to-toe with the winners in French football was massive for the club, but time was still ticking.

Strasbourg completely dominated proceedings in the second 45 minutes. Effort after effort and huge chunks of play with the ball at their feet, wearing down PSG who had to chase and chase, but the visitors couldn't find a way through goalkeeper Dominique Baratelli or the back four of Jean-Marc Pilorget, Thierry Morin, Éric Renaut and Jean-Claude Lemoult, all of whom started their professional careers with Paris Saint-Germain. When the final whistle blew, there was pure jubilation after three successive wins for PSG and a debut victory for Peyroche, who was keen to deflect the praise on to Alonzo and Choquier, saying, 'Bravo to Pierre Alonzo and Camille Choquier, who had filled in before my arrival. It's their victory, they're the ones who put together the team to face Strasbourg. I'd also like to thank the players:

there's courage to burn, heart, determination and great individuals in this Paris team.'

Peyroche may have pushed the praise elsewhere but the following week against Bordeaux saw the winning run stretch to four games. The sequence had seen PSG fly up the table into eighth, on the cusp of going higher if they managed to stretch the run further. With just five games left until the winter break, it became paramount that PSG finished the year strongly.

Three wins from their last five games of 1979, including an impressive 2-0 victory against Marseille in front of just over 5,550 fans at a dark Stade Vélodrome, put PSG fifth as 1979 drew to a close, a position they hadn't been in since January 1977. Peyroche had worked some magic on this side and kept their momentum going in this mini run, losing just once since taking over as manager. Mustapha Dahleb was playing arguably the best football of his career so far while Sarr and Beltramini were providing enough support up front to get the victories when needed. Abel Braga, although severely hampered by injuries meaning he wouldn't make as many appearances as he would have liked, was contributing as well, while the group of youth academy players like Luis Fernández were making their presence felt too. There were still areas that could be improved on but, on the whole, PSG looked like they had the foundations of a strong team growing.

Returning from the winter break with a loss at Laval wasn't ideal but once again they bounced back with strength thanks to four straight wins against Monaco, Brest, Nantes and Lens. Fifth place remained in the hands of PSG, but the toll of the games was slowly catching up to them. Sarr and Fernández were out injured with fibula and tibia issues respectively following the Monaco game, which put PSG eight players down. Dahleb was still producing his magic but the team were slowly fading away. From March up until the end of May, PSG recorded two wins and four draws, and were knocked out of the Coupe de France by Lens, even losing the first leg 2-0 at home. The collapse saw them fall to seventh, certainly not a bad effort (their highest-ever league finish at this point) but disappointing knowing what could have been. At the start of the season, Paris Saint-Germain would have snatched at the chance to finish seventh in a year that was essentially meant to be one of rebuilding and looking at how to attack the future. But given the way the season went and the fact that as late as mid-April they were in fifth, it could have been so much better.

The base for a solid, competitive team was in place with a president who was patient, clear and direct in spreading his message and a manager who knew how to get over the line and understood what it took to be a manager but, perhaps most importantly, also knew what it took to win Division 1, alongside the fact that – slowly but surely – more Parisians were supporting the club. By no means was it like an English club where thousands would flock to the ground every weekend, singing for 90 minutes, or like Germany where the fans become more involved in how a club operates, but it was becoming a place for supporters in Paris to go. They weren't Real Madrid or Liverpool, but they were Paris Saint-Germain and the fact that younger players who were coming through the youth academy were being integrated into the squad was a huge matter. Players like Fernández knew the club, they understood what it meant to shape its history and the fans recognised this and appreciated them for it.

Before the 1980/1981 season, PSG only brought two players in to help push their squad on. Nambatingue Toko, a solid but rather unspectacular striker who scored a handful of goals for Valenciennes prior to his move to Paris, but added depth and tackled the issue that, while PSG were more than adept at creating chances, finishing them was a completely different matter. Toko, while not a superstar name, could be used to shake things up a bit. But it was another forward who signed that summer who really stole the headlines and would be the main superstar for PSG.

Known as 'L'ange vert' because of his iconic spell for the great Saint-Étienne sides in the 1970s, Dominique Rocheteau was blessed with success. Making his debut for Saint-Étienne in the 1971/72 season, Rocheteau was a winger who could twist and turn like no one else in France and was blessed with not only success but the talent and intelligence to go along with it. Being known primarily as a winger didn't stop Rocheteau from scoring plenty of goals, being a great mix of serial goalscorer and creator from the flanks. His first trophy would come at the age of just 19 when Les Verts won the Division 1 title in 1974, keeping hold of it for the next two seasons. The 1976 championship could have been made all the more historic had they triumphed on the continent.

Meeting at Hampden Park in Glasgow, many expected Bayern Munich to beat Saint-Étienne given that they had defeated them in the previous year's semi-final and the fact that Bayern had so many world-class players in their ranks. Sepp Maier was in goal with Hans-Georg

Schwarzenbeck and Franz Beckenbauer at the back while Karl-Heinz Rummenigge, Uli Hoeneß and 'Der Bomber' Gerd Müller provided the attacking threat. Saint-Étienne were still confident of leaving Scotland with the trophy, but the war of words between the two sides started way before the build-up to the game with Bayern complaining about fixture scheduling, suggesting that the Scottish public would save their money and go to the Scotland vs England friendly three days later, instead of going to the European Cup Final. Saint-Étienne president Roger Rocher said in response, 'Bayern are interested in making a profit from the final. Saint-Étienne are merely interested in winning the final.'

Ultimately, Bayern were winners despite an impressive and unlucky display from the French club. Chance after chance passed them by but the experience of Bayern was enough to give them the trophy and send Saint-Étienne back to France empty-handed.

The following season, the sole trophy for Rocheteau would be the Coupe de France, his final piece of silverware for Saint-Étienne before L'ange vert would depart for the capital, promised game time and a role as the focal point of the PSG attack by boss Peyroche. And it wasn't as if Rocheteau was winding down his career by the time he arrived in Paris; rather he was in the prime of his career. Aged 25, the perfect age for a quick and skilful winger, the Green Angel had been let down by his body far too many times. His injury problems were hampering his time on the field and he only managed eight minutes on the pitch during the European Cup Final loss to Bayern Munich after being chucked on at the end to try and salvage something. The following season, when Liverpool knocked Saint-Étienne out in the quarter-final, was more heartbreak, but as Saint-Étienne appeared to change their policy from promoting youth academy stars like Rocheteau in favour of major signings such as Johnny Rep, Jacques Zimako, Bernard Lacombe, Patrick Battiston and Michel Platini, Rocheteau found himself out of luck and out of favour, despite having the confidence of his manager.

There simply was no place left in the Saint-Étienne line-up for him and, while he excelled on the wing, Rocheteau wanted a more central role, which simply wasn't available due to the acquisition of Michel Platini, so PSG offered Rocheteau something he had been looking for. They promised him adequate game time – as much as you could give someone with an injury track record like Rocheteau's – and the chance to play down the middle. Peyroche was the man who was able to convince the forward to join and it was Francis Borelli who initially wanted to bring him in, alongside Nambatingue Toko. This now gave PSG four main forwards to choose from – although it was probably the last time that Jean-François Beltramini would play even a remote part in anything meaningful on the pitch since he didn't score a single goal in any of his four appearances and was sold to Rouen the following campaign.

Rocheteau, a player with a point to prove, had become the focal point of a new-look Paris Saint-Germain side who were looking to not only dismiss doubters but to improve drastically on the field and off it. The early stages of a formidable starting line-up were starting to show through with a solid back line spearheaded by the likes of Jean-Marc Pilorget and Éric Renaut, while Mustapha Dahleb, Dominique Bathenay and Luis Fernández offered options in the middle of the field and both new signings Too and Rocheteau being the go-to guys when it came to putting the ball into the back of the net. Goalkeeper Dominique Baratelli was a pivotal part to the way that PSG was structured.

Three wins from their opening five games wasn't bad at all, especially considering that in an exciting 2-2 draw away at Lille, there was a strong case for PSG to have come away victorious. After winning at home against Valenciennes, PSG saw themselves in second place, perhaps ahead of schedule but a sign that they had the makings of a team that could at least put together a push for a trophy. However, while second was outstanding, there was still time for PSG to revert to type and drop points along the way. Losing their first game away at Monaco, who hadn't finished outside of the top four since their promotion in 1977 and winning Division 1 in 1978, was nothing to be ashamed of but perhaps it was a game that PSG imagined that they could get at least a point from. It was the kind of match that they needed to start believing they could win, although that Monaco team was always going to be far too strong on that occasion.

Aside from this and a defeat later down the line away at Sochaux, PSG were looking a lot stronger than they had done in previous seasons. By the time they defeated Lille 4-1 in early December – Rocheteau with a hat-trick, his fifth, sixth and seventh goals of the season after starting the season without hitting the back of the net for quite a while – PSG were fourth. They were looking a lot better as a team than they had done before this season and were looking like they had finally got themselves into a promising position. The fans related to the players and had fallen in love with Rocheteau, as had Peyroche who said after the Lille win, 'Not bad, our centre-forward! Rocheteau has proven that he is now a complete centre-forward.'

There were brief flashes of violence peering out from the ultras culture that was developing in the stands – for example, a rocket was launched in a game at home against Nîmes, which the club was aware of, but at this stage they felt it was something that should only be noted and not acted on – but by and large, things were developing quite nicely. That being said, the mentality and the culture from within the club still needed changing and without the experience of being this high up in the league at such a stage in the season, the fall from grace was always going to be harder than most. Paris Saint-Germain had reached a high that they hadn't achieved in their history up until this point but were about to fall quicker than perhaps they ever had done since their return to the top flight.

That win against Lille would be their last until the final day of February. They went the rest of December, the entirety of January and most of February without a victory. Throw in the winter break and that is far too long when you have the kind of ambition that Paris Saint-Germain had in this season.

Their first home loss of the campaign came in the game following the Lille triumph, a thrilling 3-2 defeat to Auxerre. Their first 0-0 of the season – a highly violent and viciously important game against Monaco – was followed up by another goalless draw at Metz which helped neither side but, when Peyroche said following the game, 'The spirit of solidarity shown by the whole team is encouraging for the future,' it was more than likely his own way of saying, 'At least we didn't lose.'

A rearranged match away at Lyon resulted in another loss, as did games against Nantes and Nîmes. At the end of the Nantes defeat, a stat revealed that PSG hadn't scored a goal in eight hours of play, but it once again all came down to a trait that they had clung on to for far too long: failing to take chances. The chances for European football the next season were fading away from Peyroche and his men, but they only had themselves to blame. The annual collapse in PSG's form was far harsher than anyone had expected, even if the fans still arrived at the Parc des Princes to cheer the team on (the loss against Nantes, their fifth in eight games, still drew a crowd of 36,208). Being without their main creator Dahleb – who had been absent since the 3-2 home loss against Auxerre – wasn't ideal but his return to the starting line-up seemed to light a spark. Given how poor their form had been, it can only be seen as either divine intervention or a brilliantly timed turn in fortunes that PSG failed to lose another game once Dahleb came back. Wins against Nice, Sochaux, Saint-Étienne, Tours, Bordeaux, Bastia and Lens alongside draws against Laval, Nancy, Lyon and Angers saw PSG go from outsiders to a European spot to finishing fifth, just three points off Monaco in fourth.

On the face of it, a fifth-placed finish wasn't the worst situation to be in and PSG actually went into the final day of the season with a chance of finishing fourth, having to rely on Monaco losing and themselves picking up a victory, but Monaco managed to win. Without Dahleb and Fernández (both suspended), PSG managed a draw at home to Angers, yet the fans still whistled, jeered and booed. Some said they were booing the players, others said they were booing the announcement that Monaco had in fact won their game. It seems more likely that the fans booed the announcement but that didn't stop Peyroche proclaiming at full time, 'After a super-season, my players did not deserve this,' very much placing his flag in the camp of the Parc des Princes booing his team.

But if the fans were booing his team then Peyroche had a point. The PSG supporters had become more and more vocal as the campaign had gone on, with the Boulogne section acting as the main core of support with the rest of le Parc still turning up to see the star teams and star names (for that important clash against Angers on the final day of the season, only 11,535 fans showed up, 10,000 fewer than the attendance for the previous home game against Lyon) So, while some sections were actually starting to get behind the team on a more regular basis – travelling the country with the team was no easy feat but some were doing it – that meant more scrutiny was to come along with it. The players were under more pressure because, as Parisians, the fans expected more. They were *the* team representing the capital but had so far failed to act like it. The violence in the stands was slowly starting to increase, with those who had grown up in what was called Kop K no longer being supervised by the Friends of PSG and left to their own devices.

Perhaps influenced by the scenes they saw on the terraces and news reports coming from fans in England, the PSG fans were not unfamiliar with fighting both in the capital and on their travels across France and became notorious for this. The far right were slowly infiltrating the Boulogne end, and while tensions certainly weren't at boiling point in the stands, it was slowly becoming a rowdy, raucous and occasionally unpleasant visit for some fans, regardless of who you supported. At this stage in Paris Saint-Germain's history, the fans were still turning up for the opposing teams, so hooliganism, songs, flares and violence were still some time away, but not as far in the distance as things would have suggested.

But on the field, there was hope and optimism. Missing out on European football on the final day of the season when you know you could have done just that little bit more to make ground on the team above you is always going to be a tough one to take, and that is only natural. For the second year of a rebuild, Georges Peyroche had done an outstanding job. The team looked as cohesive as it had done in years and was probably the best it had been since promotion back into Division 1. Three players – Rocheteau, Toko and Sarr – scored ten goals or more for the first time in a single season since the 1976/77 campaign and for only the fourth time in the club's short history to this point. That, in itself, should have been seen as a massive positive because it was a stat that acknowledged that removing the star striker and primary source of goals – in this case Carlos Bianchi – could actually be a benefit to the team. The mentality of feeding the ball to one particular player was now replaced by a mentality of trust and sense that any of the attackers could score, given the right opportunity. Rocheteau, Toko, Dahleb, Sarr were all players who had creativity, intelligence, skill, guile and a killer mentality in front of goal. They were not merely happy with padding their stats with goal after goal for their own legacy, they wanted to make sure they did what was absolutely necessary to get the win on that particular day.

The departure of Bianchi was something that did hang over the head of PSG heading into their rebuild under Peyroche, but it didn't affect them. If anything, it spurred them on. But, at this point in the PSG story, they still hadn't actually achieved anything. They had performed well in the Coupe de France once or twice plus this fifth-placed finish was nothing to scoff at, but the trophy cabinet was bare apart from the Division 2 promotion trophy. There was still that ability to push themselves over the line that was the proverbial nail sticking out of a cut of wood, tagging itself on to the Parisian sleeve and refusing to let go. The nail was holding them back, not letting them pass, but the only way PSG could unhook from the nail was to remove themselves from it. They held the keys to figuring out the next step. Yes, they had been held back by either their own lack of consistency and professionalism since the days of Hechter and Bianchi or their inexperience in tight, important situations simply because they hadn't been there before, just as the old, tired trope goes: you need experience for the role, but you can't get the experience without having the role, and the same goes for PSG here. They needed trophy-winning experience to get over the line, but they couldn't get over the line without winning a trophy.

That was the next step and everyone knew it. They were established as a Division 1 team – and a good one at that – but needed that one major moment to solidify their status as a big club in France. They were a big club in name and location but not in any other department. Would they be able to win a piece of silverware to put them at the same table as the likes of Reims, Marseille, Monaco and Saint-Étienne? After years and years of missed opportunities, it felt like the duo of Borelli and Peyroche had finally built a team that was ready to compete at the top of Division 1 and could take on challengers from wherever they may arrive from. And if they couldn't challenge for the Division 1 title and get into European competition that way, at least they had the Coupe de France to aim for.

7

L'été 1982 – The summer of 1982

IN APRIL of 1982, before the World Cup in Spain, the French national team travelled to Paris to go to the town hall for a reception in their honour. Within the town hall were the elite of French football. If you were anybody in the world of French football – whether that be on the pitch and in the squad or an owner, manager, president – you were at the town hall. So, of course, Francis Borelli found himself front and centre at the gala with only one person on his mind: Michel Platini. The France captain was preparing himself not only for the World Cup but also for his next move in football as he was seeking a way out of Saint-Étienne at the time, and Borelli was determined to try and convince Platini to leave Les Verts to join les Rouge et Bleu.

The two men met and the seed was planted in Platini's mind about how PSG were so keen to sign the great playmaker, how he would be the biggest star in Paris, but the two left it at a point. They didn't press the issue because the town hall and a gala such as that was no place to chat transfers, especially when Platini was there on national team business.

But that did not deter Borelli. He left Platini at the town hall but by the time he arrived at his home, his pen and paper were already hard at work to try and woo the star, who by this time was already establishing himself as one of Europe's top players, even if he was hitting 27 years of age. Platini was in his prime and was about to become one of the best players in the world, something that Borelli wanted a piece of. Borelli wrote Platini a letter to try and convince him to leave Saint-Étienne to join his new PSG side, to be the leader of his young club. The letter, mixed with sincerity, passion and a history of PSG alongside what the club can offer him, read something like this, as reported by sofoot.com, 'Dear Mr Platini, Paris is waiting for you. Mr Platini, what I propose to you is to enter you further into the history of our sport by becoming the builder of a destiny that is promised to Paris Saint-Germain. I have no embarrassment in telling you publicly that we need you and in declaring to you with friendly solemnity, how much the role which is given to you here seems suited to you.'

Borelli simply signed the letter off with, 'Mr Platini, become a Parisian.' The conclusion was like a call to arms but the letter itself read like a lovestruck teenager, pleading that they simply could not live without the other person and needed them in their life desperately. This, the same club that wouldn't even raise funds to sign Platini from Nancy all those years ago, was now writing footballing love letters to the captain of the national team.

But it all seemed in vain because the very same day that Borelli expressed his affection for Platini, France played Peru in a friendly at the Parc des Princes and some rather important guests were in Paris to see the game, including Giampiero Boniperti, the president of Juventus. At the time, Italy had a rule where you could only have two foreign players in your squad and Juventus had those spots occupied in 1982. One was taken up by Polish striker Zbigniew Boniek and the other by Irish playmaker and Arsenal legend Liam Brady. Juve were just about to win their second successive Serie A title but that didn't stop Boniperti looking to make a seismic change to the squad.

With three games left of the Serie A season, Boniperti called Brady into his office to inform the Irishman that his services were no longer needed and the Old Lady was looking to dump its creative playmaker. This wasn't because of Brady's ability – speak to anyone who saw him play and they'll tell you how amazing he was – and it wasn't down to his popularity among the fans – the Juve faithful adored Brady and felt that even though he wasn't a typical Irish player and his Italian wasn't pitch-perfect, they recognised that he was trying to improve and learn the language all by making his mark on arguably Europe's hardest league at the time – but simply because Juventus had their eye on a different player and needed to shift either Brady or Boniek to fit him in. Boniperti had his aim set firmly on Platini – arriving at the Parc des Princes to not only watch the great number ten play for les Bleus but also to start negotiations with him for a move (Platini was out of contract at the end of that 1981/82 season and was free to talk to clubs). Arsenal were also apparently rumoured to be interested in signing Platini in a move that would have changed English football, but his message soon became clear. He wanted to leave France and ply his trade elsewhere.

Platini had grown sick of the lack of continental success at Saint-Étienne but also the jeering and booing that met him as he walked out on to the pitch at any stadium in France so, in mid-April, he flew to Turin to seal a deal that would officially confirm him as a Juventus player, grabbing the number ten shirt that would be left for him by Liam Brady – who actually scored a late penalty to win the league for Juventus in his final game, which is about as perfect a send-off as you can get. For the second time PSG had missed out on Platini, but at least this time they couldn't really have done much more. Platini had his heart set on leaving France and the natural step up was to join a club like Juventus who could challenge for honours instead of joining a fledgling PSG side. But while Juventus were awaiting him at the end of the season, Platini still had one last game to play for Saint-Étienne and it couldn't have been written better. His final appearance before leaving France for the 1982 World Cup and then to join Juventus was the Coupe de France Final at the Parc des Princes, against Francis Borelli's Paris Saint-Germain.

For PSG, the 1981/82 season would prove to be a high point in their history and one that they would never forget. Yet, the task at hand was simple: either win a trophy or gain access to one of the three European competitions, two of which could only be entered by winning a domestic trophy. After finishing fourth the year prior, Georges Peyroche was looking for ways on how to improve the side but only made a few additions. Raymond Domenech joined from Strasbourg and, while he wouldn't be in Paris for long, his experience was deemed important. However, the main signing of the summer was of Yugoslavian Ivica Šurjak from Hajduk Split. Even though the midfielder would only spend a season in Paris, his skill and knowledge on how to deliver trophies – eight in nine years with Hajduk Split was quite impressive – was massively important. When asked on why he joined PSG, Šurjak said, 'I signed after a long reflection, because I had a lot of offers including Anderlecht and coach Tomislav Ivić, but also Italian and German clubs. Long reflection too because football as a profession is not the only thing that matters in my life. I chose Paris because it is by far the most beautiful city in Europe. There is only one thing missing: a great European club, I want that to happen and participate in that.'

Despite not being a star name, the mentality that Šurjak had was exactly what PSG needed heading into a tremendously important campaign. They had got into a position where fans, neutrals and opponents were taking them seriously. A place in a European competition, most likely the UEFA Cup, didn't seem too far out of the reckoning but the ball was in PSG's court over whether or not they could deal with the expectation. They started off the season impressively with wins over Tours and Laval, but that was about as good as it got for quite some time. From beating Laval in late July to the middle of November, PSG won just five games, losing six and drawing five.

Once again, the inconsistency bug had struck and left them eighth heading into a clash against Bastia, which ended with a 3-1 triumph. Again, the change of fortune actually favoured PSG this time as they went on an unbeaten run from mid-November to mid-February, jumping from eighth to fifth, and in with a real fighting chance of grabbing a spot in the UEFA Cup for the next season. The defensive solidity was excellent, conceding just three goals in that unbeaten run – one coming in that Bastia game – and now PSG had gone from another season in mid-table to being serious challengers to not only Europe but maybe even a decent outside shout for winning the title.

While PSG were still going strong in Division 1 and still had their eyes fixed solely on that for the majority of the season, the Coupe de France started and allowed them to change things up a bit and aim for something new. But was it worth potentially risking a UEFA Cup spot just to try and win a trophy? While sacrificing a domestic trophy to try and focus on attaining European football via the league is deemed a very modern approach, winning the Coupe de France would be a massive achievement, especially for a club like PSG and while it's been touched on briefly in previous chapters, the competition has strong ties to Paris and to have a capital team win the tournament would have been quite significant in a historical sense as well. But to understand why the Coupe de France, a traditional domestic tournament akin to the FA Cup, was so important to these clubs, you have to delve back further into history to see what makes the competition – perhaps the most exciting and unpredictable cup tournament in European football (and maybe the world) – so special.

Created in 1917, the Coupe de France is the third-oldest domestic cup competition in Europe's big five footballing nations (behind the FA Cup in England and the Copa del Rey in Spain) and was open to all clubs, amateur or professional, albeit professional clubs in France at that time were very rare. Originally the competition was called the Coupe Charles Simon after the founder of the Committee French Interfederal, the organisation which eventually became what we know today as the French Football Federation. Forty-eight teams entered the first competition in 1918 and, each year, the numbers grew and grew, with over 1,000 teams involved before 1950 and by the time of writing around 7,000 teams.

But the Coupe de France is a tournament that is, historically, quite Parisian. The very first winners were Olympique de Paris – the club that would eventually merge with Red Star Paris in 1926 – who lifted the trophy at the Stade de la Légion Saint-Michel in the capital. The following year it was an all-Parisian affair at the original Parc des Princes as CASG Paris faced Olympique with CASG taking the trophy from the holders. The first six finals were won by Parisian clubs, with two all-Paris finals, while out of the first 11 editions of the tournament Marseille were the only winners from outside of Paris.

But while Parisian clubs clearly enjoyed the Coupe de France, the capital was having a cup drought as PSG headed into the 1981/82 season, with no winners hailing from Paris since 1949. PSG had come close to reaching the final in the 1974/75 season when they got to the semi-final stage, but that was as good as it got. But the team ethic heading into the 1981/82 campaign gave off the feeling that something special was coming. No one knew when and nor could they predict how the magic would appear, but bouncing off of the fifth-placed finish the season prior meant that for the first time perhaps since their promotion into Division 1, PSG had a solid team to work around. The signings may not have been glamorous but did they need to be? Not really. They had their forward players in Toko, Rocheteau and Dahleb while defensively there was room for improvement but, in reality, what could

PSG do to improve that set-up? Michel Platini said no to a transfer while with a back four made up of Thierry Morin (a youth academy player), Dominique Bathenay (the captain, a winner and a leader), Jean-Marc Pilorget (at the club his whole career at this point, the textbook definition of reliable) and Philippe Col, and Raymond Domenech filling in the final spot from time to time, the structure was in place and the defensive unit was gelling well. Realistically, there was no real way to improve the team but by no means did that make them perfect. There were still flaws, as their form in Division 1 showed.

By mid-September, PSG were 14th and looking dreadfully inconsistent but Peyroche didn't lose faith in their ability. After a 2-0 loss at Auxerre, he said, 'I have no complaints about my players. They might as well have won this match. Roll on the next game,' and, almost as if the manager had a French football almanac, PSG went into the next game and beat Lyon 2-0. The following week saw a rain-soaked 0-0 draw at Nancy but a win against Valenciennes then saw PSG rise up to ninth. They went eighth the next week, sixth the week after, and by the time the winter break came along they were back in their now familiar position of fifth. It wasn't stagnation – to be precise, they were sixth at the winter break the previous campaign, had scored 35 goals in the previous season compared to 31 in 1981/82 and had conceded 18 goals up until the winter break in 1981/82 compared to 29 the year prior, so it wasn't that much different going forward while defensively it was a massive improvement – but this team had the potential to keep going in the league.

Five points off the top while just three points from a UEFA Cup spot was hardly a bad season for PSG but when the Coupe de France started up for Division 1 sides in mid-February, that was when their focus started to change ever so slightly. Returning from the winter break proved to be a great time for PSG in both Division 1 and in the Coupe de France, with just one loss in all competitions up until mid-March, a run that saw them into fourth place in the league and into the last 32 in the cup after a penalty shoot-out victory over Nîmes. Nœux-les-Mines were next up, this time in a two-legged affair. Located south-west of Lille, the town of Nœux-les-Mines is arguably best known for its most famous son and a hero to all involved with French football, Raymond Kopa. They weren't a particularly big club but PSG still put out a strong starting 11 in the first leg – which they won 1-0 – and treated the game with a seriousness that perhaps wouldn't be seen in a more modern setting of the Coupe de France.

You would often see a few star players rested and younger players given minutes but Georges Peyroche wanted his side to treat this game, this tie and this competition with the upmost seriousness. Qualification to the next round was imperative and eventually straightforward for PSG, who won the second leg comfortably to go through 3-0 on aggregate and advance unscathed and with form on their side. Well, at least in the cup they had form. The league, however, was a completely different matter. The win that saw PSG jump to fourth, 3-2 at the Stade Gerland against Lyon, would be one of only three after February in the league. Five losses and two draws meant that PSG had mentally gone all in for the Coupe de France but had fallen off the highest possible cliff they could find with the safety net at the bottom being a good cup run to soften the blow of any potential Division 1 woes.

The terrible run saw them drop from fourth down to seventh and out of any European competition places in the table, although they still had hopes of reaching the Cup Winners' Cup provided they actually won the Coupe de France which, judging by the form in the league, wasn't exactly a likely prospect. Injuries did play a part in the poor results, however. Both Rocheteau and Bathenay picked up muscle issues while Mustapha Dahleb injured his ankle, but while manager Peyroche was satisfied as long as the team weren't losing too much ground in the European race, Borelli wasn't best pleased following a 4-0 drubbing away at Nantes. 'We were lousy, you could even say ridiculous. I am ashamed,' bellowed the ambitious yet demanding and potentially impatient president who was eager to give managers and players time to build a solid team but was growing weary of seeing the same issues appear, season after season. The only saving grace was success in the Coupe de France and, in the last 16, PSG couldn't have been paired up with a better opponent.

In 1977/78, Marseille finished fourth in Division 1. In 1975/76, they won the Coupe de France. In 1971/72 they were French champions. But in the 1981/82 season Marseille were trying, unsuccessfully, to climb out of Division 2 to return to the top flight for the first time since their relegation in 1980. The time from that Division 1 title win to their relegation and then their meeting with Paris Saint-Germain in the Coupe de France not only meant that, for the first time in this blossoming rivalry, PSG had the upper hand but also signified the crisis that was going on at Marseille.

The starting point was when Marseille president Marcel Leclerc departed after threatening to withdraw his club from Division 1 because the French football authorities wouldn't change a rule regarding the limitation of foreign players in a squad. At the time, you could only have three players from foreign countries (however, there wasn't any limitation on players from countries that had been French colonies) and Marseille had already used up their allocation on Josip Skoblar, Lambert Verdonk and Roger Magnusson, from Yugoslavia, the Netherlands and Sweden respectively. Leclerc wanted one more player, the Hungarian Zoltán Varga – who would actually go on to play for Aberdeen instead – but the powers that be did not change their rule. Leclerc, incredulous at not being able to get his own way, did what any normal president would do and threatened to boycott the Division 1 season. Of course, the club as a whole wasn't exactly keen on missing out on an entire season, so add in the fact that Leclerc was already walking a tightrope following his decision to announce a new sporting director without telling anyone (Leclerc would eventually undo his own decision due to board pressure) and, soon enough, Leclerc would resign from his position.

Under Leclerc, Marseille actually did the double but would find themselves slowly dropping down the table as each season went by. Relegated in 1980, the club had lost a lot of its aura and glamour, with PSG no longer worried about having to be fearful of their rivals. Skoblar was long gone and the squad of 1981/82, with all due respect to them, wasn't going to be something that PSG had sleepless nights over. Marseille's last win against PSG was in 1978 and they hadn't played each other since 1979, but in March 1982 PSG were absolutely ready to make their mark on a fixture, with animosity between both clubs and the two sets of fans in plain sight. You simply could not lose this game.

The last 16 was yet again a two-legged tie with PSG making the trip south to a raucous Stade Vélodrome. Some reports say that 35,000 were in attendance, others go with 45,000, but either way the atmosphere was ready for a game of this magnitude. Missing Bathenay, Rocheteau, Dahleb, Col and Pilorget, PSG and Peyroche had to change things up a bit and included a few youngsters, such as Didier Toffolo and Alain Préfaci, to keep the team healthy and fresh. Marseille, on the other hand, were bleeding their own youngsters into the squad, more out of necessity than anything else. Now known as the 'Minots' (minnows), mainly because of the fact that PSG – and a lot of other clubs – enjoyed reminding Marseille of what division they were in).

Marseille actually had a few decent chances in the game. It was far more back and forth than perhaps PSG had expected but, with their star players missing out, it seemed only logical that they themselves were not going to be at full throttle. It was a tense game with neither side looking to make the first move in fear of making the first mistake, but when the only goal of the game did come it was quite a bizarre one that requires you to watch over and over again to try and figure out exactly how the ball went in. Luis Fernández picked it up around 20 or 25 yards out from goal in a fairly safe area from a Marseille perspective. He wasn't going to dribble past the defenders and it would take a mighty fine effort to beat the goalkeeper from that distance, so the Marseille players backed off, affording the central midfielder time to look up, assess his options and make his decision.

He could put his foot on the ball and wait for his supporting cast to catch up and give him options, or he could try and pick out Toko in the box, although it would have been a superb cross to land perfectly on his head. The shot seemed off the cards but Fernández must have been feeling lucky because he hit an effort from distance that, as soon as it left his boot, wasn't going to trouble anyone. It was either going to be an easy gather for the goalkeeper (if it was even on target) or it would fly harmlessly wide. However, to the surprise of perhaps everyone in Marseille and in the Vélodrome, the shot did neither. Fernández's strike bounced just before the goalkeeper could save it and it must have hit a divot in the ground because it took the wildest of wild deflections and bounced over the diving stopper, who was left helpless. The divot, precisely on the six-yard line, flat-footed everyone and the PSG players wheeled off in celebration even if they weren't exactly sure how the shot went in.

Advantage PSG after the first leg, but there was still a lot to play for as the two sides went back to the Parc des Princes, which was still having trouble with the rise of violence and hooliganism in the stands. Both Peyroche and Borelli denounced the trouble with Peyroche using the matchday programme to urge supporters to stop, while Borelli acknowledged that while the Boulogne end of the stadium was known for being passionate, loud and enthusiastic, the disturbances had to stop. It didn't seem to be possible for a minority of PSG fans – both home and away – to not get into scraps with either opposition supporters or one another, but at least things on the pitch were going in the team's favour. A strong and clinical performance saw PSG through 4-1 on aggregate and into the quarter-final without breaking too much of a sweat, and welcoming back Rocheteau and Bathenay, making them just that little bit stronger for the latter stages. The performance pleased Peyroche, and the team, eagle-like in their vision to take the Coupe de France, felt like no one could stop them.

The next challengers were Bordeaux, who travelled to Paris for the first leg a week after beating PSG 2-0 in le Parc. They now had to pull that kind of result off again to ensure that, on their return leg, they had the advantage. But Coupe de France PSG was proving to be a different animal to Division 1 PSG. The PSG that Bordeaux had faced a week earlier were drifting away from the European spots in the table and were slowly putting their entire focus on the Coupe de France. Coupe de France PSG had that determination and extra sharpness for these games. It sounds quite redundant to put it this way, but they just wanted it a bit more than anyone else and Bordeaux felt that in the first leg. Rocheteau and Bathenay were back but Dahleb and Domenech were out, but those changes did not seem to bother the Parisians. It took them slightly longer to get in front but two goals from the returning duo gave PSG the win in front of just under 35,000 fans. However, the second leg was far from the cakewalk many expected it to be.

After being 2-0 up from the first leg, to require extra time to qualify for the semi-final wasn't ideal, but at full time no one in that red and blue shirt cared. Rocheteau suffered a groin injury quite early in the second leg and had to be replaced later on, while it also didn't help that Bordeaux scored just three minutes into the game. All signs were pointing towards a PSG capitulation and another season where they could see the light at the end of the tunnel but couldn't quite get there, especially when Bordeaux levelled the tie overall. But when Sarr popped up with a header deep into extra time, PSG exploded with pure joy. The players celebrated, the travelling fans who made the trip celebrated with them and a place in the semi-final was booked.

They had come up against Tours in Rennes but only in a one-off match because, due to the 1982 World Cup, semis were reduced to single-leg ties. On the final day of the Division 1 season, just four days prior to the semi-final, PSG and Tours met at the Parc des Princes. An exciting 4-3 victory sealed PSG's seventh-placed finish, but the league was secondary at this point. The only thing on the mind of Paris Saint-Germain was the Coupe de France. But, in typical fashion, they couldn't just win normally. They had to do it the hard way and make everyone anxious, sitting on the edge of their seat. They could just use their attacking talents to score more goals and to get games won early on, but where was the fun in that?

A crowd of 22,300 fans was in attendance in Rennes, with at least 2,000 Parisians travelling via train thanks to the offer of 50 francs for both a train ticket and a match ticket initiated by the Friends of PSG group. The game itself had drama, tension, suspense and even prompted *L'Equipe* to title the headline of the match report 'What suspense, Mr Hitchcock' in reference to the fact that only a story brought to life by the great film director could bring out such emotions in a viewer similar to this semi-final. Yet the game ended 0-0 and, despite the attacking talent on show, including former Monaco striker and multi-time golden boot winner Delio Onnis for Tours, there weren't all that many clear-cut chances. Between the two teams, only about seven chances in 90 minutes could be labelled as potentially 'good' chances, but on a poor pitch like the one in Rennes the attacking line-ups couldn't do much even if they tried.

As the tie trickled into extra time and with a few chances falling to the likes of Rocheteau, nothing would pass either goalkeeper. Eventually the game would be decided via a penalty shoot-out, the ultimate test in football. The shoot-out arguably has less than nothing to do with skill and more to do with mental strength, ability to perform under the most intense of pressure and, of course, a hint of luck. Skill plays a part, but sometimes it isn't the be-all and end-all of a shoot-out. Either you're a hero for scoring or saving a penalty or you're the villain for missing with your kick. There is no in between. So for PSG and Tours the chance to reach the final was right in front of them, but one of them just had to keep their nerve.

Bruno Steck, Jean-Philippe Dehon, Dominique Marais, Yves Devillechabrolle and Delio Onnis all stepped up to take penalties for Tours. Steck scored but the others had their efforts saved by Dominique Baratelli, who pulled some incredible stops. Rocheteau and Renaut scored for PSG to send them through to the Coupe de France Final but it would be Baratelli who would rightly be lauded as the hero of the day. For the first time since 1950, Paris would have a representative in the Coupe de France Final and there was a chance that the city would have its first winner since 1949 but it wouldn't be straightforward at all.

PSG may have progressed in dramatic circumstances but would have to face Saint-Étienne, led by their departing leader Michel Platini. On paper it looked like an incredibly difficult task for PSG and looking at the Division 1 fixtures wouldn't help matters either: two 0-0 draws had been recorded. PSG had to win the final to deliver their first piece of silverware and slowly start to establish themselves, finally, as a truly top club in French football. Les Verts, on the other hand, had their own reasons for wanting to win it badly. Having missed out on retaining their Division 1 title to Monaco by a point – and thus not winning a place in the European Cup – Saint-Étienne were desperate to at least lift the Coupe de France to put some shine on a season that ended on a low note. Platini wanted to go into the 1982 World Cup with a good memory in his final game for the club and wanted to depart French football as a winner in some regard considering that, in his three years at the club, he had one league title.

To make matters worse and slightly more ominous for PSG, Saint-Étienne and Platini were out for revenge after not only losing their Division 1 title but also losing the previous season's final to Bastia, so they were heavy favourites before a ball had even been kicked. But PSG did have an equaliser. It wasn't a secret weapon because everybody knew heading into the final that it was going to be used, but PSG had more experience of how to use it to their advantage: the Parc des Princes.

After the finals had previously alternated between the Stade Olympique Yves-du-Manoir in Colombes and le Parc, the Parc des Princes had by this time now become the main host stadium since 1972 had hosted each one.

The second Coupe de France Final had been hosted in the very first incarnation of the Parc des Princes so there was quite a strong history between the stadium and the occasion, but you could definitely argue that there hadn't been a final quite like the one in 1982.

Much like in England, the Coupe de France Final was set at one particular ground and, on the odd occasion, would be swapped around for when the neutral stadium was being renovated or out of use. The FA Cup Final at Wembley meant, in theory, no team would have an advantage because it was the national stadium rather than belonging to a club. The venue of the Copa del Rey in Spain was voted for by the Spanish federation prior to the final, while the DFB-Pokal in Germany was held at various stadia in places like Hanover, Frankfurt, Stuttgart, Ludwigshafen, Gelsenkirchen, Düsseldorf and Cologne before eventually settling down in 1985 at the Olympiastadion in Berlin, the home of Hertha. The Stadio Olimpico in Rome was the predominant venue for Coppa Italia finals despite being home to both Roma and Lazio, before two-legged finals meant both teams would enjoy home advantage and two shots at winning the trophy. Even the Dutch KNVB Cup used Feyenoord's De Kuip for its final. In these countries, the venues' home teams would eventually play in the final on home turf on a few occasions apart from in England where it wasn't possible.

With the final being based in Paris and the distinct lack of successful Parisian sides in general meaning that very few even reached the latter stages of the tournament, let alone the final, and with the exception of Racing Paris, no capital team had been able to reach the final on their now turf (Racing Club were based at the Stade Olympique Yves-du-Manoir but were the only pre-PSG side to play in Colombes, so they're out on their own in this conversation). Marseille had won two Coups de France at the Parc des Princes before PSG or any Parisian club reached the final to challenge them, so the need to change that image of Paris clubs was in the background as PSG got closer to the final. But while the pressure was on both PSG and Saint-Étienne for different reasons this time, at least the Boulogne end would be packed in favour of les Rouge et Bleu.

On one side of the ground there was a wall of green and white. Green flags, green wigs, green shirts, green hats, green flares, green everything. On the other, there was red and blue everywhere, but with a bit more verve behind it. Red and blue flags, red flares, you name it. The Saint-Étienne fans were instead placed in the Boulogne end, cheering their team on after a long journey, but one that they were hopeful would be worthwhile. The Auteuil end was occupied by the Paris Saint-Germain fans, a spot opposite where you would usually find the more rowdy and passionate supporters, but it didn't stop their voices from being heard, hence why the singing, chanting and most of the general noise was created from that end.

For PSG, this felt like a home game, just with more visitors from the opposition. There were over 150,000 ticket requests for this historic game but only 46,160 people were able to get their hands on one. France historically didn't treat football the same way that other countries would and it was treated as a hobby, something that was a bit dangerous but acquired the perception that it was something that didn't require you to use your brain all that much and was rife with violence in the stands. Football wasn't the arts, it wasn't the theatre and it wasn't something that would be the talk of Paris in the 1980s, but you wouldn't have guessed that during the final. The stadium was packed and there was a sense of excitement in the air.

Every Coupe de France Final is special in its own way but this one felt like it had something different about it: Platini's farewell, the chance for Paris's new club to really stamp its mark on to French football, played out in front of their own fans, while potentially putting an end to the reign of success Saint-Étienne had enjoyed for many years. It was a showdown that had huge symbolic meaning but also had huge permutations riding on it. It was also the first time that a Paris Saint-Germain game had been broadcast live on television, with TF1 showing the final. Also, due to the 1982 World Cup, there would be no replay if the match was a draw at full time. It would instead go into extra time and then penalties to try and reduce the games for the French stars who were likely to be going to that World Cup, such as Platini for Saint-Étienne and Fernández for PSG.

PSG, wearing their white shirt with a blue and red stripe going down the left-hand side of the torso, came out alongside some star names for Saint-Étienne. Platini, in his final game for the club, Patrick Battiston and Johnny Rep were names that most of the world had heard of or would become quite familiar with in the next few years, but the focus on the faces of the PSG players was unmatched. Yes, there were nerves from the players, the fans and Francis Borelli himself but there was a determination to make history. They just had to get past the green monster first.

The low hum of noise emanating from the stands was the soundtrack to the game, with the occasional rise in volume when either side came close and the odd 'oohh' when Platini performed a back-heel or a flick or a beautiful pass, but the first half was relatively well balanced. Both sides restricted one another to long-range shots and half chances, but nothing of any meaning. It was a battle between two sides who tried first not to lose, rather than to go for the win. Or, at the very least, they were biding their time, conserving their energy and not letting the occasion get to them.

The teams went into half-time level but PSG felt like they should have been ahead after a goal was disallowed for offside, despite not touching the ball in from Šurjak. Nevertheless, they were still in the game. They weren't exactly hanging on for dear life but the fact they weren't behind was a positive. After 58 minutes life got even better for them when Šurjak floated a ball in from the left and after a bit of a penalty-box scramble, it reached the feet of Nambatingue Toko, who didn't need a second opportunity to smash his into the back of the net and put his team 1-0 up. The goal seemed to wake Saint-Étienne up, prompting them into action, and Les Verts decided to take control of the game with prolonged periods in possession, Platini and the long figure of Rep with his untucked shirt and languid running style posing a constant threat to PSG's reliable defence. Time after time, Saint-Étienne would threaten but they were either denied by goalkeeper Dominique Baratelli or saw their efforts fly wide of the mark.

But the crosses kept coming in, and when Jean-Louis Zanon floated one up into the Paris box on 76 minutes, Raúl Nogués flicked the ball to the back post where an unmarked Platini was on hand to level things up with a half volley. Just four days earlier, PSG had gone the distance against Tours in the semi-final and were slowly starting to labour on the field, with Saint-Étienne occasionally playing circles around them. It looked like a certainty that Saint-Étienne would win the tie but PSG held on and forced the final into extra time, where they would then have an extra 30 minutes to try and stem the tide. At first, extra time looked like the perfect time for PSG to catch their breath, refocus and regroup and try to win the game but, not even ten minutes into the extended period, Platini scored his second. All it took was a long ball over the back line to find Platini, open in the box, and it was the kind of chance that France's captain just did not miss.

Saint-Étienne knew that they had to see out the game, not concede possession or chances and just win. PSG were looking weary but the fans kept singing and chanting, they still had life left in them and as the clock slowly started to tick down they started to gain a bit of momentum. Saint-Étienne still had the advantage but PSG were getting themselves on to the ball and were getting into the box. There weren't any clear-cut chances created but it was a good starting point to build from late on in the game. Toko looked dangerous, Saar and Šurjak were always capable of producing something and Rocheteau was lurking around the action, waiting to pounce whenever he could.

Saint-Étienne goalkeeper Jean Castaneda attempted to launch the ball as far down the pitch as he could. One long punt towards the forwards, then straight into the corner flag. If they could do that then Les Verts would win the Coupe de France. But the goal kick was flat and poor with not enough height to evade the PSG back line and the Parisians were on the attack. Toko skipped past one man and tried to play the ball out wide to Michel N'Gom, who was quickly closed down by two defenders, but found Šurjak, who finds a drop of energy deep inside to skip his way into the right-hand side of the Saint-Étienne penalty box. He took a look up to spot five PSG players inside the area and one just outside. One of those penalty box Parisians was Rocheteau, who was just ahead of the penalty spot. Šurjak lifted a ball delicately into his path, Rocheteau swivelled his legs to catch it on the half volley and crashed it into the net for 2-2. Madness. An equaliser in the 119th minute of play, and chaos ensued. Fans rushed on to the field to celebrate with the players, who themselves just ran off in whatever direction their body took them in. Some followed Rocheteau, others tried to evade the pitch invaders.

Francis Borelli, who had been sitting alongside Jacques Chirac (the mayor of Paris at the time), François Mitterrand (the newly appointed president of France) and Roger Rocher (the Saint-Étienne president), leapt from his seat, ran down to pitch side, jumped the gated barriers and kissed the pitch. Borelli, a superstitious man, was clutching his lucky satchel as he got on to his knees and would later explain why he kissed the ground, 'Rocheteau's goal is the most intense moment of my life. I did not believe it anymore. It was cooked, jokingly I was saying to the people next to me, "We can't help but equalise!" And then Rocheteau scored … It was deliverance! The explosion of joy! Unthinkable … So, I kissed the lawn, this blessed land of the Park, to thank the sky … like the

Muslims I saw in Tunisia, who embraced the earth to thank their God.'

At least he had a good reason for it, but the moment was captured on camera and became an iconic scene for Paris Saint-Germain and their history, a symbolic moment of what it meant to be in a position to win the Coupe de France. Of course, the game was still going on. Rocheteau had equalised, but there was still a minute left of extra time to play plus a probable penalty shoot-out. The fans just refused to leave the field, and a 30-minute delay was needed to get everything back in order. 'It's such a shame,' proclaimed a rather annoyed Michel Platini, who had just witnessed his fairy-tale departure slam shut in his face. In Platini's world he would have scored both goals to win the cup in his final game before going to the 1982 World Cup with France and eventually going to Turin to finally join Juventus. Rocheteau had different ideas, and wanted some of that glory for himself. And rightly so.

Eventually, the match got back under way and the referee blew his final whistle to signify the end of extra time. PSG had already got through one shoot-out in the past seven days and now they had to do it all over again, so that victory over Tours gave them hope. Baratelli was clearly a fans' favourite and some just had so much confidence in the goalkeeper. They had seen his saves against Tours and knew he was capable of being the hero. Captain Bathenay stepped up first and placed the ball down on the spot, knowing he was going to put his foot through the ball with as much power as his legs could muster. His effort went over; not the best start. But just when Saint-Étienne were readying their penalty taker, the referee blew his whistle. Jean Castaneda was off his line before Bathenay shot so a retake was ordered. The captain converted his second spot kick, starting off a slew of perfect penalties. Renaut, Rocheteau, Šurjak, Fernández all scored for PSG while Patrick Battiston – with the help of yet another retake – Jean-Louis Zanon, Johnny Rep, Jean-François Larios and Michel Platini scored for Saint-Étienne.

Up stepped Christian Lopez, a French international born in Algeria who had risen up the Saint-Étienne ranks to become a first-team mainstay. He was a part of the fabric of the club for the best part of a decade, but he arguably never had as much pressure on his shoulders as he did in this shoot-out. He needed to score to keep his side alive and kicking. Baratelli was equal to his effort, diving to his left to keep the ball out. Advantage Paris Saint-Germain.

Jean-Marc Pilorget was given the responsibility of scoring the winning penalty. Born in Paris and playing for PSG for his entire career up to this point, there was no one better to do the honours. He stepped up, gave the goalkeeper the eyes and sent him the wrong way, winning Paris Saint-Germain the 1982 Coupe de France after an unbelievable game that produced magic. The team and Borelli mobbed Pilorget as Platini slithered off down the tunnel, off to the World Cup and off to Serie A, but at that moment no one was thinking about Platini, only Paris Saint-Germain. Their moment had finally come and the image of captain Dominique Bathenay lifting the trophy is iconic in the history of the club. You never forget your first trophy and PSG made sure that no one in the future ever would. For a club formed in 1970 and knocked down to Division 3 to start all over again in 1972, to win the

Coupe de France a decade later was simply incredible. Two promotions and a trophy in ten years is something that shouldn't be frowned upon especially when you consider the enforced presidential change a few years previously.

PSG were now up and running and the cup win signified a crossroads for both clubs. PSG, clearly on the rise and about to enjoy a sustained period of success, had defeated the once strong and imperious empire that was Saint-Étienne, who were losing their star player, a man brought in to dominate French football and make the team a force on the European stage, neither of which happened. Platini left for Juventus, Roger Rocher resigned the next Monday as president and they won nothing until 2013. Christian Lopez, the man who missed their penalty, also left while, just two years later, Saint-Étienne were relegated into Division 2.

This was more than just a cup final, it was a symbolic changing of the guard in French football, ushering in an era where PSG were taken a lot more seriously than before and challenged for multiple honours while Saint-Étienne were resigned to losing their stars and either being mid-table or relegation-threatened. Whatever way you look at the 1982 Coupe de France Final, there is at least one thing that is crystal clear from it all. It was the first time that Paris Saint-Germain were truly put on the footballing map.

8

La prochaine étape – The next step

THE SUMMER of 1982 thrust French football into the limelight, mainly due to the departure of Michel Platini from Saint-Étienne to Juventus but also due to the national team reaching the semi-final at the 1982 World Cup in Spain. Dominique Baratelli and Dominique Rocheteau were the only two Paris Saint-Germain players in the squad but Division 1 was well represented. Only Didier Six of German Bundesliga side Stuttgart wasn't plying his trade in France.

While the finals didn't entirely affect Paris Saint-Germain directly, they signified a change in France regarding football and the success of the national team. The sport has forever been linked closely with immigration in the country, with some of the biggest and most important stars for the national team being subjected to xenophobic and racial abuse. Raymond Kopa, the standout figure of French football in the 1950s and arguably one of the country's first superstar players, was born Raymond Kopaszewski and was from Polish heritage, while he did actually work in the coal mines before becoming a footballer, which led to him hearing abuse such as 'Kopa, go back to the mines!'.

The middle classes would often look down on football, seeing it as nothing more than a game for the working classes. Businessmen on the Paris Metro would buy *L'Equipe,* only to hide it out of embarrassment, fearing that they could not bear to be seen with a newspaper based solely on football and not finances or current affairs. Football was associated with immigrants, the working classes and anybody else who didn't consider themselves to be part of the elite. Throw in the slow rise in hooliganism seen in the stands at football matches – which was starting to grow at the Parc des Princes – and more people started to look away from football in France.

That being said, the game itself did look like it was moving in the right direction in 1982. Platini was the star and was one of the best players on the planet, Paris had a club that was on the rise and stars like Jean Tigana, Luis Fernández, Patrick Battiston and many more were slowly starting to form a cohesive team around Platini, giving him a platform to work his magic (although Fernández didn't become a key player until after this World Cup, his emergence into the national team certainly helped Platini and France).

A 4-4-2 diamond with Platini in the central attacking midfielder spot just behind Six and Rocheteau while Bernard Genghini sat in front of the back line, which was anchored by Marius Trésor and Gérard Janvion, was on paper a good side with a sprinkling of star players but it didn't quite have the start that was becoming of World Cup challengers. Three group stage games produced one win, one draw and one loss, which saw France finish second in the group behind England, meaning they would go into a second group stage against Austria and Northern Ireland. This next stage was effectively the quarter-final and France topping this group saw them move on to the semi-final to face an outstanding West Germany side filled with the likes of Paul Breitner, Karl-Heinz Rummenigge, Pierre Littbarski, Klaus Fischer, Felix Magath and goalkeeper Harald Schumacher – a man who was 120 minutes away from being public enemy number one across France and perhaps even the world.

Known in Germany and France as 'Nacht von Sevilla' and 'Nuit de Séville' respectively, this game was not only one of the greatest in World Cup history but also one of the most controversial too. Littbarski opened the scoring for Germany before Platini levelled from the spot in a tight encounter between two incredibly talented sides. The winners would face Italy, who had knocked out the great Brazil side of 1982 and were rigid in a stereotypically Italian way. Just before the hour, Platini spotted a gap between two central defenders. Making his way through that gap was Patrick Battiston, Platini's now former team-mate at Saint-Étienne. Platini wasn't the only one to spot the gap as West German shot-stopper Harald Schumacher started to rush off his line, anticipating taking both the ball and Battiston. As you watch the moment unfold, you know that there will be a coming together because that kind of thing just always seems to happen in football, especially in a scenario like this one, but no one expected it to play out as it actually did.

Battiston was the first to reach the ball and got a slight touch on it, with the effort going just wide of the goal. Battiston didn't know the ball had gone wide, and neither did Schumacher, who had decided to turn his body ever so slightly in his jump, and when he made contact with Battiston, it would be Schumacher's hip into Battiston's head. Battiston was knocked unconscious while the referee blew for a goal kick. He didn't award a foul and nor did he issue a card of any colour to Schumacher. Platini raced over to check on Battiston and said afterwards that he was sure that his colleague was dead. Schumacher never went over to check Battiston, instead waiting with his hands on his hips, chewing on his gum in an irritating fashion, ready to take the goal kick. He would later say that the reason he didn't go over to check was because the French players looked at him in a threatening manner. Battiston lost a few teeth, dislocated his jaw, had a damaged vertebrae and cracked a few ribs, yet Schumacher, whether he meant it in a sincere fashion or not, offered to pay for the dental surgery.

West Germany would eventually go on to win on penalties, but an all-time classic World Cup game – and a historic one too, as it was the first World Cup tie to be decided via a penalty shoot-out – was remembered for one incident. The loss was heartbreaking for France and any neutral who wanted West Germany to lose but the tournament as a whole helped establish France as a nation that was ready to really make an impression on the international stage after years of not being relevant at all. They finished fourth in 1982, their best result since 1958 when they finished third, but sandwiched between those two tournaments were group stage exits in 1966 and 1978, while they didn't even qualify for the 1962, 1970 or the 1974 World Cups at all. They may have returned home from Spain without any silverware or medals but the right people knew that the national team – and in turn the domestic game – was about to be put into a good place.

As for Schumacher, his status in France was sealed forever. A man, who apparently once put out a cigarette on his arm to show a girlfriend how much pain he could take and who would punch sandbags after defeats until his knuckles would bleed, had no regrets over what happened to Battiston. 'I did not want to hurt him but I would do the same thing again if the action were to recur,' Schumacher told *Le Figaro*. 'It was the only way to get the ball.' The days after the game were when the rage from the fans and public went to another level. A poll was run in a newspaper asking who the most unpopular man in France was. Adolf Hitler came in second, with Schumacher being voted ahead of him. That's how he was viewed. The incident was so bad that the chancellor of Germany and the French president issued a joint statement to try and defuse the situation. If France hadn't cared about football, it certainly did now.

So while the nation was slowly hating Harald Schumacher more and more as each day went on, 1982 was a big year for French football and things were changing. However, not everything was for good, as the crowds in that West Germany game would show. Off the field, fans were following the English influence perhaps too well, with PSG fans, in particular, embracing the term 'hooligan' over anything else and, slowly, groups of far-right skinheads were taking parts of the Boulogne end of the Parc des Princes and making it their own. Thus began the first incidents of racism in the stands, something that progressed throughout the 1980s and continued into the 90s. But on the pitch for Paris Saint-Germain, things were only getting better.

After riding the high of winning their first Coupe de France and preparing for their first season in a European competition, PSG knew they had to keep their momentum going. Dutchman Kees Kist was the major addition who could immediately help the side during the summer, arriving from AZ Alkmaar and replacing the outgoing Ivica Šurjak who was on his way to Udinese after just a season in Paris. But Kist, despite his outstanding goal record, perhaps wasn't the most glamorous marquee name entering the Parc des Princes. That honour went to someone else who had to leave England due to issues in Argentina and found himself on loan in France to bide his time and hopefully return across the Channel.

Ossie Ardiles was – and still is – one of the most loved and respected Tottenham players of all time and, given the famous FA Cup Final song 'Ossie's Dream' and his appearance in the film *Escape to Victory*, his popularity was at its peak. But when the Falklands War broke out on 2 April 1982 and with Spurs playing Leicester in the FA Cup semi-final the next day, everything changed for Ardiles and his Argentine team-mate Ricky Villa. Ardiles noticed the increased amount of reporters at training the day of the declaration of war and recognised that not all of them were sports-based, and it didn't get much better at the semi-final either. Fans booed Ardiles and occasionally you could hear chants of 'England, England, England' and, despite winning the game, both Ossie and Villa would eventually return home with only Villa playing in the final. Everything Ardiles said was being twisted by both countries to suit their own agendas, something he found incredibly difficult to deal with. Ossie's brother José was the first Argentinian fighter pilot to lose his life during the conflict and, before the 1982 World Cup in Spain, the player said he couldn't return to England and he 'cannot play in a country that is at war with my own country'. What happened next was a six-month loan move to PSG, which hurt Ricky Villa after the pair had been inseparable at Spurs and helped one another settle in London.

If you're reading this and wondering how Ardiles in Paris had slipped your mind, it's not a part of his career he speaks about often. Given the tremendous stress he was under and the fact he was essentially forced out of a country he loved by a conflict that struck his family to the core, Ardiles's time at PSG wasn't what many had hoped it could have been. He would later say, 'I never played worse than there,' when quizzed on his Parisian adventure years later and, by the start of 1984, he was back in north London wearing the white of Spurs, leaving French life behind. However, the departure of Ardiles allowed PSG to bring in another potential star who they had been looking to sign since the summer, but due to the strict rules regarding players from Soviet countries moving on they had been forced to wait until December 1982 to introduce their latest recruit to their fans. It isn't an exaggeration to say that perhaps the greatest Paris Saint-Germain player had just arrived in the French capital.

Safet Sušić had actually made his first appearance for PSG before he made his official debut. The Tournoi de Paris, a regular pre-season friendly hosted by the club, saw them go up against Atlético Mineiro and Cologne, with Sušić in Paris for both games. The first, against Brazilian side Mineiro, was too early for Sušić as he wasn't able to get permission from the Yugoslav federation to play, so he had to watch on in the stands as Ardiles made his first appearance in a Paris Saint-Germain shirt. Against Cologne, Sušić was able to feel the Parc des Princes pitch for the first time. The Yugoslav impressed and the prospect of him working alongside Dahleb and Rocheteau had PSG fans dreaming, at least until his country's federation had a change of heart. They cancelled Sušić's transfer, wanting him to stay on home soil apparently as a punishment to the internationals who were in the Yugoslavia squad for the 1982 World Cup. Sušić was one of the key men of the team as they failed to get out of a group alongside hosts Spain, Northern Ireland and Honduras and, as a result, the Federation cancelled the move – or at the very least delayed it.

A star in his country and the star of his Sarajevo side but relatively unknown to the rest of Europe (he never played in the European Cup and those outside of Yugoslavia would have only seen him at international tournaments), Sušić joined PSG despite the interest from plenty of other clubs. He told magazine *Onze Mondial*, 'I should never have found myself in Paris. I had contacts with two Italian clubs. With Inter Milan I had just laid down my conditions on a piece of paper that I had signed, without going any further. And then I spoke to Torino and there I signed a contract. For me, as for the Torino board, it was a real contract. But the next day, the two clubs went to present their document to the federation. So I was suspended for a year without the possibility of playing in Italy. But I really wanted to leave Yugoslavia, I was already over 27 years old and therefore allowed to "leave" the country. This is where PSG contacted me. Šurjak told Borelli about me and they came to get me. The choice was between Italy,

Germany and France. But it was the city of Paris that attracted me. And then when I saw the Parc des Princes, I was immediately won over.'

The playmaker was clearly enamoured with Paris but would have to wait until December to make his debut off the bench against Monaco. PSG lost 1-0, their final game before the winter break, leaving them seventh in the table. Domestically, things weren't exactly going to plan, but their first European adventure was well under way in the Cup Winners' Cup. At the time, UEFA viewed the Cup Winners' Cup in higher regard than the UEFA Cup with teams who won their domestic cup and finishing in a UEFA Cup spot in the league being placed into the former competition, due to it being seen as more prestigious. For PSG, they didn't really care if it was the UEFA Cup or the Cup Winners' Cup because, to them, European football was something they had been craving for quite a while. On a lesser scale, it put them on the map in various countries and put them in the consciousness of other nations who may not have heard of PSG prior to being drawn against them.

And it was a big deal for Paris, too. For the first time since 1965, a European game would be hosted by a Parisian club, since Stade Français played out a 0-0 draw with Portuguese club Porto and were eventually knocked out 1-0 in the second leg. PSG's first game in the Cup Winners' Cup came in Bulgaria when they faced off against Lokomotiv Sofia, losing 1-0, a result that seemed to please the Parisians with Georges Peyroche saying after the game, 'Before the match, I would have taken this result. All the players were serious and showed great determination.' A loss was still a loss but it was slightly different given that a packed and rowdy Parc des Princes was waiting for PSG back home in the second leg.

Francis Borelli managed to get the return televised, with a few million viewers on TF1 – only the second PSG game to be screened – and the Parisians romped through without a problem. Despite being without Thierry Morin, Dahleb and Rocheteau, PSG would put on a performance that was described by some fans as 'champagne football' and proceeded to win 5-1, advancing to the second round and facing a trip to Wales to face the Welsh Cup winners Swansea City. Swansea had won their domestic cup under the stewardship of player-manager John Toshack and had just been on a meteoric rise through the English football pyramid. Toshack took over in 1978 with the Welsh club in the Fourth Division, but three promotions in four years saw them rise up to the First Division and win the Welsh Cup in 1981, retaining that particular trophy for the next two years. Just under £1m was spent on new players before their First Division campaign, plus the reconstruction of a new East Stand at the Vetch Field meant that, while the cup runs and First Division football was great, finances weren't as healthy as the product on the pitch implied.

By the time PSG faced the Swans, the latter's situation was about to become quite dire. With money not readily available, teenagers were blooded in at a time when experience was needed, while Swansea were hit with a transfer ban due to the fact they couldn't afford to pay Everton the fees for Bob Latchford and Gary Stanley. The side were looking nailed on for relegation back to the Second Division when Paris Saint-Germain rolled into town, so it wasn't exactly a welcome break from domestic matters.

A typically wet and dreadful night at the old Vetch Field ground gave Swansea an advantage, according to *Onze Mondial*. They were used to the rain, the slippery surface and, while PSG knew what to expect – Bathenay had apparently spied on Swansea – the Parisians were still more than capable of dealing with whatever their opponents threw at them. Long balls into the box and crosses from the flank were all that Swansea could muster up, while PSG just mopped up the Welsh attacks and countered time and time again. Once again without Rocheteau, PSG controlled the majority of the game and took a 1-0 win back to Paris and, perhaps rather arrogantly, were already planning for their quarter-final, feeling that the second leg against Swansea was nothing more than a formality. Usually, this kind of thinking and mindset would bite PSG in the backside faster than the speed of light but no such thing would occur. A 2-0 win at the Parc des Princes saw them through with no fuss. The sold-out crowd enjoyed the game, created a good atmosphere – loud, energetic but not hostile – and the club was starting to understand what it had to do to win huge matches. Winning was all that mattered and to win without fuss, without havoc and with talent and determination was imperative.

PSG were slowly moulding their identity, something that they hadn't quite perfected up to this point. There was no philosophy or a stereotypical 'PSG way' so to speak but now the football had to be triumphant, courageous and entertaining – in that order. Could they have beaten Swansea by more than two goals? Of course, they created the chances to do so but, either way, they were winners. It didn't matter by how many because PSG were through to the Cup Winners' Cup quarter-finals and had a lot to contemplate. As they prepared for the quarter-final, they were still fighting on three fronts. The Coupe de France last 16 against Strasbourg was approaching and they didn't want to have a weak defence of the first trophy they had won, while they had climbed up to third in the Division 1 table after a good run of results culminating in a huge 2-0 win over second-placed Bordeaux, leaving PSG a point off their vanquished opponents and eight points from leaders Nantes. It was a sizeable margin but PSG had the self-belief to feel that they could close the gap and be the nearest challengers for the title. In fact, they would only lose three more games in Division 1 that season – all away from home – but even if PSG had won them they would have still finished four points off of Nantes, who would eventually be crowned as deserving champions despite PSG's superb run of form in the second half of the season.

But PSG were still chasing their own glory in the Coupe de France and the Cup Winners' Cup. The teams in the last eight could easily be mistaken for European Cup quarter-finalists, but the French media had been giving PSG messages about each side before the draw was made. How could they not fear a Barcelona side spearheaded by Diego Maradona? Would they be able to go toe to toe with European Cup-winning giants such as Inter Milan or Real Madrid? With players like Karl-Heinz Rummenigge, Paul Breitner and Klaus Augenthaler, surely they would have wanted to completely avoid Bayern Munich as well? Austria Vienna had their superstar in Toni Polster and, while the likes of Waterschei from Belgium and Alex Ferguson's Aberdeen weren't in the same bracket as the big names, the French press warned PSG that they could not underestimate the rest.

The Parisians were drawn against Waterschei, and Peyroche had spent the days prior to the game urging his charges to attack, to not be afraid by the occasion and to carry on making history (even before a ball had been kicked, PSG had become the only Paris club to reach the quarter-final of any European competition). As Jean-Marc Pilorget said before the match, 'We have not come this far to stop there. We have waited too long for this moment to miss it.' The players knew the significance of the game, as did the 49,575 fans who packed themselves into the Parc des Princes, a figure that remains the record attendance for a PSG game at the stadium and probably won't be beaten for quite some time. Fans on the Kop of Boulogne were waving their flags as the players walked out of the tunnel, drowning out the 2,500 visitors from Belgium, knowing how they could influence the game with every cheer, song, jeer or scream. PSG dominated the first half and went into the half-time break thanks to Luis Fernández's strike on 43 minutes, a move that was both beautiful in its build-up and clinical in its execution. They doubled their lead in the second half when Pilorget tapped in from inside the six-yard box just after the hour. PSG were quicker to every ball and seemingly had more energy than the entirety of Paris put together on that night. They looked unplayable and unstoppable, at least until the second leg in Belgium.

Seventeen coaches of Paris Saint-Germain fans crossed the border in hopes of catching the game live and, with everyone at the club hoping for and expecting a straightforward tie and a rollover from the Belgians, what followed must have been a huge shock. Fernández was already eyeing up who he wanted in the semi-final after the first leg, saying, 'The dream continues! If we could play against Real Madrid or Barcelona, that would be a dream,' but Peyroche was slightly more cautious than his star midfielder, predicting that, while he was satisfied with his team's performance in Paris, 'The return leg may be difficult, even if we do have a good chance of qualifying.'

The second leg was refereed by Welshman Clive Thomas, who once disallowed a goal for handball despite saying, 'In no way could I have seen the ball make contact with his hand or his arm.' He once blew the whistle for full time during a World Cup game between Brazil and Sweden with the ball in the air from a corner, a fraction of a second before Zico headed what would have been a winner for Brazil. Thomas blamed the Brazilians for taking too long with the corner rather than the fact he turned away once the kick was taken. He was also once seen singing along, to fans praising his performance during a game he was officiating – a prototype for Mike Dean, if you will. Thomas was a referee who was loved by some for his officiating style and hated by others for his attitude and his ability to make the occasions all about him. One English writer once said of him, 'The star performer before an audience of 50,000 and millions more peering through the keyhole of television was unquestionably Mr Thomas. It was the *Clive Thomas Spectacular Show*.' Whenever a referee is described like that, there is a high possibility that he's going to be the centre of attention at some stage during the game. And in a hostile Belgian atmosphere, it was going to be a night on which PSG needed to embrace their new-found identity of being brave, courageous and strong in the face of adversity.

Two thousand Parisians arrived with the team, flares in hand and making up ten per cent of the attendance, most of the Boulogne stand coming over to lend their support. In the early stages, that was needed. Waterschei surged time and time again towards Dominique Baratelli but PSG held firm. The Belgians knew they had to start fast and hard, and they did just that. The bar was struck early on by Waterschei and they just kept on coming. PSG's defence, not in any kind of structure, was slowly being exposed. The attack tried to use pace to get involved and stretch the game in their favour but they couldn't find any momentum. On the half-hour mark, Waterschei struck first through Icelandic forward Lárus Guðmundsson, who poked the ball past Baratelli from a corner. First blood to the Belgians and they were looking the more likely to grab that all-important second goal. PSG reached the half-time break just a goal down but the Belgians still needed to score at least one goal to stay in the tie. A 2-0 win would take it to extra time whereas 3-0 would knock the Parisians out.

It was more of the same when the second half restarted; wave after wave of Waterschei attack, with their players camped in the PSG box. The hour arrived and the Belgians got their second goal, but it wasn't without controversy, centred around referee Thomas. He invoked rule XII of the laws of the game on Baratelli and awarded Waterschei an indirect free kick in the PSG penalty area. The law stated at the time that after controlling the ball and after four steps, the goalkeeper should pass it before receiving it back and kicking it upfield. Thomas felt that

Baratelli broke this law, as did the Waterschei players, but Baratelli felt that by pushing a shot that he saved to the side, he didn't technically have control of the ball, therefore the rule shouldn't have applied in this instance. That didn't concern the referee and Roland Janssen tucked the free kick away to bring Waterschei level on aggregate.

PSG woke up a bit once the tie was level, but it went into extra time and that was when – already tired, demoralised and feeling unfairly treated – they caved in. Having held on for a while, Waterschei found themselves gaining more and more ground. Janssen crossed in from the left and forward Eddy Voordeckers flicked the ball on with a delicate back-heel to the onrushing, unmarked Pierre Janssen, who didn't need a second invitation to score the winning goal. PSG were broken. Jean-Claude Lemoult was sent off for a second yellow card (some reports suggesting he was shown his marching orders because he smacked a fan) and Boubacar Sarr also left the game early thanks to the referee, with PSG being eliminated in a way that was unbefitting of their new-found mentality. This was the old PSG, the one that would always find a way to defeat themselves when it truly mattered, but it was a learning curve for the team and for the club. Peyroche acknowledged Waterschei's performance and also said, 'We have fallen into a great trap. The referee is one of the big people responsible for our elimination.' Dominique Rocheteau, who had a great chance in the dying minutes of the game to send PSG through, didn't blame Thomas at all, 'We did not expect to meet such a good team. Waterschei has been superior to us tonight. Overall, this coronation is deserved.'

To make matters worse for PSG fans back home, they didn't even watch the game live. Due to a strike by workers from French television, the second leg wasn't shown live like the first leg, so the following day the channels had to use Belgian footage (with excitable Belgian commentary) to explain how these minnows had taken down Paris Saint-Germain. The only possible crumb of comfort for PSG was the fact that Waterschei were knocked out in the semi-finals by Alex Ferguson's Aberdeen, who would eventually win the competition.

With PSG's European adventure over in the middle of March, it's easy to forget that they were still fighting on two more fronts at this point. They were third in Division 1, and in the last 16 of the Coupe de France, where they would dispatch Strasbourg with relative ease, especially when winning 5-2 at le Parc in the second leg. Brest awaited them in the quarter-final and posed a much tougher test. Despite taking the lead, PSG dropped the first leg 2-1 but came back to win 2-0 at the Parc des Princes. Clearly, playing at home was proving to be a massive advantage, PSG losing just twice in front of their own fans all season across all competitions. A second semi-final in two years showed that cup runs were starting to become a speciality.

Yet again, they faced Tours over two legs. Their opponents were fighting against relegation and a split in their club between striker Delio Onnis and manager Hendrikus Hollink, with players either taking the side of one of those two or just staying out of trouble. Clearly focusing more on their bid to avoid the Division 1 drop, Tours seemingly threw in the towel in the first leg, losing 4-0 with barely a whimper. With Luis Fernández and

Sušić grabbing a goal each before ten minutes were on the clock, it became startlingly obvious that it was going to be a long night for Tours and a coasting one for the hosts. With Tours already relegated after losing the play-off to Nîmes, they were demoralised and demotivated and wouldn't pose a threat to a PSG side who were feeling like they had already booked their place in the Coupe de France Final, a potentially historic one at that. Jean-Claude Lemoult even said before the game, 'If I had to choose between a place in the cup final and the assurance of playing the following season among the elite, I would rather drop the cup.'

Between the UEFA Cup and the Coupe de France, followed by another season in the Cup Winners' Cup, Lemoult and PSG clearly had their eyes set on the UEFA Cup instead, which they had already qualified for by the time they lined up against Tours for the second leg. A 3-3 draw was enough to send PSG through in a game that lacked any kind of suspense once they decided that they had to actually try after going 1-0 down after five minutes. Awaiting them in the final was a team looking to make history and set to dominate for the next few seasons. Nantes were dangerous, with goals spread across their team, and defensively were solid, functional but viciously effective. Led by the Yugoslavian talisman Vahid Halilhodžić, scorer of 32 goals across Division 1 and the Coupe de France, Nantes romped their way to the championship with a hefty ten-point gap over Bordeaux and 11 points ahead of PSG. Nantes scored more than anyone else with 100 goals in total and had the best defensive record. They went into their Coupe de France Final as heavy favourites. PSG's experience in the final the previous year and their star creator Safet Sušić meant that it would be foolish to completely rule them out but the wise money was being put on Nantes to win the double.

With around 50,000 in attendance at a sunny Parc des Princes, it had the makings of a classic. The champions vs the 'home' side, both of whom were guaranteed to be playing in Europe in the following season, with some wonderful players on display to please those watching at home or in the ground. A fast start was what was needed and it was exactly what happened. PSG won a free kick around 25 yards out, not quite in typical shooting range but central enough to perhaps test the goalkeeper and sting the palms of his hands. Up stepped defender Pascal Zaremba, often used as a central midfielder or even as a sweeper, and on the odd occasion in the *libero* position, demonstrating that he was a man of great talent but also of great versatility and had earned the trust of Peyroche. One of the more unsung members of the PSG squad, Zaremba strode into the path of the ball and leathered it into the bottom-left corner past the diving Jean-Paul Bertrand-Demanes in the Nantes goal.

It was the perfect start for PSG, but it invited pressure on to them and Nantes levelled just before the 20-minute mark. Bruno Baronchelli's first touch to take him clear of two defenders was exquisite, as was his little dinked finish over Baratelli, and just like that it was game on again. Nantes kept pushing forward looking to take the lead but the Parisian rearguard held firm until five minutes before the half-time interval when they conceded what could only be described as a goal of sheer class and pure magic. Seth Adonkor clipped the ball into the PSG penalty area, hoping to find the technically gifted José Touré. Touré had his back to goal and was surrounded by Franck Tanasi to his left and Jean-Marc Pilorget to his right, but he controlled Adonkor's pass with his chest in mid-air, took a touch with his right to steady himself and, just as the PSG defenders looked set to win the battle, he flicked the ball past the pair of them into the air, where he connected with a left-foot volley past Baratelli into the far corner. It was an absolute delight of a goal to watch, one you could see over and over again and never tire of it. Baratelli watched on as Bathenay screamed at his fellow defenders for not doing more, but the goalkeeper knew that not much could have prevented the end result. Once the ball left Adonkor's boot, it was just unstoppable.

On commentary that day was Jean-Michel Larqué for Antenne 2, who simply said, 'More goals like that please, gentlemen,' and it was looking more and more like Nantes were ready to complete a famous double, something that seemed even more on the cards when Bathenay went off injured and was replaced by Mustapha Dahleb after half-time. If anything, however, the substitution kick-started PSG. The extra attacker gave them confidence and they kept piling on the pressure, pushing Nantes back and creating chances that excited the crowd but also worried the Division 1 champions. PSG had the experience of being in this kind of game in this kind of atmosphere before, an experience that could only be obtained in a cup final. Most of the time it was about talent and who had the better team but, when it came down to the crunch, the ability to read a situation and play to the moment was arguably just as important, and PSG were head and shoulders the better side in the final 45 minutes.

With 65 minutes on the clock Nantes still led 2-1. PSG had been knocking on their door but Nantes weren't answering, much to the frustration of the Parisians, but they kept their head and kept their mentality the same. They had to keep plugging away because their experience the year prior told them that the best things, sometimes, come to those who wait. Just as time was ticking down, a Yugoslavian magician appeared in the middle of the field. Twenty yards from goal, he lured in Adonkor and within seconds Adonkor vanished. The magician managed to drag the ball back and past the Nantes man without Adonkor realising. The magician twisted, turned, checked back on to his right foot and hammered the ball into the back of the net. While it wasn't an actual magician, Safet Sušić was about as close as you were going to get, and Sušić probably delivered more magic than an actual magician anyway. The talisman of the PSG side, who was signed for big moments and to deliver when the club needed him to, popped up exactly when he was required. Sušić had seen what Touré had done and decided to try and go one better with his goal, but, regardless of the battle between those two, PSG found themselves level and ready to win the cup, in 90 minutes this time rather than on penalties.

Their experiences from the season prior had them in the superior position and their play on the day had them as favourites, with the pendulum flowing in their favour. Borelli, looking nervous compared to the ice-cool Peyroche on the bench, urged his charges forward whenever they had the ball and told them to retreat whenever Nantes had possession, acting more like a fan than a chairman, but Peyroche remained steady, hunched over on the bench, staring intently at what was transpiring on the field, almost like he knew what was going to happen and had no worries. With ten minutes left Sušić dropped deeper to pick the ball up around the centre circle, inviting his teammates to rush forward to offer him any attacking outlet possible, with two running down the right flank, one down the middle and one on the left, all unmarked. One of the players on the right was Nambatingue Toko, who had laid the ball off for Sušić on the halfway line. Toko continued his run, then Sušić took a look up and threaded an inch-perfect through ball into his path. The forward from Chad didn't have to break stride but kept galloping forward to reach the ball on the right-hand side of the box. With the ball running away from him, Toko had to get a shot off as quickly as possible, and calmly side-footed the ball past the desperate Bertrand-Demanes, who could only watch from the prone position as it trickled across the line. For the second year in a row Paris Saint-Germain had won the Coupe de France, triumphant again on their own turf, in their own city and in front of their own fans. Francis Borelli rose from the bench to embrace the Parc des Princes pitch again, and it would prove to be the perfect send-off for the ever-calm Georges Peyroche, who announced prior to the game that he would be taking a sabbatical at the end of the season. 'I'm going fishing in the Dordogne, but it's not a goodbye, it's only a meet again,' was the Peyroche au revoir, rather than a big song and dance, probably the way he would have liked it to have been.

But perhaps the most emotional reaction to the day wasn't the departing manager or even the roaring fans in the stands, but that of stand-in captain and the receiver of the trophy on the day. Goalkeeper Dominique Baratelli was not only incredibly happy to win yet another Coupe de France, he was seemingly overwhelmed by the fact that *he* was the captain and the one to hoist the trophy into the air, following the injury to Bathenay. Baratelli said after the bells and whistles had quietened down, 'I felt one of the deepest, most interior joys of my footballing life when the president of the republic handed me the Coupe de France. I was not prepared for this kind of ceremony. Everything was spinning in my head. Mr Mitterrand said a few words of congratulations which I barely heard. The crowd was raving. I held up the cup towards the audience. What joy! Coming down from the presidential platform, I thought of Bathenay, who should have been in my place. Regarding the match, I was flabbergasted by José Touré's technical feat on the second goal. But I reassured myself by telling myself that he could not do something like this again in the same game.'

If you weren't sure of how Baratelli felt about the game, these comments made it pretty clear. If you also weren't sure on how good the José Touré goal was, the use of the word 'flabbergasted' probably does it as much justice as any other word could.

While PSG's first triumph is seen as a much more iconic moment in the club's history, understandably so, the Nantes final still had a cultural impact in at least one medium away from sports. In the film *Le Fabuleux Destin d'Amélie Poulain*, there's a scene where a young Amélie is on the roof and decides to disconnect the antenna to the television in the house of Mr Collignon while he's watching the 1983 Coupe de France Final. She pulls the antenna out before the Zaremba free kick, then she pulls it out again before Safet Sušić's brilliant equaliser, then again just before José Touré's goal. If you ignore the factual mistakes, it's a good scene.

Peyroche was gone, but the cup stayed in Paris, although the fishing trip that the manager wanted didn't last too long. The new era for Paris Saint-Germain of winning trophies and contesting at the top of Division 1 was established by Peyroche but his successor, Lucien Leduc, couldn't carry it on during his brief spell in charge. At the age of 65, Leduc was always going to be a short-term appointment and was a safe pair of hands, who was famous for winning Division 1 with Monaco and also for his stint in charge of Marseille where he was sacked in March 1972, seven points clear of second place.

Leduc, translated into English as 'The Duke', tried to assert his influence on to the team but Peyroche was still lurking in the background – the former boss sent telegrams to the team before the opening game of the 1983/84 season and would be quoted in interviews as saying, 'I will be back, perhaps sooner than you think.' The rumour had been that Leduc would be a placeholder for when Peyroche decided to finish his sabbatical, but this was something Leduc denied time and time again. 'I do not know if Georges Peyroche has agreed with the board for his return. I did not come to do an interim for a few months but to fully fulfil my mission as a coach, at least until the end of my one-year contract,' said Leduc, who must have had a feeling that the lurking presence of Peyroche was too large to ignore.

It was a season of change and one that didn't feel particularly special despite a match-up against the Juventus side of Michel Platini, Zbigniew Boniek and Paolo Rossi in the Cup Winners' Cup – which PSG lost on away goals despite taking the lead in the first leg – and an early Coupe de France exit to Division 2 side Mulhouse didn't help their cause either. Peyroche eventually found himself back in the dugout in April of 1984, guiding Leduc's side to fourth and a place in the following season's UEFA Cup, their first time in the competition. However, one of the main rules in football is to never go back to your old club, which Peyroche seemed eager to break the moment he left in the first place, and it ended in predictably terrible circumstances.

PSG finished 13th in Division 1 and went out of the UEFA Cup on penalties in the second round against Hungarians Videoton, with the saving grace being the Coupe de France Final against Monaco, which Peyroche wasn't even in charge for having been replaced by interim coach Christian Coste, although PSG lost it 1-0 anyway. The season would have been worse if it hadn't been for the likes of Sušić, who actually recorded five assists in a 7-1 win against Bastia, and while relegation was never a true threat past the first seven games of the season, their form in the second half of the campaign was that of rank amateurs and relegation fodder teams.

A total of 13 wins all season, nine of which came before 2 December, was utterly woeful. Peyroche knew he was under threat for the majority of the season – Borelli even apparently said to him, 'Coach, I will not risk my place as president. I will fire you, if necessary, but I will remain president' – but even he was stunned when the announcement from Borelli came to sack him. Peyroche was on his way to have an ankle operation but saw Borelli with Coste, who was in charge of the reserves at the time. Before Peyroche went under the knife, Borelli made the announcement about replacing him, with Peyroche still bitter about it many years later and saying, 'I was so stuck before the operation that I couldn't react.'

The Peyroche era was over, but the mentality that he installed of winning and in a professional manner needed to be brought back out of the players again. It needed someone to come in and light a fire underneath the Parc des Princes to let Paris – and France – know that PSG weren't just a cup side, they were to be reckoned with. But who would be the manager to do the job that Borelli wanted, dreamed of and was starting to demand? Peyroche couldn't survive a mid-table finish despite back-to-back Coupe de France triumphs, so what would the reaction be to the appointment of someone who had never won a trophy in his career prior to his move to Paris and had only been a Division 1 manager for a handful of years?

9

Le vainqueur oublié –
The forgotten winner

VERY RARELY do you find successful coaches or managers in football who weren't professional players at some stage in their career. Some are embedded into coaching earlier than others, such as Julian Nagelsmann, but even he was on the books with Augsburg and 1860 Munich as a youngster, but never made a first-team appearance because of major injuries. There is a culture within football that's wary of 'outsiders', those who aren't within the game itself, day in, day out. To gain the trust of a professional footballer as a coach takes more than your tactical knowledge, but also what you've achieved either in your coaching career already or on the pitch as a player. Players can make an instant judgement based on your CV before you've even spoken to them, and it can be an almighty task to win them over.

Even rarer, however, is someone coming into coaching without any kind of background in football, instead coming from the world of teaching – not even teaching sport or physical education, but the English language. For someone like Gérard Houllier, being treated with a lack of respect was something he was familiar with in the early stages of his career, but despite his success and influence both in France and abroad it is perhaps his first major job and certainly his first major success in management that is often widely forgotten about. Very rarely is it spoken about in interviews, bar the few odd lines here and there, and very rarely is it eulogised about in the same way that other triumphs are, but arguably his first triumph was his greatest. But to understand why Houllier's first trophy in management was so special and extraordinary, you have to go back in time and trace the steps of an English teacher who became manager of Paris Saint-Germain.

Born in the north of France in a commune called Thérouanne – somewhere that is actually closer to London than it is to Paris in terms of miles – was a young, football-mad, Reims-supporting Gérard Houllier. Putting up posters of Reims' super team from the 1950s and writing to the club in the hopes of getting an autograph or two, Houllier was in love with football and it seemed destined that he would, at some point in his life, be fully engrossed in the professional game. Houllier's first clear footballing memory took place in Paris, the 1956 European Cup Final between Real Madrid and his beloved Reims, with the Spaniards coming out on top, but his path to Paris Saint-Germain took a few unexpected stops before it had even begun.

Most managers are players or start coaching at a young age, but not Houllier. After dropping out of university and eventually doing his English degree on a part-time basis, Houllier became a school teacher, even travelling to Liverpool and teaching French. At a young age he was showing his leadership qualities albeit in the classroom rather than on the training ground, being the deputy headmaster of École Normale d'Arras, a boys' school in the Arras region. When Houllier turned 26 he decided to leave the school life behind to take his chance in the football world once and for all. He was a youth coach with Arras before taking charge of the reserves at Nœux-les-Mines, praising the club's head coach Guy Debeugny and citing him as a major influence in his style of coaching. Houllier said, 'Guy was a great person. It was a godsend for me to be his deputy. He was ahead of his time in terms of physical, tactical and technical training. He made me progress enormously by launching me into a path of performance research.'

Houllier's time with Nœux-les-Mines was important, not only in his development as a manager but also as a man, learning what it was like to be working in the lower divisions of French football and how to communicate with players on a human level. Winning promotion from Division 3 into Division 2 was the highlight of his time with Nœux, but at that level, in any country, you're bound to be scouted by other clubs who want to learn the art of developing players like Houllier did and try to exploit his skills. RC Lens, the perennial mid-table Division 1 club, came calling for Houllier and, seeing it as a huge step up – which it was – he jumped at the opportunity and took over in the summer of 1982. Lens were keen to bring Houllier in, yet he had huge obstacles to overcome before he even stepped foot on the training ground. At Nœux-les-Mines with part-time players, his methods worked because the amateurs hadn't been treated to tactics or anything of the sort until Houllier came in. Yet at Lens, a Division 1 club with professional players, he had to hit the ground running. Louis Plet, the club's general secretary, told *The Guardian*, 'We could see he was an intelligent, rigorous coach,' and Lens were ready to back Houllier no matter what. The club knew it was a risk but all involved felt the risk had more positives than it did negatives.

As for hitting the ground running, Houllier did just that, finishing in the UEFA Cup places in 1983 and just a handful of points behind Paris Saint-Germain, the same season that PSG beat Nantes in the Coupe de France Final. Houllier was making moves and impressing those at Lens but, on a wider scale, he was going largely unnoticed, although those in the boardroom in Paris hadn't completely ignored what he had accomplished in such a short space of time.

Having finished runners-up in the Coupe de France in 1985 and 13th in Division 1, PSG knew they needed to make the next step and become consistent challengers for the title. Changes had to be made, with two positions at the back first on the agenda. Firstly, Dominique Baratelli retired as a PSG legend but also as one of the most consistent and reliable goalkeepers in French football. Totalling 593 league games, Baratelli is currently fourth on the list of most appearances made by anyone in the French top flight, an incredible statistic and one that speaks to how reliable he was. The other to depart was captain Dominique Bathenay, who was such a big part of the Coupe de France triumphs and a consistently excellent defender for PSG.

With Mustapha Dahleb leaving to join Nice the previous season, three key figures had departed the Parc des Princes but the club was still in a strong position and still had stars scattered throughout their team such as Dominique Rocheteau, Luis Fernández – who was made captain to replace Bathenay – and Safet Sušić, the driving force of the side. Jean-Marc Pilorget was still a strong asset to have in defence while Philippe Jeannol joined him after his move from Nantes in 1984 and, despite both Pilorget and Jeannol being 27, their experience would prove to be incredibly valuable. With a new captain in place, a creative spark and a supreme goalscorer to add to the sturdy defensive structure, two things were still needed: a new goalkeeper and a new manager.

Recruited to play between the posts was France's number one, Joël Bats, a poet off the field but a general and a leader on it. After being diagnosed with testicular cancer in the summer of 1982 and missing the World Cup in Spain, Bats made a full recovery following successful surgery and took up poetry as a means of therapy and a way to express his thoughts and emotions through the recovery, even recording and releasing an album in 1986 called *Gardien de tes Nuits,* meaning 'Goalkeeper of your Nights'. Pierre-Etienne Minonzio wrote about Bats in his book *Petit Manuel Musical du Football* – (The Little book of Music and Football) – and suggested, 'Goalkeepers – like drummers in a rock band – are often very strange people, sometimes lunatic, or shy or egocentric. Bats was shy, a bit uncomfortable with the pressure of his status as goalkeeper of the French national team and he apparently recorded this album as a way to take his mind off of the pressure.'

It would be easy to categorise Bats as a goalkeeper who was a bit eccentric or took a trip to the wild side from time to time, but he was far from that. He wrote his poetry to keep his mind at ease rather than to show off. He was someone who took football seriously, but also was acutely aware of how important it was to unwind and step back from the sport at times, for example when he decided to go on an impromptu fishing trip the night before the 1984 European Championship Final. Bats wasn't someone who misbehaved or snuck out from the team camp to go and cause trouble, but he was a free mind who knew what he needed to do to keep himself at ease.

There was a reason why he was the starting goalkeeper when France won their very first trophy in the 1984 Euros – the fishing trip worked for Bats – and there was a reason why PSG were so keen to bring him in to replace Baratelli, someone who had a huge influence on the team and the club. Not only was Bats an excellent player but he commanded his area and was the perfect base for Houllier and the back line to build from. If anyone was strong enough to replace the ever-reliable Baratelli, it was Bats. Houllier had his goalkeeper and a strong defence to start his season with, but he also had an incredible strong spine. From Bats in goal with Pilorget and Jeannol just ahead of him, Fernández and Sušić were in the middle of the park with the former providing a screen for the defenders, being strong in the tackle but also having a good eye for a pass, and the latter being the creative force and the man who linked up play from midfield into the feet of the final piece of the Parisian spine, Rocheteau, who was still hitting the back of the net on a regular basis.

Yet, despite the clear quality in their squad, PSG weren't seen as favourites for the Division 1 title. Nantes and Bordeaux were the strong contenders alongside

Monaco, but PSG were almost viewed as the best of the rest. With the team having the ability to challenge but with two key players departing in the same window and a relatively unknown and untested manager taking the helm, many saw their chances as fairly slim.

Their opening game against Bastia offered both the new-look PSG and Houllier the chance to impress, albeit not on the island of Corsica – where Bastia usually play their home fixtures – but in Reims, just 150km from Paris. The sky was blue, a beautiful kind of day just made for football, in July, but while Houllier smiled his way through the pre-match preparation he struggled to hide the nervousness. He needed to get off to a good start. Being 4-0 up before the half hour was about as good a start as he could have hoped for and even though Bastia grabbed two goals before the half-time whistle, Houllier was thrilled with the result. 'First victory, it was the beginning of a beautiful page which is beginning to be written. It's funny but in Reims I've always been happy, I never lost, I always had good results, maybe it was a little sign of fate,' he said after the match.

The manager's mood got even better when his charges put three past a Lille side that were chasing shadows rather than the ball. 'We immediately felt that the team had a different look, we played the match with a different device compared to what PSG used to do in previous years, and things were going well, because the players were ready to adhere to what we set out to do,' said Houllier, not long after his debut in front of the Parisian public at the Parc des Princes, but clearly he felt his side were already a different proposition to the one that he took over a few months prior.

The two wins to start the season had PSG in second place but the third game against Toulouse, a 3-1 victory, put them top of the table. Despite the fact that it was still very early in the season, the improvement in PSG was remarkable. Following up the Toulouse result with a confident and impressive 1-0 triumph over reigning champions Bordeaux in front of just under 45,000 fans was extraordinary. Perhaps it was Houllier's influence, perhaps it was having Fernández as captain, but PSG looked confident. They looked like they felt they could hold their own against the title contenders, the pre-season favourites, and they weren't intimidated by their opposition. Bordeaux couldn't get into the game and it must have felt like fending off a tidal wave with a fishing net, because there was nothing they could do to bring PSG to a halt. The 1-0 scoreline made the match look a lot tighter than it was, but it did send out a message to the rest of France that PSG were not messing around.

Laval were the only side to take a point off PSG but Houllier's first clash against Marseille was the perfect chance to get back on track and to show that, even though they had suffered a slight setback, PSG weren't going to let it derail them. If you were late to the game you probably missed the first goal. Not even 50 seconds were on the clock and PSG had taken the lead, captain Fernández stooping down low to turn Sušić's free kick home. Some 20 minutes later Robert Jacques made it 2-0 and gave PSG a massive win in a footballing as well as a psychological sense.

The victories just kept coming, with Bats giving an incredible performance against his former side Auxerre in a tight yet exciting 1-0 result. Yet Houllier noted the way that PSG won. 'I think everyone wanted to give Joël [Bats] a nice gift and they couldn't give a better gift. There we discovered something that the team had not yet shown, and that is that they are able to resist before winning. Often she prevailed because she was brilliant, but didn't show that quality,' Houllier said.

Not only were PSG winning, but they were learning to do so ugly and grind out as many points as possible. By the midseason break, PSG were not only top of Division 1 but were unbeaten too, six points clear of their nearest challengers Nantes. They had the best goal difference, the joint-best defence and by far the leading attack in the league. PSG weren't just top of the league, they were absolutely running away with it and deservedly so. The ability of their players was never questioned but the shift in mentality was massive, as was Houllier's ability to take the team to a new level in a tactical sense. He had managed to turn this talented group of players into a talented team who found ways to win. Not every game was a masterclass in football, but a victory is always a victory.

PSG's rise up the table also coincided with the increase in hooliganism in the stands, with more and more violent and controversial incidents occurring every week. In a post-Heysel world, hooliganism was on the minds of everyone who went to games across Europe. The Kop of the Boulogne end was the area that was seen as the hub of hooliganism at the Parc des Princes, with the Commando Pirate hooligan firm forming in this season. Filled with far-right extremists and skinheads, the firm would travel to games and deface away ends and even towns and cities, writing to opposition fans and exclaiming that they were '100 per cent nationalists'. On the walls of Stade du Ray they wrote 'Hitler is our master' and proceeded to break into the stadium, destroy the changing rooms, executive lounges and set the telephones on fire. According to a member of the Paris Casuals group, 'A group of PSG supporters ransacked the offices of the Union of Journalists in Paris, to protest against the media hype against English supporters, following the Heysel disaster,' because a certain section of these hooligan firms also believed that the 'aggressors of the Heysel disaster should be decorated'.

It all became quite unsavoury quite quickly with the police not being able to fully investigate and arrest those who took part in the attacks because some information said they were coming from the Boulogne end, while others claimed the skinheads were 'for the most part, too intellectually limited and too short-sighted to organise such operations hundreds of kilometers from home'. The fact of the matter was that these firms were organising attacks away from home and no one knew how to prevent them.

At one game, PSG hooligans were arrested as soon as they got off the train into Le Havre while the club reduced its stadium's capacity from 17,000 to 12,000 with hope of being able to police the stands better with a fewer amount of people on the terraces. Some PSG fans who bought tickets for behind the goals were moved into a small corner of the ground, even gaining the attention of Francis Borelli who said, 'Guys, I'm so sorry they put you here, but there's nothing we can do. I will compensate you, I will give you places for the next game.' According to a fan who wrote an article for *PSG Mag* about this game, Borelli eventually did do, with a signed note attached too.

While PSG's hooligan firms seemed to be causing trouble off the pitch wherever they went, on the pitch the players kept collecting win after win. They went into the second half of the season unbeaten and still top of Division 1, in a remarkable feat of consistency. The first concession that PSG could possibly win the title was made by the Toulon manager Alain Rey, who put it rather bluntly in his post-match interviews, saying, 'PSG will be champions.' That Toulon game, their first in a run of three consecutive draws, was marred by even more fan trouble, but from the Toulonnais, who – according to reports from the time – sent a bomb threat to PSG's plane, delaying its departure, sent death threats to their hotel, and blocked the team bus to the extent that the squad had to get off the bus and walk the rest of the 200m to the stadium.

Hooliganism was rampant across France, affecting every club, and at what appeared to be every possible opportunity. These hooligans weren't 'fans' but rather they were hoodlums looking for an excuse to write right-wing, offensive drivel across the walls of an unsuspecting town and used football as their get-out. The 1985/86 season was perhaps one of the first where hooliganism in football became a massive issue in France just as it had done in England and in Italy. It wasn't non-existent beforehand, but the incidents during this season highlighted the issue further and the fact that Heysel became such an impactful moment was even more reason to keep a close eye on fans, at least in the eyes of the law.

Floodlight failure in Lille caused PSG's visit there to be postponed in the 86th minute, a game that they would eventually lose because the authorities felt that, even though there were only four minutes to complete, the whole 90 minutes had to be replayed. To some it seemed fair, but to PSG captain Luis Fernández it seemed rather pointless, telling media after the game, 'When I think that for such a short time the game has to be replayed ... It's a shame because the draw suits everyone,' while Houllier didn't quite mince his words, 'I will no longer have any respect for these men huddled in their office, who decide the fate of athletes. I do not want to believe in such an outcome and I hope that reason will prevail.'

Houllier wasn't pleased with the decision, and he couldn't have been happy when the rearranged fixture ended up being the first game PSG lost in Division 1 that season, dropping their unbeaten run in a cold, dark and dreary night in northern France. Up until that point in January 1986, PSG had been invincible and were comfortably ahead in the title race and had even broken the record for longest unbeaten run in the French top flight, going 26 games without defeat and beating Saint-Étienne's record of 21. But with Lille beating them, and then with losing the following game away at Nancy in the thick, heavy snow, opponents of Paris Saint-Germain no longer saw them as untouchable or as invincible. With some losses on the table, PSG had been brought down a peg or two but, with the title more or less theirs to lose for the majority of the season, those two defeats probably served as timely wake-up calls.

Houllier's men would lose three more games before the end of the season – away to Nantes, Strasbourg and Metz – and a theme crept into their performances after the winter break. Yes, they would win multiple games and ultimately that was all that mattered, but the general performances weren't those of a team going in the right direction. Fernández often spoke about his displeasure of some performances and said after the loss to Strasbourg, 'I think tonight we hit rock bottom. We can't do worse. We often think it's an easy game, we lose our focus ... and we lose.' He would, however, always end his statements by acknowledging that his side had gained two points. The two points were key, but the standard of performances had dropped and Fernández couldn't have been the only one to have noticed.

While standards had been slipping on the field, the fact remained that PSG needed to win on the final day of the season to secure their very first top-flight title. The championship could have been wrapped up weeks earlier but the various hiccups meant that PSG had the chance to win the championship at the Parc des Princes in front of their fans, and a sell-out crowd of just under 45,000. There was still a chance that Nantes could pip them to the title but the likelihood of that happening was next to none, hence the joyous mood from the Parisian fans. Pink and white balloons were set off prior to kick-off and the festivities prior to the game almost stopped you from thinking that PSG still had to get a victory to officially be crowned champions.

After four minutes they were already 1-0 up. A scramble in the six-yard box was finished off by Robert Jacques with a low, stooping header. Jacques then grabbed his second on the 20-minute mark with a powerful and wonderfully driven header past the hopeless Bastia goalkeeper. With no change in score by half-time, the festivities in the stands continued but everyone and their dog knew what the outcome was going to be. It was predicable but, from a PSG point of view, that was ideal. Bastia did pull a goal back before the hour but Fernández, the undisputed leader of the team, the man who would be crowned French Player of the Year for 1985 – the first PSG player to win the award – and finished 12th in the Ballon d'Or voting of the same year, stepped up to take a spot kick. He scored with ease as PSG went on to claim the win and their first Division 1 title.

Their 1-0 win at home to Monaco was when the championship was almost certainly wrapped up in the minds of the fans but, on paper, they could still have let it slip. After the Monaco win, PSG had a four-point gap on second place, in the era of two points for a win, with two games to go, and while they lost to Metz their confirmation as champions soon came along.

Fireworks lit up the Parisian skies while Houllier and Borelli embraced, with the duo managing to conjure up a spectacular title. This was a PSG side not expected to achieve much in Houllier's first season but they pulled off something remarkable. Not only had they won their first league title but they dispelled the old trope of being scared to win and managing to find a way to lose when it looked easier to win. PSG teams of old had always fallen at some kind of hurdle whether it be in the league or in the Cup Winners' Cup, with the Coupe de France victories proving to be vital in the change of mentality. The cup wins showed that PSG had the quality to win multiple one-off matches but, over the course of a 38-game season, it took more than just that. It took hard work, trust, intelligence, skill, heart, desire, mental and physical toughness and this PSG side possessed it all. Bats in goal proved to be a calming and reliable presence while the spine of the team remained consistent and excellent throughout the season. Rocheteau was top scorer with 20 goals and the creative genius of Sušić was instrumental on countless occasions. The decision from Houllier to give Fernández the captain's armband was borderline genius, transforming the midfielder into a star and giving him the confidence to lead PSG to glory and be a leader in France's 1986 World Cup squad, helping form part of 'the magic square' for Les Bleus along with Platini, Jean Tigana and Alain Giresse.

Champagne was generously flowing wherever you looked, mixing in with sweaty PSG players and the flashes of the photographers' camera bulbs, while le Parc treated the fans – who were allowed in for free to watch the game, hence the high attendance – to a superb fireworks display, and if you were lucky enough to find yourself on the Champs-Élysées in the next few days you would have seen the trophy parade. Paris was in full-blown party mode. PSG had become the first capital club to win the top flight since 1936, prompting Houllier to let everyone know how he felt about the occasion and about the achievement, 'It's the greatest reward of my career. To put in such a performance, you have to have quality men. The Paris Saint-Germain players are talented and deserve the title.' Houllier was set to be the man to lead PSG forward in a bright, new future and Luis Fernández was set to be his general on the field. But things didn't quite go to plan. In fact, things went wrong very quickly, starting with their captain.

In the summer of 1986, following PSG's Division 1 triumph and France's road to the World Cup semi-finals at Mexico, Fernández decided it was time for a change of scenery. He had achieved what he had wanted to with Paris Saint-Germain and moved on to another French club: Matra Racing, formerly known as Racing Paris. In 1982, Jean-Luc Lagardère, an industrialist who had been rather successful in the auto and horse-racing worlds, turned to football in a bid to add another arm to what he considered to be a rapidly growing sporting empire. Initially he wanted to merge Racing with Paris FC, although the Racing members turned that down due to a lack of information regarding the finances of Paris FC. So Lagardère simply bought Paris FC, renamed it Racing and merged the two Racing clubs together a year later.

Starting in Division 2, Lagardère was an impatient man who wanted nothing but success and he wanted it yesterday, sometimes unable to fully grasp that teams needed time to build. They did gain promotion to Division 1 in 1983/84 but were swiftly relegated in the following campaign. In the year that PSG won the Division 1 title, Racing won promotion yet again to return to a Division 1 run by a Parisian club, with Lagardère determined to make his the superior outfit. It was in this summer that Racing made their biggest splash. Just before the 1986 World Cup, they brought in two Uruguayans – Rubén Paz from Internacional, and Enzo Francescoli, the superstar of River Plate. West Germany forward Pierre Littbarski signed for the equivalent of more than €1m from Cologne, then, rounded off the spree was by snatching Fernández from their city rivals. Victor Zvunka was the player-manager initially but Porto coach Artur Jorge soon took over, immediately after guiding the Portuguese club to the European Cup by beating Bayern Munich in the final.

On paper, Racing looked like a huge threat. World-class players with a European Cup-winning manager usually equals success. They even tried to sign younger French players like David Ginola from Toulon (who they would eventually land) and Eric Cantona. Yet, while the outsiders felt that Racing was the glitz and glamour that Paris demanded of anything that was popular, the club was a complete mess on the inside. The training facilities weren't up to standard, the wage differential between the superstars and the rest of the squad couldn't have been good for team morale and even the stars were looking for ways to escape. Littbarski even paid his own transfer fee to return to Cologne (the German club eventually managed to find ways to pay Littbarski back), while Francescoli stayed for three miserable years before departing for Marseille (where he would inspire a little boy named Zinedine).

Jean-Luc Lagardère eventually pulled his investment out of the club a few years later after just surviving relegation on goal difference in 1989. Racing had changed its name in Lagardère's time to Matra Racing, named after his 'sporting empire' that he so dearly craved, but were called Racing Paris once again after he left. The right to buy Racing Paris cost Matra 300m francs and it brought them absolutely nothing, but it took PSG's influential captain away from them and also taught the rest of French football a massive lesson. If you're going to invest heavily into a football club, spend wisely, look towards the future while keeping an eye on the present and, perhaps the most important factor, win. While Racing's experiment did not completely ruin PSG, it did serve as a reminder of a club that didn't think too fondly of Paris Saint-Germain could do if they were given tonnes of money to spend, which brings us neatly on to the second reason why things didn't go to plan for PSG.

Bernard Tapie was a Parisian by birth, growing up in the northern part of the city while Paris was still under the occupation of Hitler's Third Reich. His wealth, gained by his forays into business specifically specialising in saving bankrupt companies and turning them around, saw his own personal wealth to two billion francs (around €760m) by the mid-1980s thanks to 'a fierce desire to earn lots and lots and lots of money' as a younger Tapie stated in the documentary *Bernard Tapie: A Free Man* by *L'Equipe*.

Tapie's first dabble into sport was via the Tour de France, with the 1985 and 1986 winning team *La Vie Claire* sponsored by and named after his food stores business. The man was eccentric, addicted to success and was loved by some, despised by others over the years. Tapie felt, as did many others at the time, that his strategy in business was perfectly suited to football. Buy a struggling outfit for a relatively low price, spend big to improve them over the course of time and mould them into a successful operation, heralded across the country and the envy of others.

His rise to prominence came at a time when Marseille were in desperate need of a spark to take them from relegation struggles and mid-table obscurity back to the top, to challenge the likes of Bordeaux and Paris Saint-Germain. They were relegated from Division 1 in 1980 and by 1984 they hadn't caught back up with the top teams. Mid-table finish after mid-table finish meant it was hard to envision Marseille challenging regularly any time soon, until the board and the mayor of Marseille had the idea to try and convince Tapie to invest into the club and eventually take it over, then proceed to build Marseille back up to where they felt they belonged. Tapie at first refused and dismissed the idea, claiming to know nothing about football, but was eventually persuaded and had his takeover confirmed in April 1986, just as Paris Saint-Germain were wrapping up their first Division 1 title and Marseille were floundering in 12th place.

Tapie's first action was to bring in a director of football who would essentially act as a right-hand man and guide the owner on the right footballing decisions to make while Tapie handled the financial side. And it wasn't just any old face; France's 1984 European Championship-winning manager Michel Hidalgo was the first big-name star to be attracted down south by Tapie. 'I would not undertake anything without having the certainty that Michel Hidalgo, recognised as one of the best coaches in the world, would be with me,' said Tapie to the club's general assembly, before telling the local press, 'When I start a business, I always want to have the most qualified people by my side. Michel Hidalgo will be with me in Marseille to build this new OM of which we all dream.'

The second action was to invest heavily into the transfer market. Jean-Pierre Papin and Alain Giresse became the two marquee signings for Marseille in 1986, alongside West German defender Karlheinz Förster. Marseille were forcing people to take them seriously, and the rest of France was forced to do just that when they managed to fire themselves up to second, just four points behind Bordeaux. Marseille looked like a team on the rise while

PSG's defence of their title was mediocre at best. Having been so dominant in the 1985/86 season, Houllier's side fell into the trap of inconsistency and their form from the latter stages of the previous season crept in to the entirety of 1986/87, leaving them in seventh place, knocked out of the European Cup in the first round, and a tepid attempt at the Coupe de France saw them bettered by Strasbourg.

It got even worse in 1987/88 as PSG saw themselves slip into the relegation zone for the majority of the second half of that season, saving themselves only by winning their final three games – one of which was a huge 2-1 victory at the Stade Vélodrome against Marseille. While PSG were struggling to maintain any good form for a prolonged period of time, Marseille were on the ascendancy. Finishing second in Tapie's first season was followed up by a disappointing sixth, but it set the scene perfectly for 1988/89. Marseille, now boasting players such as Klaus Allofs, Abédi Pelé and the most sought-after young talent in French football at the time, Eric Cantona, felt they had the perfect chance and opportunity to strike for the title. PSG, on the other hand, were more than happy to take a back seat and let Marseille and Tapie have the spotlight because they knew they had an outside chance of upsetting them down the stretch.

Houllier had departed PSG at the end of the 1987/88 season to join up with the French national team as technical director and assistant manager under Michel Platini before taking up the role as manager in 1992, and was replaced at PSG by Tomislav Ivić. Ivić was a Yugoslavian who was known as a master strategist and someone who was incredibly successful, seemingly wherever he went. There's a chance that Tomislav Ivić could be the greatest manager you've never heard of. He was more than happy to bounce from job to job and country to country – he totalled 30 different jobs in 14 different countries by the time his career came to an end – and his inability to stay anywhere for longer than three years (three years was his maximum period at a club, Anderlecht in the early 1980s) is perhaps why he isn't as celebrated as he should be.

A thorough trainer and a meticulous thinker on the touchline, PSG hired Ivić off the back of his incredible stint at Porto where he took over the side left to him by Artur Jorge – who had left to take over Metra Racing – and managed to win the Primeira Liga, the Taça de Portugal, the UEFA Super Cup and the Intercontinental Cup in one season. That sounds incredible and to really emphasise just how impressive the feat of winning four trophies in one season was, it was a Portuguese record that stood for 23 years until a young André Villas-Boas did it for Porto with the incredibly fun Hulk and Radamel Falcao sides from the early 2010s. On paper, PSG looked to have made a smart appointment. Ivić's résumé made him look like a trophy-winning machine and, to be fair to him, he had won everywhere he had been.

PSG weren't perceived to be as strong as Marseille or as strong as reigning champions Monaco, who were now managed by Arsène Wenger and had an array of talents such as Mark Hateley, Patrick Battiston, topped off with the incredibly gifted Glenn Hoddle and had just added Liberian striker George Weah to their ranks, yet they weren't too far removed from their Division 1 title win. The likes of Fernández and Rocheteau had departed but Bats, Jeannol, Pilorget and Safet Sušić remained as influential players, who were now captained by Senegalese midfielder Oumar Sène. Being the first season in French football where a win was worth three points made things seem just that little bit more exciting. And, rather ironically, the title would actually be decided by a three-point margin.

An impressive start to the season saw PSG reach the summit after just seven games, with their first defeat coming in the fifth match, away at Monaco, an 88th-minute winner for Wenger's side being the difference. It took Marseille until their fifth game to pick up a first win, but PSG kept on racking up the victories. Seven of their first eight were won and by the time PSG and Marseille met for the first time, PSG were top of the table and one point clear of their rivals, who had lost just one of their last 12 Division 1 games. With such importance riding on this encounter, it was expected to be thrilling, exciting and entertaining.

Unfortunately, none of the fans who were at the Parc des Princes that night could claim to be thrilled, excited or entertained, with perhaps the only exciting part of the match being the full-time whistle or the fact they knew they were on their way home. You could count the chances both teams had on one hand and the importance of the fixture actually meant that both sides tried not to lose, lining up to cancel one another out.

PSG's tactic of playing on the counter-attack may have been effective in terms of getting results, but the fans in the stands were voicing their opinions even without saying a word. The attendances fluctuated across the first half of the season, with just over 9,000 showing up for a 1-0 win over Strasbourg while more than 38,000 were present to watch a draw with Bordeaux. The fans weren't exactly flocking to le Parc to see what Paris Saint-Germain had to offer, despite their good run of form.

PSG were top at the winter break, two points clear of Auxerre and three clear of Marseille and they were looking in a fine condition to suggest that they could actually win the title. But when the team were back in action following the break, it all fell to pieces. Between returning in February and the end of the season in May, PSG picked up just four wins. They were knocked out of the Coupe de France and, to make matters worse, Marseille kept on winning, going 11 unbeaten after the winter break. That end of the run would prove to be one of only two losses in the second half of the season. PSG also only lost twice, but struggled massively to turn draws into wins. They only conceded nine goals in the second half of the season but scored just 13 of their own.

Eventually PSG and Marseille had to face off once more, this time in the south of France and in front of a rowdy Stade Vélodrome crowd who were ready to shout whatever they wanted to at the Parisians. And with PSG fans banned from travelling to Marseille due to persistent crowd violence throughout the season and the club's inability to ensure the safety of those travelling, it was like walking in to a cauldron of fire for them. Both teams were level on points at the top of the table. Marseille drew their game heading into this fixture while PSG beat Racing Paris. Fans had learnt the lesson from the last time these two met and their expectations were more than likely dampened down, but at the very least everyone knew that this game was going to be huge.

The action was intense, with both sides being cautious but also knowing that a win was imperative, not only for the end of the season but to the fans, because the rivalry was developing into the biggest in France, if it hadn't already. Before this season – and before PSG won their first title back in 1986 – the only main reason for these two clubs to dislike each other was the north–south divide in France, a sporting version of the rich, middle-class Parisians vs the working-class Marseille citizens. Yet there now seemed to be a real footballing rivalry to add to the mix. The two clubs were going head to head for a league title and this match meant more than just football.

The 90 minutes on the pitch were tense and nervous. The accusations of PSG being a defensive team weren't dispelled, eventually getting under the skin of Ivić, who said, 'You tell me that Paris Saint-Germain is a defensive team which has not played to its full potential. I answer you: where did you see that? You tell me that Paris Saint-Germain cannot win if it does not attack. I answer you: I saw three Parisian attackers on the pitch,' while even Marseille's Jean-Pierre Papin had sympathy for the forwards of PSG, confessing, 'I could not play in a team like that.' The verdict was damning for PSG and their style, but playing like that occasionally wielded results. It needed to on this occasion in the Vélodrome, but it became clear that, while the tension was palpable all game – understandably so – PSG came to not lose rather than to win.

And for the 90 minutes, their plan had worked. It wasn't a classic match but that was what PSG wanted: to get a point and move on to the final three winnable games against Laval, Lens and Metz, which would give them the best chance to at least take the title race down to the wire. Then Franck Sauzée, a French national team star who joined Marseille from Sochaux prior to the start of the season, picked the ball up on the left-hand side. PSG's players desperately tried to race back to get bodies behind the ball to block a shot or intercept a pass, but their energy was drained from them. Sauzée passed inside, remained unmarked and eventually received the ball back about 25 yards out. He took a touch with the instep of his right foot, didn't even look up to see where Bats was standing and fired a bullet of a shot directly towards the PSG goal. As soon as that ball waved its goodbyes to the boot of Sauzée, it was a goal. He struck it so perfectly that it was only going to end up hitting the back of the net, which it duly did. Marseille won 1-0 and put themselves into the driving seat to win the championship. A bit like when PSG beat Monaco in their own title-winning season, this victory didn't give Marseille the Division 1 crown mathematically, but it almost felt like it did. They weren't champions but they must have felt like it after that win.

PSG beat Laval but drew against Lens and Metz to give Marseille the championship. Tapie's transformation had been complete and PSG were left distraught. In reality they had no right to be in the title race but, after getting so close, they couldn't help but wonder, 'What if we had just beaten Lens and Metz?' The Lens game is one of interest simply because of the controversy that surrounded it at the final whistle. Ivić decided to drop Safet Sušić and play central defender Philippe Jeannol in the attacking trio, a decision that made sense to absolutely nobody and even prompted concerns of a potential match-fixing scandal. A mediocre and toothless display handed Marseille the title, gift-wrapped with a bow on top, with Ivić seemingly the only person that night pleased with the result because it assured his club UEFA Cup football for the following season (although he was sacked at the end of the season and never got his chance in the UEFA Cup). President Borelli slipped away out of the stadium at full time but, while he contemplated saying nothing to the media, he changed his mind. 'Bernard Tapie bought the match,' he declared.

According to some reports, this wasn't the first example of Borelli accusing Tapie of such a thing. Apparently Borelli felt the same way about Tapie and potential match-fixing prior to Marseille's 1-0 win over his side. *L'Equipe* investigated the claim and spoke to a Lens player who remained anonymous. He told the newspaper, 'The night of the match, we received double bonus and I do not know why. Usually, when we get a draw, we get a bonus, but now it has been doubled.' A lot of fingers were pointed in the direction of Ivić for his dropping of Sušić, his strange team selection on the day of the game and the defensive tactics he employed all season. No one in Paris was happy, yet Marseille were winning the league and cup double to properly usher in the new era of French football. Tapie wanted to take over French football for good and he had done it perhaps a lot quicker than he expected. He threw money at his club and built a good team with some outstanding players who were on the verge of unprecedented heights, some of which still haven't been reached in the 2020s. Yet in the capital, things were looking very different.

From winning Division 1 in 1986, PSG were struggling. Poor results and poor transfers coupled with debts that kept piling on top of one another meant Francis Borelli was close to running PSG into the ground. In a bid to ensure nothing but success for the club, Borelli had nearly killed it and nearly ruined his own legacy. By the end of the 1980s, Paris Saint-Germain were in desperate need of financial help and it isn't a stretch to say that, if they hadn't received it, the club may have changed completely. But what happened next completely changed the face of French football. To put it simply, it revolutionised the way the game was seen in France.

10

Le Classique – The Classic

AFTER WINNING the title and the Coupe de France in 1989, Marseille were moving like an unstoppable force both on and off the pitch. On it, they retained their title in 1990 with Jean-Pierre Papin scoring 30 goals – the most in the French top flight since Carlos Bianchi's 37 in 1977/78 – and they made it a hat-trick of titles in 1991. Off the pitch, things were flourishing as well.

In 1989, Bernard Tapie won a seat in the French parliament to be the Marseille representative under the socialist banner during François Mitterrand's presidency, eventually joining Mitterrand's cabinet as minister for urban affairs. A year later, Tapie acquired 80 per cent of Adidas, eventually putting in place a plan that would save the brand while, in football terms, Michel Hidalgo was building a super team in the south.

Enzo Francescoli – formerly of Racing Paris and hero of Zinedine Zidane – joined the Marseille empire alongside Jean Tigana, Alain Roche and Manuel Amoros, while the most expensive and perhaps most audacious capture was the £4.5m the club spent to bring Tottenham and England winger Chris 'Magic Chris' Waddle to the Stade Vélodrome. Waddle would eventually go on to be a huge fan favourite and arguably his most iconic moment came when he scored with an outrageous back-heel after a deft flick over the head of Joël Bats against Paris Saint-Germain.

Marseille even tried to sign Diego Maradona in 1989 with Tapie telling Hidalgo to go incognito in a bid to get the deal done, but *L'Equipe* heard about the potential meeting, splashed it across its front page and the story eventually put El Diego off any move that may have been in the offing, opting to stay at Napoli and become an icon of Italian and world football.

Tapie's Marseille were built not only to succeed but to dominate at the expense of teams like Paris Saint-Germain and Arsène Wenger's Monaco, who fell victim to one of Tapie's more dishonest moments of transfer dealing. Mulhouse of Division 2 had a Ghanian forward called Abédi Pelé, a talented player who was sought after by both Monaco and Marseille. Tapie then 'leaked' that Pelé had once tested positive for HIV and told the player to refuse a blood test at Monaco during his medical. That refusal caused the transfer to Monaco to collapse, only for Tapie's Marseille to swoop in and pick him up.

Marseille were building a team for domestic and European dominance in the future, which was where their real ambitions were. They were a cut above the rest in France, leaving the likes of PSG to sit and twiddle their thumbs for a potential Marseille setback. So what did any of this mean for PSG? Having finished second in 1989, did they go on to challenge Marseille for honours? Well, no. While Marseille flourished, PSG were left behind and had to bide their time to mount any kind of challenge for whatever silverware was on offer.

The year after the nail-biting title race, PSG finished fifth and 11 points behind Marseille. Monaco and Bordeaux had almost usurped PSG in the race to be Marseille's closest challengers, but Bordeaux were actually relegated in 1991 due to financial difficulties despite finishing tenth and one point behind PSG. By 1992/1993 Marseille had established themselves as the superior force in France and had built a team focused solely on capturing the European Cup. In 1991 they had reached the final only to lose to Red Star Belgrade on penalties, but it was to be a learning curve for the club, with Tapie determined to win the trophy by any means necessary. Marseille were *the* stars of French football at this point in time. They had the money, they had the trophies, and they had the stars to back it all up as well. They even had pop stars in their ranks with Basile Boli and Chris Waddle releasing 'We've Got a Feeling', which ended up being a huge hit in France, proving that Marseille had the capability of boasting not only the best footballers in France but also the best singers in the charts as well. In the space of a handful of years, Bernard Tapie had built perhaps the first Galácticos team – but on the south of France rather than in Spain. What he and Marseille did was quite influential when you consider how the likes of Silvio Berlusconi and Florentino Pérez would soon run their respective clubs. At this point, Marseille were on top of the world and seemingly no one could bring them down. But, as is the case with most rapid ascents to the top, they're usually followed by equally fast descents.

An aerial view of the Parc des Princes velodrome in Paris, 1919. (Photo by Maurice Branger/ Roger Viollet via Getty Images)

A view of the Parc des Princes and Paris, circa 1970, France. (Photo by MOPY/Gamma-Rapho via Getty Images)

Fans of PSG during the Division 1 match between Paris Saint-Germain and RC Lens, at Parc des Princes on 25 January 1976 (Photo by Michel Piquemal/Onze/ Icon Sport)

PSG captain Dominique Bathenay lifts the Coupe de France after beating Saint-Etienne in the 1982 final (Photo by Joel Robine, Philippe WOJAZER/AFP via Getty Images)

The first board, coach and captain of Paris Saint-Germain (Photo by PSG)

PSG players Mustapha Dahleb (L), François M'Pelé (C) and Carlos Bianchi (R) shaking hands on 13 July 1977. (Photo by AFP via Getty Images)

The great George Weah during the Champions League match against Bayern Munich, moments before scoring a thunderbolt into the top corner. (Photo by Alain Gadoffre/Onze/Icon Sport)

Ronaldinho celebrates after scoring two goals against Marseille in Le Classique in October 2002. (Photo by AFP via Getty Images)

Pauleta, one of PSG's greatest goalscorers, celebrating yet another goal against Marseille. (Photo by Eddy Lemaistre/Corbis via Getty Images)

Zlatan Ibrahimovic is unveiled as a Paris Saint-Germain player after signing for the club, posing at the Trocadero. (Photo by Marc Piasecki/Getty Images)

Nasser Al Khalaifi and Leonardo – the new faces of the Qatari PSG (Photo by Jacques Demarthon/AFP via Getty Images)

Nasser and Neymar, the biggest transfer in the history of football (Photo by Catherine Steenkeste/Getty Images)

Kylian Mbappe and his already trademark celebration – the next best thing in football (Photo by Jean Catuffe/Getty Images)

Lionel Messi celebrates scoring against Manchester City in the Champions League (Photo by Aurelien Meunier - PSG/PSG via Getty Images)

PSG still chasing that Champions League glory (Photo by Matt Childs/Pool via Getty Images)

The 1992/1993 season changed everything for both PSG and Marseille. As time went on for PSG, who could only sit back and watch on as Marseille swept all who came to battle them, their debts kept rising and rising, with Francis Borelli resigning due to the poor financial state of the club. Fluctuating positions in the league table certainly didn't help, and the situation looked dire for the Parisians. Alain Juppé, one of the men close to Jacques Chirac during Chirac's time as mayor of Paris, decided that he was no longer going to help ease the debt at PSG, but he still didn't want to see the club sink into the ground. Juppé didn't want to pay the debts but he helped assemble a town hall meeting to try and find a way to save the club before the financial situation got to a point where it simply wasn't possible to save them anymore.

The idea of Berlusconi buying PSG was floated but didn't come to fruition. Then Canal+, a TV company in France well known for holding rights to show the top-flight games, came in with a bid and a plan to buy a percentage of the club. On 31 May 1991, Canal+ bought 40 per cent of Paris Saint-Germain, with 51 per cent going to the PSG Association and the other 9 per cent to Alain Cayzac, Bernard Brochand and Charles Talar. But even though this takeover had nothing to do with Marseille, Tapie decided to stick his nose in and actually take credit for it. Talking to Daniel Riolo, Tapie said, 'Everyone has forgotten that I pushed Canal toward PSG. I talked about it with [Canal director Charles] Biétry for a long time, I convinced him that it was a good thing for everyone. Canal and Paris, but also Aulas and Lyon, it was I who brought them in, there was no point in being alone [at the top].'

Charles Biétry, the man who Tapie says he persuaded to buy PSG, simply dismissed the claims as 'pure megalomaniac delirium'. By this point Tapie had become engrossed in success, even when it had nothing to do with him or his team. He essentially claimed that he was the reason why Canal took over PSG and thus laying claim to Le Classique because, without it, Marseille wouldn't have had any 'real' competition. Due to the fact Bordeaux had fallen away in recent years, Marseille were left with nobody to challenge them in Division 1, winning the title at a canter for the past couple of years. However, Tapie's undeniable will to win and thirst for the European Cup would be what eventually brought this incredible team down.

PSG, now funded by Canal+, overhauled their squad and in 1991, it was all change. Henri Michel left as manager, being replaced by Artur Jorge, the European Cup-winning coach of Porto and formerly of Racing Paris. The appointment signified that the new ownership were focusing on European glory. A successful manager for Porto both domestically and on the continent, Jorge seemed to be the right man for the job and was given a clear plan of what needed to be achieved in a three-year span, so said Jorge's assistant at the time, Denis Troch, 'We arrived at a period when PSG did not have many results and had very few players. Canal+ having European desires, you had to be European from the first year. The second, you had to win something and the third, to get the title. These were the objectives that Canal+ had set for us. Behind that, with Artur Jorge, it was very simple.'

Indeed, it was simple enough to understand but not so simple to achieve. Jorge's first job was to ensure that PSG learnt to not lose. It sounds simple enough but creating a solid base and a tough core was what helped bring PSG success in the 1980s and Jorge felt that the key to a successful team was a strong core. Paul Le Guen was brought in from Nantes while both Ricardo Gomes and Valdo joined PSG from Benfica, two players who Jorge trusted to build a spine around. It also meant the end of the era of Safet Sušić, who departed at the age of 36 without being offered a contract by the new ownership, two years after turning down a move to Marseille – which Michel Hidalgo had all but confirmed before PSG gave Sušić a new two-year deal to keep him in the capital. It was a changing of the guard, but perhaps the most exciting signing happened midway through the season and was designed to take Paris Saint-Germain to another level.

David Ginola, a man who had been flamboyant since the day the sun had contact with his skin, was lighting up French football. After the failed experiment of Racing Paris, Ginola moved on to Brest where more and more people took notice of his performances to the point where he played to such a high standard that even if you wanted to ignore him, you simply couldn't. Ginola was a free spirit. He would be spontaneous and could change a game with one kick. He wasn't afraid to take on his direct opponent and he was the kind of player who fans paid good money to see and loved to watch. If you didn't enjoy Ginola, you didn't enjoy football.

Performing at a high level for Brest attracted interest from numerous club but it would be PSG who would take the leap, and bring Ginola to le Parc. The story around Ginola's move to PSG evolves around an outstanding performance he put in against them for Brest in a 3-2 win, yet if you look at the record between Stade Brestois and PSG, Brest didn't beat the capital club while Ginola was in their ranks. Ginola left Brest at the end of 1991 due to the club declaring bankruptcy, but he left them in Division 2. PSG were clearly keen on Ginola but perhaps not in the way that the story goes.

The signing of Ginola was a statement for PSG. It was the kind that Marseille would make, spending big to sign a top-quality player from a domestic rival in order to boost their domestic campaign. PSG were hovering around the UEFA Cup spot, leaving Wenger's Monaco to battle it out with Marseille for the title. Of all the games Ginola could have made his debut in, it was against Marseille just before Christmas, coming off the bench in a 0-0 draw; yet what stunted PSG was their form at the end of the season. Losing twice and drawing the other two of their final four games saw them finish five points behind Monaco, who themselves were six behind Marseille. Normal service resumed on that front, but those at the Parc des Princes were feeling optimistic about the future. Making the jump from ninth to third in a single season, thus attaining European football for the following campaign, was huge for the plan and project that Canal+ set out for Jorge and his staff. Yet while Monaco and PSG had been building to topple the Marseille machine that Tapie had built, it was all about to change in an instant, and would affect football in a far greater way than perhaps many people realised. And it was all because of greed, arrogance and a desperation to win at all costs, regardless of the consequences.

Heading into 1992/1993, PSG, Monaco and Marseille were all building towards different goals. PSG, who had now added the likes of George Weah, Bernard Lama and

Vincent Guérin to their squad, were looking for silverware and a consistent approach to European football. Monaco, armed with Lilian Thuram, Emmanuel Petit, Jean Tigana, Youri Djorkaeff and Jürgen Klinsmann, were determined to beat Marseille to the Division 1 title, while Marseille themselves were looking to conquer Europe. They had reached the European Cup Final in 1991 despite having two key players out injured, but lost on penalties to Red Star Belgrade, and Tapie said he did not want a repeat of that defeat in the future. Provided Marseille reached the final again, Tapie did not want to go in with anything less than a fully fit squad.

In an ideal world, Tapie and Marseille would walk to the Division 1 title with no fuss, brushing aside their competition and have a free run at the European Cup. But PSG had other ideas. They were unbeaten in the league up until the end of November and occupied top spot for most of the first half of the season, dropping as low as fourth before the winter break following a 1-0 defeat against Marseille where PSG displayed their talent and their ability to hold their own against a title rival. It was also in this game where the rivalry between the two sides went up to another level. Ginola proclaimed beforehand that 'it will be war' while Jorge chose to up the ante by saying, 'We are going to walk on them! OM are going to go through hell.' That might sound quite dramatic – dramatic enough for Tapie to take those quotes and quite literally stick them on the Marseille dressing-room wall to motivate his players – but when you watch the highlights you'll understand exactly what kind of game it was.

It was 90 minutes of late tackles, outstretched elbows and enough confrontations to warrant the game being played in a boxing ring. In between the rough and tumble there was some football too, albeit very little, but that didn't stop PSG throwing a few accusations of referees favouring Marseille (following on from what Francis Borelli had said back in 1989). With 50 fouls, the match earned itself the nickname 'The Butchery of 1992' and rightly so, but it also intensified the rivalry to unthinkable levels and thus made that year's title race even more exciting. The two would trade blows week in and week out, constantly jostling for attention and to be the leaders of the pack, but Marseille's know-how and talent shone through at the end, winning the title by four points ahead of PSG, who qualified for the Cup Winners' Cup after an impressive and comprehensive 3-0 Coupe de France Final win against Nancy.

But while PSG were celebrating that triumph, Marseille were preparing for their second European Cup Final – the first of the newly revamped 'Champions League' era – and had a fully fit, fully prepared and fresh squad at their disposal. They would be going up against the formidable AC Milan side containing the likes of Paolo Maldini, Franco Baresi, Marco van Basten, Frank Rijkaard, Roberto Donadoni, Alessandro Costacurta and Jean-Pierre Papin, led by Fabio Capello from the touchline. It was going to be the toughest take of Tapie's reign at the club, to guide them past this star-studded Milan line-up, but he was his usual optimistic self and was more than confident of his side's chances. Tapie was completely obsessed about this occasion, yet couldn't take his mind away from PSG breathing down Marseille's neck in the title race and was hugely concerned about going in to the final with injuries to key players. So Tapie did everything he could to make sure his team was at 100 per cent for the final and to ensure that they didn't lose the Division 1 championship. Unfortunately for Tapie and Marseille, it was a move that would change their history forever, and forever stain French football in ways that no one could have imagined.

While a huge clash against PSG was scheduled for three days after the European Cup Final, all eyes in Marseille turned to Munich. It was Tapie's Marseille against Berlusconi's Milan, both filled with stars and both determined to stamp their mark on European football history. For Milan, a win would give them their third European Cup since the start of the Berlusconi era and their fifth in their history. For Marseille, it would be the crowning moment of Tapie's reign, using the model that Berlusconi had put in place in Milan to bring success to the south of France, while Tapie himself knew how much it would mean to become the first French team to win the most prestigious competition in world club football. It would justify the spending that Tapie had pumped into Marseille, while it would give Marseille dominance over every other French club.

The great Reims side of the 1950s couldn't win the European Cup, nor could Michel Platini's Saint-Étienne, but Marseille could make history. They were built to win and simply had to succeed in this game, but it would be no easy task. Fabien Barthez, Marcel Desailly, Didier Deschamps, Alen Bokšić, Rudi Völler and Abédi Pelé were a star-studded team in their own right, but none would have the honour of scoring the winning goal. That would belong to Basile Boli, the outstanding defender who was as reliable as he was talented and scored what can only be described as a 'bullet header' to give Marseille the trophy that they had been desperate to win. All the years of spending, dominating French football and near misses on the continent were over. Marseille were the kings of European football. Nothing could take that away from them or even sour the mood or devalue the triumph, until something came to light that no one could hide from. There had been accusations thrown at Marseille and Tapie before, but this one never went away. No one could ignore this claim.

In their title race against PSG, Tapie was convinced that something was going to halt his side's ascent to the top of the European mountain. He was having flashbacks to the 1991 final when Marseille were without key players due to the tough tackling nature of some Division 1 games and when he said he wouldn't let that happen again, no one was quite sure what lengths he would go to. Before the 1993 final, Marseille travelled to relegation-threatened Valenciennes who should have posed next to no threat to his all-conquering team, but Tapie was to take no risks, and on Wednesday, 19 May the deal was sealed. Jean-Pierre Bernès, the general manager of Marseille, asked Marseille midfielder Jean-Jacques Eydelie to get in touch with his former Nantes team-mates Jorge Burruchaga, Christophe Robert and Jacques Glassmann. All three were at Valenciennes and were offered large sums of money from Eydelie on behalf of the Marseille hierarchy to take it easy and to not go into tackles with as much ferocity as normal. They weren't approached to throw the game or to purposefully lose; rather they were paid to not try as hard as they usually would. Burruchaga and Robert accepted the proposal while Glassmann rejected it.

The night before the game, Robert's wife met with Eydelie in a hotel car park to receive a brown envelope. Marseille won the game 1-0, with no injuries or suspensions, yet many felt suspicious. Marseille winning 1-0 wasn't controversial, it was expected, but the attitude of some Valenciennes players raised the alarm of the referee Jean-Marie Véniel, who told *L'Express*, 'Burruchaga usually changed everything; however, that evening, not only did he not dispute anything but he asked his team-mates to be silent. Conversely, Jacques Glassmann ran everywhere, as if he was trying to prove something.' Glassmann had explained the situation before the game to the Valenciennes coach Boro Primorac but when the two told the club president, he did not believe them. He had no reason to. At full time, Glassmann told Véniel, and players were questioned in the dressing rooms afterwards.

Tapie, his usual bombastic self, denied the accusations immediately. 'Who could believe that Marseille have so little confidence in their team that it is necessary to buy the players of Valenciennes to win? In my heart, I don't believe it,' he told TF1. A few days later Marseille were crowned champions of Europe, but the rumours of match-fixing and what would become known as 'L'affaire VA-OM' simply would not go away. By February 1994, deep into yet another title race with PSG, Tapie was charged with corruption and witness tampering, being sentenced to two years in prison with a year suspended, although that was reduced on appeal to four months, with Tapie serving just two months for his crime. The Valenciennes players involved were suspended from football while Glassmann was awarded the FIFA Fair Play Award in 1995, once the trials were over.

As a result of the scandal, Marseille were stripped of their 1992/1993 Division 1 title and their spot in the following season's Champions League. The title and place in the competition were offered to runners-up PSG, who declined. Apparently, as the story goes, the Canal+ owners refused to accept the offers due to fears of angering fans of Marseille and running the risk of losing their subscriptions and viewership. It was a stain on French football that it has never been able to shake. Whenever a French team reaches the final of the Champions League – admittedly not a common occurrence – the story of Marseille always gets brought up.

The fact that they remain – at the time of writing – the only French team to have won the competition is always shortly followed by the stories of match-fixing and tampering. It was an affair that was completely unnecessary, driven by greed, paranoia and obsession with success and control. The match against Valenciennes would prove irrelevant to the title race and Marseille's squad was strong enough to rest star players ahead of the Champions League Final. And from a Paris Saint-Germain point of view, it completely overshadowed their excellent season which, in any other year and any other campaign, would be remembered as something extraordinary, the spark that ushered in a new era in the French capital. They had swagger, class, flair, toughness and, most importantly, they had success.

PSG fell short to a talented Marseille side in the league table but that doesn't mean the season wasn't a success. It was a magnificent campaign led by magnificent players across the board. Bernard Lama, Alain Roche, Paul Le Guen, Vincent Guérin, David Ginola, George

Weah were a line-up worthy of defeating the evil empire that Marseille had become. In Weah, PSG had a player who was on the cusp of entering his peak. He had been superb for Arsène Wenger's Monaco and successful, but he took his game to another level in Paris, despite the fact he wasn't the first choice to join the club that summer. In fact, he wasn't even the second choice.

Prior to the 1992/1993 season, PSG and their new owners wanted to bring in a star striker to rival the star names in the south of France. First on their list was Bulgarian superstar Hristo Stoichkov, who was looking for a new challenge away from Johan Cruyff and Barcelona, and was set for a pre-contract transfer to PSG after a meeting with Michel Denisot. Stoichkov had agreed the deal, as had PSG and his agent, but Joan Gaspart, the head honcho at Barcelona, refused to sanction it and the move was off. PSG were left without Stoichkov and the Bulgarian would later win the European Cup in Cruyff's 'Dream Team' in Catalonia before forming a formidable partnership with Romário and eventually claiming the Ballon d'Or in 1994 after a great showing at the World Cup in the same year. It's funny how so much could have changed in football had this deal gone through.

Next up on the shopping list of PSG was German striker Jürgen Klinsmann, then plying his trade in Serie A with Inter Milan alongside fellow 1990 World Cup winners Lothar Matthäus and Andreas Brehme. In an era when Serie A ruled the world, it proved quite hard to pry Klinsmann away from Milan as PSG would find out. Klinsmann had a year left on his contract and Inter were more than happy to do a deal for around 25m francs (around £3m), but PSG felt they were priced out because of the demands of the German. However, everyone outside of Paris and Milan believed that Klinsmann was on his way to the French capital, until the morning of 21 July. Fans were greeted with the front page of *L'Equipe* saying Klinsmann had joined Monaco while Monaco had sold George Weah to Paris Saint-Germain. 'We were putting pressure on Klinsmann when we learned that Monaco would let Weah go. So we jumped at the chance,' said Michel Denisot to *France Football* magazine, describing it as a 'perfect situation'. Klinsmann's salary added with Artur Jorge's preference for Weah over the German sealed the deal from PSG's end, while for Monaco and the principality's relaxed tax laws, Klinsmann's demands weren't a problem.

Arsène Wenger felt it was time to bring new blood to the Stade Louis II, letting Weah go in favour of Klinsmann. The Liberian wished to make the move to Italy and Serie A but had only attracted the interest of Pescara and Ancona, two newly promoted sides, with the more established clubs not willing to take the risk on him. PSG knew all about Weah's quality and were more than aware of his talent, so felt it made more sense to sign a top-class striker at an affordable fee, who didn't need time to adapt to the French top flight. Partnering up front with David Ginola, it seemed like an ideal blend of technique, pace, strength and skill that would put fear into any opposition defender. The team hadn't been completely built at this point, but Jorge had a group that was dangerous, exciting and willing to be as successful as possible.

While the Division 1 title race went down to the wire and was ultimately won by Marseille, PSG also had the

Coupe de France and the UEFA Cup to focus on. Their UEFA Cup campaign would begin in Greece against PAOK Salonika and, of course, it wouldn't be Paris Saint-Germain without some controversy involved. In the first leg at the Parc des Princes they ran out comfortable 2-0 winners thanks to two wonderful headers from Weah, with PAOK putting up less than no fight, something their fans didn't let them forget in the second leg back in Greece. It was a boiling hot day in Thessaloniki but PSG were yet again 2-0 up by half-time. It was comfortable and PSG should have had a few more goals, but the tie was effectively over by the time the two sides went in to their respective dressing rooms, but it wouldn't even finish due to what was going on at the interval.

The PAOK fans were furious with their team's display, and tried to storm the pitch. With very few security guards on hand to prevent them, there was essentially a stand-off and it didn't look like calming down any time soon. Dutch referee John Blankenstein decided the best course of action was to call the game off and awarded PSG the 3-0 win. PSG had their qualification, but in circumstances that Jorge had never been a part of, saying after the final whistle, 'I have seen a lot of things in my career, but not up to this end! As for us, there is every reason to be satisfied. We were able to manage this trap match [known in Britain as a banana skin] with a lot of calm and lucidity.' With PSG gaining the win, they moved on to face former winners Napoli in a tight but tough and tricky affair.

The trip to Italy offered PSG the chance to show what they were made of against tougher opposition. Granted, this wasn't the same Napoli side that contained the likes of Diego Maradona and won the UEFA Cup a few years prior, but it was still talented with Gianfranco Zola, Careca, Ciro Ferrara, Daniel Fonseca and a young Fabio Cannavaro. Coached by Claudio Ranieri until his sacking in early November, Napoli weren't having a great season in Serie A but felt the UEFA Cup could be a platform to reignite their faltering form. The first leg at the San Paolo was going to be a game where the toughest shone through and where victory would require more than just talent and skill. What came next was perhaps the most perfect performance under Jorge at PSG.

As a team, PSG were immovable. Individually they were irresistible and even though Weah had a bout of the flu, the decision to start him proved to be a masterstroke. For a player who had a dream of playing in Serie A, Weah showed Napoli how good he was over the course of the game. His volley in the first 15 minutes was too powerful for anyone to deal with, and he wheeled away in delight despite his illness. From that point on, the game was PSG's to lose. They had control and dictated the play in a performance where everyone could be graded at least eight out of ten. For his second, 20 minutes later, Weah showed his prowess in the air, rising above everyone in the box to power home from around the penalty spot. It wasn't even half-time and PSG had the game wrapped up, and thus the final score remained 2-0 in their favour. Jorge, a manager who was more cautious than most, even took time at the end of the match to enjoy how good his side were, saying, 'I had imagined a lot of scenarios, but this one, no. We were almost perfect in the first half and excessively rigorous in the second. We were strong. Very strong.' The second leg at the Parc des Princes finished 0-0 and PSG were starting to believe that they could really challenge for the UEFA Cup. They had dispatched a talented yet out-of-sorts Napoli side, but had far tougher games ahead, starting with their next opponents: Anderlecht.

A crowd of 45,000 visited the Parc des Princes to see what PSG would do against the Belgian giants, and very few came away from the game fully satisfied. A goalless draw with David Ginola being shown the red card in the first half wasn't ideal, but Alain Roche left still in high spirits and confident of what the second leg would bring them, 'I remain optimistic for the return leg in Belgium. While I realise that nothing is easy in the UEFA Cup, it would be serious not to be confident with a team like ours, given the game they play. Paris is able to win at Parc Astrid.'

Confidence from Roche but, without the suspended Ginola and an injured Weah, it wasn't going to be straightforward. John Bosman opened the scoring for Anderlecht just after half-time, guiding home a header that put PSG on the back foot. All the visitors needed was a goal to advance to the quarter-finals on away goals but without Ginola and Weah they were looking short of options, so Jorge looked to his bench for a game-changer. It was there he saw Antoine Kombouaré, a talented defender who was finding it hard to break in to the starting line-up. He was frustrated, and told Michel Denisot that just a day before the second leg against Anderlecht, 'I want to leave, I can't take it anymore. It's too hard to be a replacement.' Denisot replied with a reassurance that he would find more game time soon. And, to Kombouaré's luck, he did. Jorge put him on in place of Jean-Luc Sassus and it wouldn't be long until he made his impact.

Kombouaré's main position was as a centre-back who didn't take any prisoners during the 90 minutes but he had found himself usurped by the imperious duo of Ricardo and Alain Roche, prompting him to work on making himself a right-back. With Sassus suffering from injuries, Kombouaré felt retraining himself as a full-back would be the best chance to get back in to the starting 11, but it wasn't the case when Jorge announced the team to face Anderlecht, as Sassus started, and Kombouaré was left on the bench. 'Antoine chained the tenure [put together a run of games for teh team] since the injury of Sassus on the right, it seemed natural that he started the match,' said Alain Roche, who started that game at centre-back. 'Then during the talk, Artur Jorge announces the starting 11 and it is the late Jean-Luc Sassus, who comes out of three weeks of injury, who begins in place of Antoine. You have to see him, Antoine, to understand his anger. His frustration. There, we talk to him, we keep him in the match, because we know that otherwise, he can unpin.' At this point, Kombouaré felt like he had had enough. He wanted to leave to play football and not to be dropped for someone who's just returned from injury.

After Bosman's goal, PSG went into a bit of a mini crisis until Kombouaré came on. Sassus went off injured and for the short period where the team tried to get back into a shape, they were down to ten men until Jorge sent Kombouaré on. PSG found their rhythm and tended to the mission at hand: equalise, hold on to the draw, advance to the quarter-finals. Simple. PSG won a corner just after the hour mark. The 18-yard box was pretty packed but there was enough room for Kombouaré to make a darting run to the front post. Valdo floated the ball into the box and

Kombouaré, running at full speed, flicked it on into the top-right corner. Parisian pandemonium ensued. The PSG players all rushed over to the defender, who barely 24 hours ago was asking a director of the club if he could leave, and the feeling was that this goal was what PSG deserved. They had been pushing away to get an equaliser and, when they finally scored, it grabbed the air out of the Anderlecht players, fans and coaches. They were demoralised while PSG were on the opposite end of the spectrum.

PSG hung on and advanced to the quarter-finals, thanks to the man who had to be calmed down by his team-mates in the dressing room when finding out he was starting on the bench. To show that level of mental strength was incredible in its own right, but to score the goal that saw your team qualify? That was even better. But with PSG through, their focus turned to their quarter-final opponents and perhaps the biggest, most glamorous fixture in the history of the club: Real Madrid.

Fixtures like the tie against Real Madrid were exactly why Canal+ invested into Paris Saint-Germain. The name of the Spanish giants alone is enough to grab the attention of any football fan, and for PSG, this was the first time they had a glamour tie, the sort that people would go out of their way to watch. They'd had huge games before but never a bigger one in Europe and certainly not one that would be as historic as this. Even when they reached the European Cup they were knocked out in embarrassing fashion by Czechoslovakian outfit Vítkovice in the first round. Even in the Cup Winners' Cup in 1982/1983 they avoided Barcelona, Real Madrid, Inter Milan and Bayern Munich.

Up until this point in their history, PSG had never been in a game like this. Real Madrid had the upper hand in that regard and the Parisians were firmly underdogs in this tie. Madrid may have sold the likes of Gheorghe Hagi and Hugo Sánchez but they were still blessed with immense talent in the shape of the Chilean goal machine Iván Zamorano, youth academy graduates such as Míchel and Rafael Martín Vázquez, alongside Luis Enrique, Robert Prosinečki, Fernando Hierro and their star man – 'The Vulture', Emilio Butragueño. Madrid were going through a barren spell when it came to winning La Liga, having not finished top since 1990, while it had been seven years since their last UEFA Cup triumph, and the European Cup had eluded them since the mid-1960s. It wasn't vintage Real Madrid, but it was still a talented Real Madrid. It was still a Real Madrid that many felt would push PSG aside to usher in a new era of European success in the Spanish capital.

In the first leg at the Santiago Bernabéu, PSG were outclassed. It was as simple as that. Real Madrid waited until the 30th minute to open up the scoring through Butragueño after capitalising on a lapse of concentration from the Parisian defenders, with Bernard Lama leaving his goal more or less unmanned as the ball floated in from the corner. The cross caught the goalkeeper off guard and Butragueño couldn't miss from about two yards out. The second was another tap-in, this time for Zamorano, and at that point it looked like Madrid could stroll away with the game and the tie. David Ginola did pull one back for PSG early in the second half but, if anything, that just woke Madrid up from their half-time rest. Míchel added a third late on and gave PSG an uphill task heading in to the second leg. PSG had their chances and held themselves well considering who they were up against but it was simply a case of one team being well versed in intense European ties and the other being talented and creating a few chances here and there but very much experiencing a European tie like this for the first time.

Some may have questioned whether this PSG side had looked out of their depth in Spain, which no one would have liked to have heard but it must have crept into their minds at some point. Yet the Parisian players knew that at 3-1 the tie wasn't over. They had only lost once at home all season in all competitions – against Marseille, of all teams – and a packed Parc des Princes could make all the difference. The surroundings, the feel of the Parisian air; it sounds minimal in the grand scheme of the tie but it is the marginal gains that can decide such ties. Paris Saint-Germain's players knew this, as did their fans. And if they felt the Bernabéu was raucous, le Parc was about to take it to another level.

The Parc des Princes, when it wants to be, can be a cauldron of noise. The stadium itself shakes when the atmosphere gets to a certain level, to the point where, if you stand still and just take in the moment, you can feel it. PSG fans will tell you stories about how incredible the atmosphere can be inside the ground, and undoubtedly they will tell you about 18 March 1993. Real Madrid were in town and, while it's one of the oldest clichés in the book, the PSG fans knew they had to act like a 12th man to help their team come back from the two-goal deficit. The tifos from both the Auteuil and Bolougne ends of the ground brought an incredible display seen by all in the ground, and the atmosphere was electric. Were the fans filled with hope? Expectation? Or were they just looking to create as difficult an atmosphere for

Real Madrid as possible? To win by a three-goal margin is tough regardless of who you play but that didn't seem to bother PSG. To them, the task at hand was simple. They knew how they were going to do it and they knew that, with the likes of Ginola, Valdo and Weah, they had the firepower to pull off a comeback.

But actually pulling off this miracle turnaround, against a team that beat them not so long ago, was going to be a tall order. And it was crucial that PSG started off well. They needed an early goal, not only to bring the tie to life and to offer themselves a lifeline, but also to calm their own nerves. In their white kit, with Commodore sprayed across the abdomen, PSG and their faithful were ready. It took a full 30 minutes for PSG to make the breakthrough but there was only one man who could have done it. A flicked header at the near post from a brilliantly delivered corner led to Weah giving PSG the 1-0 lead on the night, though they were still 3-2 down on aggregate. By half-time the Parc des Princes was pumping. It was hot, like a furnace, but mainly from the sheer atmosphere. The sun was not out on that March evening, but the floodlights and the fury – in a positive sense – from the stands were driving the temperature up. Madrid had weathered the storms that came towards their goal, but the sense and feeling among both the fans and the players was that, at some point, their resistance would have to blow over.

But as the second half dragged on, Real Madrid stood their ground. PSG came out from the half-time break believing that they could complete their turnaround and were expecting that early goal out of the interval. It never came. As the minutes ticked away so did Paris Saint-

Germain's hopes of completing the comeback, and when the 81st minute hit there was a feeling that the miracle was not going to happen. The belief swung into Madrid's favour. The longer it took PSG to score, the more hope it gave the visitors, and time was running out quickly for the hosts. But, seemingly out of nowhere, PSG had a moment of magic. Valdo passed forward to Weah, who was holding off his marker expertly and managed to flick the ball up and knock it goalwards towards Bravo, who had his back to goal but was still determined to do something productive. Knowing it was near-enough impossible to get off a good shot on goal, Bravo headed the ball downwards, timed perfectly to meet the onrushing Ginola who unleashed a piledriver into the back of the net for 2-0 on the night and 3-3 on aggregate. The goal was a thing of beauty, with each individual artist adding their own unique twist to the movement. Valdo's initial pass, Weah's glorious piece of skill and improvisation, mixed with Bravo's intelligence and Ginola's technique, power and ferocity had put PSG level and sent the Parisian crowd wild.

And just like that, the game completely flipped on its head. Madrid were retreating as the Parisian cavalry pushed forward with pace. Weah, Ginola, Bravo, Valdo; the onslaught just did not stop. The 89th minute arrived as the game was destined to head into extra time, but PSG had other ideas. Breaking at pace again, Weah flicked the ball infield to Ginola who had time and space to pick out the right pass. He could have returned the ball to Weah on the right or play in an unmarked Valdo to his left. Ginola looked up, passed to Valdo and let the Brazilian work his magic. Valdo took a touch to steady himself and moved to shoot but feinted a couple of times before tucking the ball away to make it 3-0 on the night and 4-3 to PSG over the two ties. Denisot had his hands over his head in the crowd, mouth wide open in amazement, shock, awe and glee, but those around him did not keep their composure in the same way. Fans were jumping, running, hugging, screaming, cheering, you name it. They were doing the absolute lot. All in the name of joy.

But it wasn't over just yet. There was still stoppage time to be played and, while the PSG fans had lost themselves among a pile of delirium, Real Madrid had a dangerous-looking free kick on the left-hand side of the pitch. The ball was thrust towards the back post, hoping that someone in blue would get a touch on it and put it back into the danger zone, which was exactly what happened. A knock-down fell into the heart of the six-yard box where master poacher Zamorano was waiting to tap home. Real Madrid, at the death, had pulled a vital away goal back, that, as it stood on 91 minutes, was enough to send them through to the semi-finals and PSG out. Le Parc was stunned into silence. The sheer drop in noise from the home fans was almost as deafening as their celebrations just moments before. The audible cry of desperation was heard as the ball connected with Zamorano's boot but there was nothing anyone in the stands could do. With one kick, the entire atmosphere had changed. Surely, despite PSG's heroic efforts, it would be one hurdle too many for them?

With PSG out on their feet, exhausted mentally and physically, Ginola tried in vain to push forward to create something, but he was going nowhere. He was heading down a cul-de-sac until Zamorano decided that the smartest thing to do would be to barge the Frenchman 25 yards from goal to give away a free kick. Valdo stood over the ball, waiting for the referee to blow his whistle. Some in Spanish blue argued that, with six minutes of added time on the clock, the referee should have already blown for full time but, nevertheless, it was he who everyone was waiting for. He signalled for the game to resume and Valdo whipped the cross in. Just as the Brazilian went to connect with the delivery, you could see a tall Parisian defender dart into the front-post area, completely unmarked and at a pace where, if the ball was to make even the slightest contact with his head, it would be a goal. It was Antoine Kombouaré.

Valdo's ball went straight to where Kombouaré was heading to and, with the deftest of touches, the finest of glances, it went into the bottom corner to make the score 4-1 on the night and 5-4 on aggregate. The Parc des Princes erupted. Bedlam ensued. The Parisians in the stadium had a mixture of shock, elation and just unbridled joy on their faces, and Kombouaré, who earned the nickname 'The Golden Helmet' after this game, ran off with sheer joy on his face. From asking to leave before the last round to scoring the winner in the UEFA Cup quarter-final against Real Madrid, he had etched himself into the history books of this young club. Even Artur Jorge, a typically calm manager who gave nothing away regarding his emotions, tried to keep a straight face among the celebrations but he couldn't resist a look of astonishment. To put it simply, it was historic and incredible. No one quite knew how to react afterwards, with Paul Le Guen giving his thoughts, 'This match is crazy, crazy, crazy. An extraordinary match to play in. We must savour this victory all the more because it was so difficult, and we really went looking for [the result]. We lead 3-0, we get brought back to 3-1. There, I think I released a whole series of insults. I was angry with myself, I was angry with us, I cursed everyone, the sky was falling in on our heads. The disappointment was enormous. I immediately got it into my head that we were going to play extra time. And then, the fourth goal came in an incredible way. Antoine's goal is my strongest emotion on the pitch. It's wonderful that he's scoring the same goal as he did at Anderlecht and at Parc des Princes. I'm happy for him! The happiness I feel is a rare moment in a career, sometimes never experienced. I already know that it cannot be erased from my memory.'

Perhaps it was only the second great night in the history of Paris Saint-Germain (the only other one that could come close was the Coupe de France Final in 1982) and yet they still had a semi-final to play. It almost got lost in all the emotion and drama of the Real Madrid tie, but PSG were still in the UEFA Cup and still had to make the journey to Turin to face the Italian giants Juventus, who themselves staged a comeback to defeat Benfica in the quarter-finals, albeit their turnaround wasn't quite as dramatic as the one that took place in Paris. After avoiding fellow French side Auxerre, who were just about to enter their golden years under Guy Roux, and Borussia Dortmund, PSG were drawn against the favourites and perhaps the most star-studded team in Europe at the time. Angelo Peruzzi, Jürgen Kohler, Dino Baggio, Antonio Conte, David Platt, Andreas Möller, Gianluca Vialli, Paolo Di Canio, Fabrizio Ravanelli and their superstar captain Roberto Baggio made up most of PSG's opponents for the semi-final, and manager

Giovanni Trapattoni, who had returned to the club after leaving Turin in 1986 to take charge of arch-rivals Inter Milan, was determined to add more silverware to the Old Lady's trophy cabinet. This wasn't the first time these two had met, with Juventus and Michel Platini knocking PSG out of the UEFA Cup Winners' Cup back in the early 1980s and the UEFA Cup in 1989, so effectively PSG were playing the one side who seemingly had their number in European competitions. They also boasted world-class players and arguably the best player on the planet at the time in Roberto Baggio.

In the old Stadio Delle Alpi, PSG went to nullify the vast attacking threat that Juventus posed but also to use their own attacking talents on the typically strong Juve back line. With Valdo, Ginola and Weah all starting, PSG were confident that, if they hit Juventus in the right areas at the right times, they were vulnerable. PSG knew that Juve were not invincible. Even Platini said, 'PSG have all the qualities to eliminate Juventus ... but beware, an Italian team remains an Italian club.' It's a saying that sounds quite obvious, but Platini meant that Italian clubs were smarter than anyone else in Europe, certainly at that stage of the 1990s. They had outstanding flair players but they were laced with tactical discipline, defensive rigidness and a dogged determination to not let the opponent even score a goal, let alone win the game. So when PSG managed to take the lead after 23 minutes through Weah, it should have come as a shock. But, thanks to how Jorge set his Parisians up, it didn't feel like a goal that went against the run of play. PSG knew that defensively they had to be watertight and, while they did concede a few chances, with Ravanelli going close, they largely held Juve to half chances and hardly anything to make the Italians feel like they should be ahead.

PSG could have gone on to push for more goals after going 1-0 up, but they decided to sit deeper and get some rest in their legs, in preparation for the onslaught from the Old Lady that was likely to follow. Going into the break PSG were ahead, an ideal situation to be in. It meant Juventus had to push forward and had to leave gaps in behind, which PSG planned on exploiting and in the same way that they had in the first half. But what they didn't plan for was the sheer brilliance and game-changing ability of Roberto Baggio. 'Il Divin Codino', or 'The Divine Ponytail', levelled with a shot from around 20 yards and from that point on, PSG struggled to get a foothold on the game. Juventus's tails were up and they were pressing with more purpose, pushing PSG further and further towards their own goal, thus restricting their attacking opportunities. Time went on, and while PSG weren't happy with their style and how they were hanging on, 1-1 with a vital away goal was a good result for them.

At least, until the 88th minute. Baggio, who was on course to win his one and only Ballon d'Or later in 1993 – to put the dominance of Italian football into perspective, 13 of that year's top 30 players plied their trade in Serie A – stood over the ball, not too far from the spot where he scored the equaliser. Bernard Lama set his wall up and gave Baggio just one option. He could only really score if he hit the ball into the top-left corner. He did exactly that to make it 2-1 to Juventus, and PSG were flat out. They had fought for 88 minutes against some of the best players football had to offer, but they still had the second leg to play and, more importantly, they had the away goal.

Yet, Juventus were in the perfect position, with a one-goal advantage and knowing that if they sat back they could go through without even having a shot on goal. Like Platini said, an Italian team remained an Italian team. In truth, PSG should have scored in the first half of the second leg. Weah forced a wonderful save from Michelangelo Rampulla in the Juventus goal, as did Alain Roche who was back in the defence after missing the first leg through suspension. The French press said that Juventus travelled with a plan to implement the famous *catenaccio* style but PSG did have a few chances of their own. To be level at half-time wasn't a bad thing, but PSG would have been kicking themselves for missing those chances. The game remained the same throughout the second half, with PSG pushing and pushing but Juve resisting. However, it all turned on a controversial penalty decision that went against the hosts. The ball was played through to Weah, who had Massimo Carrera grabbing him around the waist but outside the penalty area. As Weah went for the shot, Carrera appeared to get the slightest of touches to the ball but Weah fell to the ground. The Parc des Princes, Weah and the rest of the PSG team turned at once to see what the referee would do. He did nothing. Dutch referee Uilenberg waved play on and insisted, despite the rather loud Parisian protests directly to his face, that nothing had happened. Carrera had won the ball and no penalty was to be given. Jorge was furious but even the commentators on French television admitted that Carrera had got a touch on the ball, so play continued.

But in the stands and on the pitch, it felt like the air had been let out of the proverbial balloon and PSG looked deflated. In some games you just get the feeling that it isn't going to be your night. The ball falls the wrong side of the post, your shots take a deflection instead of heading on target, decisions don't go your way at key points and the opponents score with one of their only opportunities of the match. That was exactly what happened to PSG. On 77 minutes, Baggio managed to flick home a shot that was going to be comfortably saved by Lama and, just like that, in the blink of an eye, PSG were heading out of the UEFA Cup.

Juventus went to Paris with a plan to sit deep, absorb pressure and strike at the pivotal moment. They did just that. The Italian team remained an Italian team and played in the stereotypical Italian way and their experience and game management saw them over the line and into the final to play Borussia Dortmund. Both French clubs, PSG and Auxerre, were left thinking what could have been – either one would have been the first from their country to reach the UEFA Cup final – but while there is no shame in losing to such a good side, PSG felt that with a bit more luck and a bit more know-how of the big-game experience on the European stage it could have been them in the final.

Nevertheless, it was still a season to celebrate when all was said and done. A vastly improved Division 1 campaign, marred by Marseille's controversy and European Cup exploits, could not overshadow what had been achieved in the cup competitions. A fantastic run in the UEFA Cup was coupled with their third Coupe de France triumph, a 3-0 win in the final against a talented Nantes side, who had players such as a 23-year-old Christian Karembeu, a 20-year-old Claude Makélélé and another 23-year-old called Patrice Loko in their ranks. For PSG, it marked the start of what would be a golden period in the history of the club. By the end of 1994 Marseille would be in Division 2 and their vast riches would be taken from them as punishment from L'affaire VA-OM, leaving PSG and Canal+ as the main players in the top flight of French football. The mid-1990s for PSG were destined to be memorable and historic and there was no better way to kick off a new, special era than with what they achieved in the 1993/94 season.

11

Championnes – Champions

WITH MARSEILLE now in free fall and Paris Saint-Germain entering their first golden era, all sights were set upon the goal of conquering Marseille and becoming French champions. There were other long-term ambitions, such as dominating on the European scene and making a splash in the newly named Champions League. Marseille were about to lose Bernard Tapie – he was being forced to step down as a result of the match-fixing scandal, eventually leaving his post when charged with complicity in the corruption case in February of 1994 – and the threat of relegation to Division 2 of French football was looming over them as well. They still had their star players but, with their leader on the verge of vanishing, their hopes of long-term success looked like they were hanging by a thread.

For Paris Saint-Germain, on the other hand, it was looking like the complete opposite. They and Monaco had both benefited from Marseille's fall. PSG were now favourites to take the Division 1 crown while Monaco had been awarded Marseille's place in that season's Champions League. Yes, Marseille still had players such as Fabien Barthez, Basile Boli, Didier Deschamps, Alain Boghossian, Rudi Völler and Sonny Anderson, but the aura around the club had changed. PSG's attacking talents of George Weah, David Ginola and the others were viewed in a different way. They were producing free-flowing football, the kind that you would go out of your way to not only watch but pay good money to do so. Of course, PSG were backed well by Canal+ but it was viewed in a different way to how Marseille were. Marseille were the team that cheated – even if they technically didn't cheat – and PSG, alongside Monaco, were the fresh new faces that were ready to take over. PSG had all the tools on hand to enter a special period in their history but they just felt like they needed one extra piece to try and take them over the edge. It wouldn't be someone like Hristo Stoichkov or Jürgen Klinsmann as they had been close to bringing in before. In fact, they decided to sign the brother of a doctor, even though he wouldn't be able to join up with the team in Paris until the following year.

Sócrates, one of Brazilian football's most coveted and lauded superstars, was actually a doctor, a physician to be more precise. To be a footballer and a physician is incredibly impressive but imagine having to be his younger brother. Imagine growing up in the same household as the great Sócrates who oozed coolness with whatever he did and became a cult icon after his performances at the 1982 World Cup, even if he didn't actually win the trophy. Sócrates was loved and admired, even until this day, but Raimundo, he almost blocked out what his older sibling had achieved.

Raimundo, simply known as Raí, was a silky playmaker adorning jet-black hair who made his debut with Botafogo in Brazil at the age of 19. He was one of those players who had the ball attached to his boot like it was on a string, such was his ability. And there was no doubting that his talent was there for all to see, although the only issue that some had with the attacking midfielder was his lazy demeanour and the general look of disinterest he had during games. This was a criticism labelled at him during his time at São Paulo, constantly being reminded of his brother and always told that he lacked the consistency that Sócrates had to be a truly top player. With the arrival of Telê Santana as head coach, Raí completely changed. As captain, it was up to him to display the right level of consistency that many had said he had been lacking for so long and also to set an example for the rest of the squad. He was becoming a star of a team that had swagger, skill and ability but was slowly adding trophies to the mix.

By 1992 there was hardly anyone better in South American football – and perhaps world football – than Raí. He was named as South American Player of the Year and by the end of his incredible season, where he would win the Copa Libertadores and the Intercontinental Cup, almost every major club in Europe had their eyes on his signature. He could have signed for anyone given his natural talent and ability, but Raí wanted a lot more than just football from whomever he signed for. He wanted a good team to play for but Raí also wanted a city that oozed with history, style, elegance and culture. And when you put all of those aspects together, it left the Brazilian with only one choice: Paris and Paris Saint-Germain.

The Brazilian joined PSG for a fee believed to be around the £5m region, pennies in modern football but, for a player who was untested on the European stage and for a club in the French top flight, it was a lot of money. Bearing in mind that the world-record fee at one stage in 1992 was £10m, for Jean-Pierre Papin, who departed Marseille for Milan, the price tag for Raí was a hefty sum. A lot was to be expected of the Brazilian considering the attacking force he was about to be linking up with. Weah, Valdo, Ginola and now Raí gave PSG a threat in every single attacking position, but how would the new signing transition into European football? Would he slot right in or would it take time for him to immerse himself into this highly talented and already well-formed PSG team?

He scored on his debut against Montpellier and it looked like a match made in heaven. Yet things didn't quite kick into the gear that many had expected. Raí struggled to match the high expectations that were set on him when he arrived in the capital and also found it a struggle to oust Valdo from the starting line-up with manager Artur Jorge opting for a player he was more familiar with. Raí would score just eight goals over the course of the season in 36 appearances, but while he was the new acquisition, PSG's focus remained on dominating domestically and Jorge felt the best way to do that was by trusting those he already had in his ranks. Raí added to the firepower and was a good weapon to have in reserve, but PSG's success came from familiarity more than anything. The team remained the same for most of the campaign. Lama, Ginola, Weah, Le Guen, Guérin, Colleter and Roche all made 40 or more appearances while Valdo made 39. The core of this side was good enough to win Division 1, or so Jorge and the hierarchy at PSG thought and, to their credit, they were proven right almost immediately.

From October onwards, PSG were dominant in Division 1. The familiarity of the team came in handy when all was falling around Marseille and this gave the Parisians a massive advantage. While Marseille were losing their president and all kinds of rumours were floating around about their own future, PSG were winning game after game. In the first half of the season they only lost twice in the league. One was on the opening day at Bordeaux (with the only goal scored by a young midfielder by the name of Zinedine Zidane) and the other, rather ironically, was away at Marseille in the fifth game of the campaign. That match was going rather well for PSG until the 88th minute when Alen Bokšić capitalised on an error by Le Guen, who was one of only two members of the squad who was authorised to speak to the media (the other was Jorge). No fans travelled to Marseille and, apart from the result, everything went smoothly. It was also a wake-up call for PSG that came at arguably the perfect time. If you speak to anyone about winning leagues or trophies, they will always talk about wake-up calls; those games where you're reminded that you are beatable and do have weaknesses and that it might be in your best interests to look at how to solve those problems before they happen again. After that Marseille defeat, PSG wouldn't lose a competitive match – in any competition – until early April. It was to say that they learnt from that mistake and decided to embark on a truly incredible run of form.

PSG started collecting win after win in Division 1, the Coupe de France and the Cup Winners' Cup, as the team clicked into place seemingly at the perfect time. A run of 27 games unbeaten wasn't a bad response to the two early defeats and, despite it being interjected with ten draws, it was still mightily impressive. Weah's development into a truly world-class player was evident for everyone to see, and Ginola was playing some of the best football in the world at the time, even if the Ballon d'Or rankings in 1993 and 1994 didn't recognise that. Valdo and Raí – who wasn't setting the world alight at this point but still played an important role – showed that competition in the squad was healthy and added to the attacking offerings that PSG had while their defence boasted the toughest, most secure back line in Division 1. It was, without being as star-studded as some other clubs, the makings of a perfect team. An incredibly robust defence, a creative midfield, an elite-level forward in Weah and a maverick who was a match-winner at the drop of a hat in Ginola made this PSG side not only must-see but also incredibly effective, ruthless and worthy of lifting the Division 1 championship after 38 games.

Having been top since matchday 13, it's not exactly a secret as to what happened at the end of the campaign. PSG would win Division 1 officially following a 1-0 victory at home to Toulouse. The fans on either side of the Parc des Princes were singing before, during and after the game, and the explosion at the final whistle was almost as if any tension that may have been creeping into the back of their collective minds was released. For the second time in their short history, Paris Saint-Germain were French champions. Artur Jorge, who had announced prior to the end of the season that he was going to be departing for a return to Benfica, had achieved what he had set out to achieve from the very beginning. He had delivered a league title and had made PSG a team that no one on the continent wanted to face, despite the fact no actual continental silverware was won.

PSG's name in Europe was growing, and having talents like Weah, Ginola and Raí meant they were must-watch. But with Marseille gone, relegated to Division 2 as a result of their match-fixing/corruption investigation, and a championship to defend, there was no obvious challenger, with Monaco also seemingly in a bit of disarray. Arsène Wenger's side had reached the semi-final stages of the Champions League, crashing out to eventual winners AC Milan. Bayern Munich, who had just been guided by Franz Beckenbauer to the Bundesliga title for the first time in four years, were looking for a new manager after Der Kaiser went upstairs to the boardroom. Uli Hoeneß was keen on Wenger and approached Monaco in April, enquiring about the availability of the Frenchman. Monaco swiftly shut down any talk of Wenger leaving and, rather than resign to take the Bayern job, Wenger remained loyal and stayed in Monaco.

In September 1994 Wenger would resign from his job, citing his disillusionment at how the Marseille controversy transpired, believing Monaco had a potential dynasty ruined by the corruption at Marseille. So while Monaco were looking for a new manager to replace the man who resigned due to poor form and his own detachment from French football at the time, due to the acts of Marseille, themselves relegated as a result, PSG were on the lookout for two things. They wanted a new manager who could push them in the right direction in Europe while maintaining the potential dominance domestically that was in front of them. They were also looking for a title rival. The search for both was on and it saw the return of a club legend to Paris Saint-Germain and the restoration of a former French football powerhouse to the top of Division 1 standings.

Luis Fernández was the first PSG captain to win Division 1. He never got the chance to retain the title. Leaving to join Racing Paris before ending his playing career at Cannes meant that the championship-winning captain was shipped off before the defence had even begun, so he had to wait until 1994 to get the chance to defend a Division 1 crown. While he had been retired as a player for a year or so, Fernández became manager and an impressive one at that. Former PSG head honcho Francis Borelli was instrumental in the appointment. Fernández initially didn't want to be a player-manager and requested that Pierre Alonzo, another former PSG employee, be alongside him in the dugout. He took over at Cannes as player-manager and guided them to promotion into Division 1 prior to his retirement in 1993. Then, in his first season as a boss in the top flight, he guided Cannes into the UEFA Cup with a sixth-placed finish ahead of the likes of Lyon and Monaco and earning the Manager of the Year award for the 1993/94 season, beating Artur Jorge to the gong. The CV that Fernández was building up was massively impressive and had all the hallmarks of him becoming a top manager in the game. So with PSG looking for a new boss, preferably one who played a style of football that was more visually pleasing than Jorge's sides, it seemed like a no-brainer. Fernández was appointed and finally had his chance to retain the Division 1 title. He was blessed with a squad that was very talented but wasn't without its ups and downs.

For example, look at two of his most prominent attacking stars in David Ginola and Raí. The Brazilian was selected for the 1994 World Cup and captained the side for the entire group stage before being dropped completely for the rest of the tournament. He had come off the bench for the quarter-final and the semi-final, but never kicked a ball in the final. As described by *The Guardian* in 2008, Raí was 'Brazil's poster boy' heading into that tournament. Fresh off the back of becoming a champion in France, Raí was set to be the star for Brazil. He wanted to do what his brother Sócrates couldn't and lift the World Cup as captain of his country. It was set up to be that way, but with Raí underperforming and Brazil opting for a more defensive leader in Dunga, the PSG man was dropped to the bench and lost the captaincy to the diminutive defensive midfielder, who would wind up lifting the trophy above his head in California later that summer. Raí achieved what his brother couldn't by becoming a World Cup winner but to Raí it was an anticlimactic way to win a tournament that was supposed to belong to him. Did it help that Raí's flair and guile was more suited to the Sócrates-led 1982 side as opposed to the pragmatic and (to be quite frank) unloved 1994 side? Of course not, but returning to Paris as a World Cup winner but also as a member of the squad who was pushed aside couldn't have been a positive at all.

As for Ginola, his 1994 World Cup journey ended before the tournament had even started. In fact, his World Cup ended before 1994 had even started. On 17 November 1993 France faced Bulgaria at the Parc des Princes, Ginola's own backyard. The situation was simple. France needed to draw to go through to the World Cup and Bulgaria needed to win. Heading into the 90th minute, the score was level at 1-1. Ginola received the ball close to the corner flag by Bulgaria's goal. If he kept it in the corner then France would get their all-important point. Instead, Ginola decided to fire a cross into the box which evaded everyone and was massively overhit. A few seconds later, Bulgaria scored a winner. France had failed to qualify and the blame was laid at the feet of Ginola by France manager and former PSG title-winner Gérard Houllier.

Houllier had accused Ginola of being 'the murderer' of France's World Cup dreams and stated, 'He sent an Exocet missile through the heart of French football and committed a crime against the team.' The feud between Houllier and Ginola carried on for years after the incident and Ginola even admitted in his autobiography, 'It is something which will haunt me for the rest of my life. I believe a weaker person would have been destroyed.' So Fernández was walking into a job where he had to defend the French Division 1, tackle the club's first campaign in the newly rebranded Champions League, deal with a disappointed and almost ashamed World Cup winner in Raí and a potentially mentally broken David Ginola. It could have been an easier start, but every manager loves a good challenge. It could have gone one of two ways. Either the duo returned under new management looking to prove a point to the new boss, the club and their nations that they were still top players, or they could be dragged down by either the expectation or, in the case of Raí, the disappointment in not living up to expectations set on to him.

After an indifferent start to the campaign which saw PSG win just one of their opening five games, Fernández found a formula that worked in the sixth match, at home to Monaco, which the fans made feel like a huge affair with an incredible display in the Boulogne and Auteuil ends of le Parc. In honour of the club's 20th birthday, the fans organised a showcase of banners including the names of key players in the short history of the club as well as former presidents Francis Borelli and Daniel Hechter alongside Artur Jorge and Georges Peyroche as integral managers to the success of the club. It felt like a big game and, with both Monaco and PSG needing points, it was a significant one at that for the men in both dugouts. For Fernández, it was imperative that he imprinted his own identity on to this Parisian side, and for Monaco boss Arsène Wenger it was becoming increasingly clear that his position at the club was under threat. Having rejected Bayern Munich's advances in the summer, it was looking like the gas from the Monégasque was slowly fading away.

As soon as the whistle went, it looked like only one side was in this game for the win. PSG were faster to every ball and creating more chances at a higher pace than their southern counterparts. It could have been 3-0 by half-time if not for the wastefulness of Weah and Guérin, but there were positive signs for Paris Saint-Germain and Fernández's side. It was an obvious case of creating the chances and getting into the right positions, but not finishing them off. Weah did eventually get the goal he was after and PSG strolled to a 1-0 win, impressing fans with their verve and swagger on the ball, having confidence to try any pass and almost be certain that it would come off. It was the polar opposite to Monaco's performance, but no one in the capital would care.

Paris Saint-Germain would lose two more games in Division 1 in 1994 – both away from home, at Lyon and Cannes – but their impressive form in the back end of the year saw them jump up to second and challenging for the title with an impressive Nantes side. But while targeting the championship was important to the club, their performance in the Champions League was seen as the real big objective for the season. PSG had already delivered the Division 1 title and, after their incredible, historic and memorable run in the UEFA Cup a few years prior, the board were determined to make a name on the biggest stage in European football. It really was simple for PSG. They had to perform well in the Champions League in order to take another step forward towards being an elite club.

For Canal+, the Champions League was the holy grail. It was – and remains today – where the best of the best show just how good they are, and can go a long way to changing the perceptions of teams and players alike. If you want to be considered as an elite team, you have to play and perform in the Champions League. The same goes for individuals as well. George Weah, at this point, had been one of the leading marksman in Europe for PSG and David Ginola had earned praise from the great Johan Cruyff but, from outsiders, they weren't yet elite. They had to deliver on Europe's grandest stage.

After qualifying thanks to a 5-1 win over Hungarian side Vác FC, PSG eagerly waited to see who they would be drawn with in the group stage. The 16 teams were split into four groups and, with the likes of Bayern Munich, Barcelona, Manchester United, Ajax and AC Milan in the frame, PSG were going to be put to the test regardless of what group they were in. They were eventually drawn alongside the Germans and faced two galling trips to the eastern side of the continent to face Dynamo Kyiv and Spartak Moscow. Up first were Bayern, who travelled to the Parc des Princes looking to reassert their dominance on the European stage. The 1994/1995 season was Bayern's first in the European Cup/Champions League since 1991 when they reached the semi-final, but they hadn't won the competition since 1987, and with the likes of Mehmet Scholl, Christian Ziege, Dietmar Hamann, Oliver Kahn, former Marseille hitman Jean-Pierre Papin and headlined by captain and World Cup winner Lothar Matthäus, they felt they had a squad capable of challenging. But so did PSG and their new, exciting attacking line-up felt ready to let Europe and Bayern know what they were all about.

Bayern arrived in Paris, without Papin, struggling in the Bundesliga (they would eventually finish sixth) and looked like a team that was happy to leave the Parc des Princes as quickly as they had arrived. It wasn't a sold-out crowd in the capital but it was still a loud one, which urged PSG forward as it became clear early on that the Parisians would have the majority of the possession. The first major opportunity came when Roche fired a ball through the middle of the pitch from his own half to the feet of Weah, who flicked it over the head of Ziege but could only drag his half volley wide of Kahn's far post. PSG were pressing, but Bayern's resoluteness was winning the battle, until the 41st minute.

A corner from the left was whipped into the area by Valdo and connected perfectly with the forehead of Ricardo. The effort from the Brazilian smashed against the crossbar but the rebound fell straight into the heart of the six-yard box, where Weah was there, like a predator waiting for its prey, to pounce on to the loose ball. Weah stabbed his foot at the ball and made it 1-0 just before half-time. Le Parc erupted.

It wouldn't be until the second half when Bayern did anything of note, when they played the ball across the pitch to Jorginho in the right-wing position, but his tame effort didn't trouble Lama. PSG weathered any Bayern storm and kept pushing for a second, looking more and more like they were going to add to their lead as the clock ticked on. Again Valdo delivered a corner into the box and the ball, yet again, found Weah unmarked. The Liberian got his shot off but an incredible save from Kahn tipped it wide for another corner. It was a truly magnificent save but it was what the world would come to expect from Kahn, who hadn't long turned 25. The following corner from Valdo was headed clear for a third successive flag kick. Bayern were defending well enough to hold off PSG's wave of attacks, but the third corner was just a step too far for the Bavarians. Valdo delivered, the ball was headed high up into the air and towards the edge of the box, only to fall to the feet of Bravo, who volleyed with power, technique and control to fire it past Kahn and into the bottom-right corner to make it 2-0 after 82 minutes and the two points would be staying in Paris, together with a well-earned clean sheet.

It was an exemplary performance from an impressive side, and it sent a message to the rest of Europe and certainly to the rest of the group. PSG may not have been favourites for the Champions League heading into the competition but they were going to make enough noise for the other teams to look up and take notice. And after matchday one and the tearing apart of the

German champions, some were starting to take note of what PSG had on offer. Gone were the Artur Jorge days of winning via getting the job done and just getting over the line; the era of Luis Fernández was free-flowing, expressive and enjoyable football where dominance meant winning and winning well. PSG had done all of what was required of them against Bayern and were ready to take the trip to freezing Russia to face an ice-cold test in Spartak Moscow.

And a big test it was, at least for PSG. The conditions didn't help, but Spartak went in to win and weren't intimidated by their Parisian opponents, taking a deserved lead before half-time through Rashid Rahimov. For large parts of the opening 45 minutes, PSG were anonymous. Out of sorts, lacking a bit of spark and chasing the game, the break was needed and Fernández needed to give his side a kick up the proverbial backside to avoid another disappointing half. Whatever the coach said, it had quite an effect. Seven minutes after the restart Paul Le Guen levelled with an unbelievable long-range effort for a goal that was the polar opposite of the first-half display. A PSG corner was caught by Spartak goalkeeper Dmytro Tyapushkine, who tried to bowl the ball out for a quick breakaway, but it was intercepted by a tenacious Ginola, who moved the ball out to Weah. Weah then took his touch and avoided the awfully placed referee to spray the ball out to the right flank, finding an unmarked Le Guen. Le Guen cut in to his left foot and unleashed a bullet into the top corner. Quick passing, ferocious defending and the bit of spark that had been missing in the first half. It was like two different PSG teams had started the game, but at least one of them was back on level terms.

As PSG pushed forward and as the game went on, a winner from the French side was looking inevitable. Their task was made a bit easier when Ramiz Mamedov was sent off for dragging down Guérin on the edge of the box after he had received a ball from Ginola that was simply sublime, indicative of the swagger that PSG had in the second half. From the resulting free kick, Valdo took the opportunity to capitalise on Spartak's miscommunication when setting up their defensive wall and slotted a low shot into the bottom-right corner. It was almost hit like a pass to a team-mate rather than a shot on goal, but no one of a Parisians persuasion cared. They had turned around a game that could have been a potential piège (banana skin, or 'trap' to give the word its literal translation). It was another win for the Parisians, who applauded the effort made by their travelling fans, which provided a soundtrack to the game with whistles and cheers alike.

Up next was a trip to the Ukraine to face Kyiv, who had beaten Moscow and lost to Bayern, so were looking at this PSG game as a potential way to get themselves back into the group. With 93,000 fans packed into the Respublykanskyi Stadion, goals from Guérin and Weah either side of a penalty from Viktor Leonenko meant PSG had played three and won three, with Kyiv travelling next to Paris in a bid to actually stop the capital club from making it four wins from four.

Weah's winner in the first half put PSG in the driving seat for top spot in Group B and meant that the upcoming match against Bayern in the Olympiastadion was crucial in so many ways. First, it was more or less the clincher for finishing top of the group. Secondly, it was a fixture that PSG simply could not lose if they wanted to improve the perceptions that others had of them across the continent. To beat Bayern home and away while finishing top of their Champions League group would to turn heads and with a potential quarter-final tie against Barcelona or Manchester United on the cards (as it was, IFK Göteborg would go on to beat United the same night as PSG v Bayern, which meant the final group game would determine who qualified out of the two European giants), it was all the more imperative that PSG made it through. PSG had the confidence and skill to beat anyone, but Bayern in Munich is a different, much harder task than most other big European ties.

A harsh, cold Bavarian night greeted PSG as they walked on to the pitch at the Olympiastadion, knowing that they were already through to the quarter-finals but wanting to really make a statement to the rest of Europe and finish top of Group B. Bayern, mid-table in the Bundesliga, had already been knocked out of the DFB-Pokal by TSV Vestenbergsgreuth and had lost the German Super Cup against Werder Bremen, and were absolutely desperate for a win. They needed to perhaps kick-start their season into something meaningful rather than a scrap to even reach the UEFA Cup, but from the off against PSG you could tell that something was not right. PSG began like a house on fire, with Pascal Nouma, starting in place of the benched George Weah, taking charge and leaving defenders for dead as he and his attacking cohorts closed in on Kahn's goal, but the imposing German was a match for any shot on target. Barring one chance from a cross that went harmlessly past Lama, Bayern were a non-entity. Half-time came and went with the pattern of play remaining the same.

PSG pressed forward and forward, eventually getting their shots off (with the French commentators occasionally reacting with a high-pitched 'ooohhh' if an effort went just wide), but Kahn remaining impenetrable.

The first real big chance of the second half did in fact fall to Bayern but not to the man they would have wanted. Papin and Matthäus were nowhere to be seen when Thomas Helmer rose to meet the cross from a corner, but Lama was equal to it and calmed the situation down immediately. Just before the hour mark, Weah arrived on to the scene to replace Ginola. According to Daniel Bravo in an interview with website Paris United, the public perception of Weah was that he would 'choose his games' and essentially only show up for the big occasions and perform when it truly mattered instead of every match. Yet he was the perfect player to bring on in this situation and, even if it was the case that he chose his games, this was the scenario that would be ideal for someone of his ability.

With about ten minutes to go there was a little passage of play between Le Guen, left-back Patrick Colleter and Weah. The neat passing allowed Weah to pull off from his marker and find a slither of space in the middle of the pitch, around 40 yards from goal. Nouma dropped deep to give Weah someone to play a quick one-two with. His touch went straight back to Weah, who decided that now was the time to change the game. He received the touch back from Nouma and immediately left Helmer helpless on the ground, flailing around trying to get any kind of touch on to either the ball or on Weah. Full-back Jorge Campos slid in to try and win the ball back but failed miserably, going from right back to merely a hurdle for

Weah to bypass in a split second. Midfielder Mehmet Scholl had found his way back to the edge of the penalty box and tried to face up to Weah, but the deft drop of the Liberian's shoulder turned Scholl inside out, completely losing his bearings and losing sight of Weah.

Weah, who had shown all the poise, skill, speed and agility to evade half of the Bayern back line, had one more trick up his sleeve. When he beat Scholl there was only one option in his mind. Nouma's run into the box had been cut off so Weah had to shoot. Weah's effort left Kahn sprawling and unable to even get close to the ball, such was the ferocity in the shot. The swing of Weah's right leg unleashed an absolute bullet into the top-left corner, leaving Kahn helpless and Bayern's back line embarrassed. 'What a goal! What a goal' screamed the commentators who couldn't quite believe what they had seen.

The action replays and slow-motion shots only made the goal better, seeing Weah slalom his way through Bayern's team, and the camera angles from behind Weah and from behind the goal showed just how perfect his effort was. Kahn's right hand sprung out as far as it physically could and still that wasn't enough to stop the shot. If the public had accused Weah of picking and choosing his games before, at least he was smart enough to pick this one as the time to score one of the most iconic goals in PSG's history and in the annals of the Champions League. To score a goal like that to win any game was magical but on an occasion like this it was simply world class.

PSG ended up winning Group B and would go on to face Barcelona in the quarter-finals, looking to beat the other half of Spain's big two after their successful tie against Real Madrid in the UEFA Cup back in 1993. But this wasn't any old Barcelona. If anything, PSG probably would have preferred to be drawn against Manchester United, but to go against the runners-up from the previous season's competition was tough luck, especially considering they finished top of their group. So PSG went into this game as underdogs and had to come up against one of the greatest players-turned-managers – who had formed the Dream Team, one of the best club sides in European football history – and had to do it against a star-studded line-up.

Barcelona in the Champions League. That, for some, is the pinnacle of football. The big nights under the lights at the Camp Nou are what make the European Cup/Champions League so special but, as romantic as it sounds, PSG weren't there to admire the opposition and let them waltz past unopposed. They were ready to dispose of a once-great side who were on a downward spiral that no one could stop. European champions in 1992, Cruyff's Barcelona led the world in so many ways. They were the modern-day embodiment of the Total Football teams that Cruyff had played in for Ajax and the Netherlands and showed the way football should be played. While Catalan players were loved at Barcelona, only two of the starting 11 from their European Cup win had come through the club's youth ranks, but the plethora of immensely talented Spanish stars created a strong line-up. Coupled with the excellence of Ronald Koeman, Michael Laudrup and Hristo Stoichkov, the man whose non-arrival at PSG paved the way for George Weah to sign, Barcelona had an outstanding team worthy of being world-beaters.

Adding Romário to that team was only a bonus, but things didn't quite pan out the way many felt they would.

Domestic dominance resumed but a crushing defeat in the Champions League Final of 1994 to Fabio Capello's AC Milan side was more than just a loss. It completely crashed the club on the field. Cruyff's side were heavy favourites with Milan having both Marco van Basten and Gianluigi Lentini out injured, and Franco Baresi and Alessandro Costacurta suspended, while the likes of Florin Răducioiu, Jean-Pierre Papin and Brian Laudrup were also left out due to UEFA's three non-national ruling. Barcelona had the same issue and dropped their own Laudrup, Michael, out of the squad completely, although Capello himself later said the one Barcelona player who scared him was Laudrup. Milan won 4-0 and the aura around Cruyff's Barcelona was disappearing. It hadn't vanished completely, but they had lost any air of invincibility they had about them. The 1994/1995 season was even worse and even more embarrassing. Romário, the FIFA World Player of the Year in 1994, left midseason to return to Brazil, while Barcelona finished fourth and ten points off Real Madrid in La Liga. The only bit of hope Barcelona had left for the season was this Champions League tie against PSG. Yet it would only go to show how weak and limp the team was, despite how incredibly PSG played.

The first half of the first leg went the way most people had expected it to, in favour of Barcelona. The hosts knew they had to at least keep a clean sheet in order to be favourites for the tie and remove the away goal from the equation, and for the first 45 minutes it looked like Barcelona were going to be more than capable of that. They kept trying to knock the Parisian door down but were greeted by Bernard Lama palming away whatever the Catalans threw his way. A goalless scoreline at the break meant PSG were content, albeit not entirely happy with their performance, but they were still in the game and still able to be competitive.

Barcelona, however, wanted to go for the kill early on in the second 45. Russian forward Igor Korneev broke through on the right flank and looked to fire the ball across the penalty area, but Lama was there to gather and kill off any attack. However, it wasn't that simple for Lama. As much as he looked in control of the situation, he had fumbled the ball when coming to claim the cross and it spilled over the line and made it 1-0 to Barcelona. Some would say the goal had been coming for some time but Lama and PSG were completely gutted to have conceded that way. Alas, there was still time for PSG to strike back, and something that this side didn't lack was ability, courage and a fighting spirit. They had enough weapons to keep going and had the confidence to know that a chance would fall their way at some point. George Weah was on fire after the Barcelona goal too, deciding that now was his time to shine and to show everyone just how talented he was. His jinks past Koeman and the rest of the Barcelona defenders were such a joy to watch and they were unable to contain the Liberian, who was brought down on the left-hand side of the penalty area.

Treated more as a corner rather than a free kick, Valdo stepped up to delicately dink the ball into the area of the penalty spot where there was a cluster of Parisian and Catalan stars dotted around, but one rose highest to head home an equaliser. Weah, the man who won the free kick, had now brought PSG level and, rather than wheel off into the corner to celebrate, the star made his way to the halfway line, embracing a jubilant but relieved Lama. This goal put Weah top of the scoring charts in the Champions League that season, ahead of Milan's Marco Simone and Ajax's Jari Litmanen, and was testament to how important he was to PSG. They had many outstanding talents, but Weah was the jewel in the crown and showed his worth at the Camp Nou. With the game finishing 1-1, that gave PSG a huge advantage going into the second leg. A raucous Parc des Princes awaited and Barcelona knew they had an uphill task on their hands. The Catalans looked dead on their feet towards the end of the first leg. They now had to do it all over again in a much louder, much more intimidating setting.

There was an air of anticipation around the Parc des Princes heading into the second leg. Yes, it may have been Cruyff's Barcelona but the away goal and the advantage of the home fans was enough to give everyone associated with PSG some hope. A 0-0 draw or any kind of win was enough to send PSG through to the Champions League semi-finals to face an AC Milan side who were dispatching Benfica in their own last-eight clash. To face one star-studded line-up from Italy, PSG had to eliminate another, from Spain.

Fernández, dressed in a black jacket, looked across the crowd as if to calculate how loud the atmosphere was going to be. Fernández looked calm in comparison to his Dutch counterpart Cruyff, styled in his famous beige overcoat. The game started in entertaining fashion with Weah hitting the post and forcing goalkeeper Carles Busquets into several saves. Barcelona also got a few efforts on goal but nothing went in for either side. In a moment that wouldn't be seen in 21st-century football, Vincent Guérin was stretchered off with a shoulder injury, only to get off the stretcher and return to the action albeit while clutching his shoulder. The roar of the Parisian crowd signified their relief that the midfielder was returning to the action. Ginola hit the woodwork, Weah fired a shot wide, Raí's diving header hit the post; no matter how hard PSG tried, it just felt like the ball refused to go into the net. The first half ended level, but the second half began with a Barcelona free kick, 25 yards out and to the right of the PSG box. Ronald Koeman whipped the ball in and, unmarked on the penalty spot, José Mari Bakero connected to head Barcelona 1-0 up. PSG's defenders were left looking at one another, asking who had let Bakero free, while the Barcelona captain ran as fast as humanly possible to the corner flag to celebrate with whoever wanted to join in.

But, as the cliché goes, nothing changed from PSG's perspective. They were looking to score as many goals as possible before Barcelona took the lead, but going behind just amplified their desire to get goal after goal. Ginola hit the bar yet again after a brilliant touch and turn into space, with the winger looking completely dejected as the ball was cleared away. After 72 minutes Paul Le Guen's shot was deflected wide for a corner. Le Guen, who was moved into a more advanced position by Fernández, had started to play a huge role in PSG's emergence as the controlling team in the game. The ball was crossed into the heart of the penalty box, with Raí connected ahead of Busquets to level the game up at 1-1. Extra time was looming but there was a feeling that PSG were ready to win the tie in normal time. The fans swarmed to the front of the terrace, celebrating the equaliser with relief, joy and passion all at the same time.

But back on the pitch, it was all PSG. Ginola quite literally cursed his luck when Busquets clutched on to his shot, but Ginola was involved not long after with a wonderful flick over Sergi Barjuán before playing the ball inside to Valdo, unmarked near the centre circle. Valdo took a touch, looked up and slid the ball to Guérin, who had been in and out of the game due to his non-recovery from his shoulder issue. Guérin strode forward with purpose and found himself around 20 yards out with seemingly the freedom of the Parc des Princes. Guérin turned and fired a shot towards goal. There was next to no power on the effort, but the precise direction and placement of the shot made it nigh-on impossible for Busquets to scramble across to save.

Le Parc erupted. The fans swarmed once again, Fernández embraced his coaching staff with a look of determined joy and the actual foundations of the stadium began to shake, such was the noise created. For the first time in their short history, PSG had qualified for the semi-finals of the European Cup/Champions League and they had done it by beating one of Europe's elite clubs and one of the best teams left in the competition. Fernández, clearly overcome by emotion, completely ignored Cruyff – the man who Fernández saw as an inspiration and based a lot of his tactical ideas around – to run straight to his troops. Even Fernández and Ginola, who were going through strained times throughout the majority of the season, put their differences to one side and celebrated the monumental victory. Guérin, the match-winner, did a lap of the field with a swapped Barcelona shirt and his right arm dangling by his side, still nursing his injury from the first half.

Yet what made this result even more impressive, alongside their run in the group stage, was that all did not appear to be well in the Parisian camp at this point in the season. The issues between Fernández and Ginola started, at least according to Ginola, back in their playing days at Racing Paris. 'We played 11 against 11, the possible against the probable. He was only doing attacks and tackles on me,' said Ginola, claiming that Fernández targeted him and only him. Fernández responded, 'It was my playing side ... He was elegant, good-looking, easy and technical. I played in training as well as in matches, with my own qualities.' For Fernández, it was just a case of making his mark on the flashy winger. For Ginola, it felt targeted. When Fernández took charge at PSG, he made Ginola his captain in a bid to show how much confidence he had in him. Ginola had leadership qualities, but Fernández gave him the armband to show how much he believed in his former team-mate. But halfway through the season, the armband became front and centre of the controversial relationship the duo had.

The first suggestion that it was strained came in a Champions League group-stage game against Spartak Moscow when Ginola, annoyed at being subbed off with just two minutes to go, threw the armband at Fernández. What happened next was where things started to get a bit blurry. Ginola claimed that after the incident he was suspended for 15 days and made to train on his own. Fernández, however, remembered things differently, 'As for the so-called lay-off after the game at Spartak Moscow, that's a lie. I have never fired a player for two weeks. It wasn't in my way of thinking. David was simply suspended for the next match against Caen, which we won.' Fernández rebuffed claims that he took the captaincy off of Ginola because of that incident, instead saying that it was because of a humiliating 3-0 loss at home to eventual Division 1 champions Nantes. 'If one day he lost it, it was not against Spartak but after a match against Nantes. We lost 3-0 [on 11 January 1995]. David had not come because he was supposed to go for medical treatment. But in fact, he was gone golfing and taking pictures for a fashion newspaper. There, the armband, he was removed for his behaviour where he had only thought of himself,' said the manager. Ginola had also claimed that he had refused a move to Real Madrid to stay with PSG, declaring his love for the Parisians.

Yet Fernández's style didn't sit well with others, Ginola aside. In 2017, goalkeeper Bernard Lama did an interview where he scathed Fernández down with multiple blows, claiming him to be a 'cup coach, not a stability coach' and adding, 'Every week, he had to change the team. He's someone who didn't understand where he was. It was too high for him. Intellectually, there was a lag. In man-management, he missed the mark.' If that was how your goalkeeper felt about you over 20 years later, it can't have been a pleasant dressing room.

On the face of it, the 1994/1995 season was one of huge success. On Wednesday, 5 April PSG faced the great AC Milan in the Champions League semi-final, while getting prepared for their very first Coupe de la Ligue Final against Bastia and they had a huge Coupe de France semi-final against Marseille to look forward to as well. Nantes were taking Division 1 by storm and, while PSG were disappointed not to be ahead in the title race, it still felt like a huge amount could be achieved if things were to go as planned. To be involved in four competitions and reach the semi-final stage in all three cups was something to be proud of. But while Marseille in the Coupe de France and Bastia in the Coupe de la Ligue posed problems and obstacles in the way of domestic triumph, Milan in the Champions League was where the focus was. Rossi in goal, a back line of Panucci, Baresi, Costacurta and Maldini – with Tassotti available on the bench – with Marcel Desailly, Demetrio Albertini, Zvonimir Boban and Dejan Savićević all ahead of them. It wasn't quite Gullit, Van Basten and Rijkaard, but it was still a pretty dominant side nonetheless.

Once again, le Parc was electric. The fans were ready for arguably the biggest game in the history of the club, waving blue and red banners from the stands as is now customary for any big match. Milan, in stereotypical Italian fashion, were compact and looked to restrict PSG's attacking talents, with Rossi being on top form early on to deny whatever Ginola and Weah had to throw his way. The game plan from Fernández, according to the match report from newspaper *Libération*, was to force Milan to play at a higher pace than they were used to.

The PSG boss had spoken to the groundsman on the day of the game and said an hour before kick-off to water the pitch with the idea being that, with a slicker surface, Milan wouldn't be able to deaden the pace of the game. In theory it was a genius idea. But this was AC Milan in the semi-final of the Champions League, not some two-bit outfit from the back end of nowhere. If anything, the slick surface nearly caught Bernard Lama out within the first 30 seconds. Ricardo played a harmless pass back to the goalkeeper who got his legs completely tangled up when trying to return the ball, eventually – somehow – back-heeling it behind for a corner to Milan. The air was completely sucked out of the Parc des Princes when Lama got muddled up, before it safely returned back as the ball trickled the right side of the post, from PSG's perspective. A few moments later Lama cleared the ball directly to Marco Simone, who couldn't produce a goal. Just to up the pressure on the goalkeeper, Lama then dropped a simple-looking catch, perhaps not helped by the wetter-than-usual ball on the Fernández-manufactured playing surface.

The man-marking from Capello's side was admirable for neutrals but beyond an annoyance for the Parisians. Costacurta wouldn't let Weah's shirt leave his grasp while every time someone even considered passing to Ginola, he was surrounded by three white shirts looking to deny him any space to breathe, intercept the pass or make him irrelevant to the proceedings. PSG tried to press on for a goal but Milan's back line resisted incredibly well. PSG knew that to gain the upper hand in this tie they had to score at least once and restrict Milan to nothing, eliminating the away goal and giving themselves the lead before they went to the San Siro, but the second half started in much the same way. Milan didn't let up defensively and didn't allow PSG's key players any time on the ball.

Ginola managed to wriggle some space from Panucci and hit a strike that could only cannon back off the crossbar. That was the chance. That was the only true sight of goal that PSG had and they couldn't take it. The little details mattered against this Milan side. If you got one chance you simply had to take it. Ginola didn't and Boban, in stoppage time, made him pay. Boban found the smallest of pockets of space away from his marker and hammered past Lama at the near post to deal a sickening blow to PSG. They had done all they could have done, hitting the woodwork and ensuring that Rossi had a busy night, but they couldn't quite get the job done. Milan, a team of immense talent and knowledge at that level, did.

PSG had lost the game and lost any kind of advantage going into the second leg. They travelled to the San Siro needing to win by a two-goal margin. In Serie A, only Juventus had managed to achieve that feat, and the only team to do that in any other competition in the 1994/1995 season was Ajax in the Champions League group stage, winning 2-0. PSG couldn't cause an upset as Milan won 2-0, with Savićević grabbing both goals. Crashing out of the semi-final stage against an outrageously strong Milan side was nothing to be ashamed of, but the players and staff would rue the minor details that went against them. If only Ginola's effort was a few inches lower and if Rossi hadn't made what felt like 1,000 saves, it could have all been very different.

As for the rest of the season, whether it was a success remained up in the air. Reaching the Champions League semi-final was a superb showing, as were the triumphs in the two domestic cup competitions, but third in Division 1 behind Nantes and Lyon, losing their crown with far more ease than anyone would have liked with a 12-point gap to champions Nantes, left a somewhat sour taste in the mouth. Fernández had shown that he was up to the task of being PSG's coach, at least in the cup competitions. He had to show he was up to the task in the league. If he wasn't, then change would be afoot. The remit for Fernández was simple: win Division 1, win as many trophies as he could

315

and build his own PSG. He had inherited Artur Jorge's Division 1 champions but now he had the chance to shape his own version of Paris Saint-Germain.

12

Faire sa marque en Europe –
Making a mark in Europe

WHEN YOU'VE reached the semi-finals of the
Champions League and won both of the domestic cup
competitions, that is usually the catalyst to build upon
an already strong foundation and push on in Europe.
For Paris Saint-Germain, however, the approach was
different. David Ginola's relationship with Luis Fernández
had soured to the point of no return, and the winger was
looking for a new path, away from the Parc des Princes. In
a problem that still faces some players in France, Ginola
felt that he had achieved all he could with PSG and
needed a fresh challenge. It was 1995, he was 28 and in
the prime of his career. Why spend your prime working
under a manager with whom you don't see eye to eye with?
The first suitor for Ginola was a man who he had helped
PSG beat in the UEFA Cup a couple of seasons prior:
Johan Cruyff.

Barcelona were in dying need of fresh energy. Cruyff
wanted Ginola as much as a manager has probably ever
wanted one player before or since. Cruyff was one of

Ginola's footballing idols (Diego Maradona was the other) and to play under the great Dutchman would have been an honour. Ginola in Barcelona seemed to be the perfect fit given the weather, the historic style of football and the manager, but rules at the time meant that Barcelona already had their full quota of foreign players in their squad. Gheorghe Popescu, Gheorghe Hagi, Robert Prosinečki, Jordi Cruyff, Hristo Stoichkov and Luís Figo were all at the club when Cruyff met up with Ginola to try and persuade him to join the Catalan giants. That wasn't the real problem; it was trying to create space for him.

Popescu, Prosinečki and Figo had all joined that summer and Johan was never going to sell his son Jordi while he was in charge, which left Hagi as the one who looked likely to go. Stoichkov had already made way at this point, but Barcelona needed Hagi off the books to bring Ginola in. Meanwhile, as Barcelona were trying to find ways to create space for Ginola, the Frenchman set off on a mini European tour to try and find his new club. Bayern Munich, Inter Milan and even Celtic met with Ginola, who had made it abundantly clear that his time in Paris and in France in general was over. One club made a pitch that seemed to put them above the rest, even if their stature wasn't akin to the aforementioned European Cup winners.

In the north-east of England, while Ginola was meeting with Johan Cruyff and finding a way to leave Paris, Kevin Keegan was on the lookout for a new, exciting winger to improve his already impressive and entertaining Newcastle United side. Keegan had been working on a particular target for a while and at one point thought he had got his man. The winger in question was John Salako of Crystal Palace. The Salako deal fell through and he moved to Coventry, which left Newcastle searching for a winger who was available for a transfer.

Keegan and his assistant Terry McDermott had heard that Ginola's deal with Barcelona was off and managed to phone him up and schedule a meeting. After meeting in an Amsterdam hotel, it all seemed to be sorted until David Dein of Arsenal called Ginola to try and broker a deal between the Frenchman and the north London club. Salako later claimed that Newcastle were only after him because Ginola had demanded a wage of £30,000 a week and Keegan had moved to get Salako as the cheaper option. Other reports claimed that Ginola was signed due to Salako failing a medical. Either way, Ginola was no longer a Paris Saint-Germain player and he wasn't the only star to leave Paris that summer either. After George Weah had impressed throughout the Champions League, Parisian conquerors AC Milan swooped in to add him to an already incredible-looking side, but his transfer also represented somewhat of a double-edged sword for PSG.

Weah's performances in the Champions League were mightily impressive after finishing as the competition's top scorer, but those who watched Weah at Monaco and PSG knew that this wasn't a fluke or a run of good fortune. That was Weah's standard. He was so good that he took to Europe's elite competition like a fish to water, but it wasn't until he was part of a side that had a good run in the Champions League that some of the elite clubs in Europe began to take notice, thus presenting a bit of a problem for PSG. Their ambitions had allowed them to sign stars like Ginola and Weah, but their standing in the game meant that, during that period, there was always a destination that was deemed to be a 'step up'. PSG wanted to make a splash in the Champions League, which they did. But it also meant that their players were put out into a brand-new shop window where everyone could see their talents with ease.

Silvio Berlusconi had made a habit of buying the best players available. After seeing at first-hand the skill of Weah, Berlusconi went and got him. But if PSG hadn't got to that semi-final against Milan, would Weah have left at that point in time? Nevertheless, Weah did go and PSG were without their two star attackers. Weah would go on to win the 1995 Ballon d'Or and become the very first African player to do so, beating out Jürgen Klinsmann, the man who replaced him at Monaco prior to his arrival at PSG. Weah had started the Serie A season incredibly well and, in what was perhaps the toughest and best league in the world at the time, he was noticed a bit more than he would have been in France, plus the added factor of his productivity against tougher opponents held him in good stead, but how much of his win was down to his PSG performances? His Champions League outings were the catalyst for people to truly take notice and the fact that eventual winners Ajax had three players in the top ten of the voting shows that no matter what league you played in during that era, what you did in the UEFA competitions mattered a lot more.

But amid all the departures and the awards, what happened to PSG? They had just won a domestic cup double and reached the Champions League semi-finals, so they should have been on the road to more success. The sales of Weah and Ginola brought in a combined total of what today would be just over €10m, but where would that money be invested? The club felt that by losing two of their big players, it was only right to improve the team rather than bring in one particular superstar-calibre player. First in the door on a free transfer from Monaco was Youri Djorkaeff, son of Jean, who played for the original Paris Saint-Germain in 1970. Youri had made his name at Monaco under Arsène Wenger, who brought him in after his stellar performances for Strasbourg in Division 2, but was coming to the end of his contract at the end of the 1994/1995 season and was looking to make a move away from the principality. In came PSG with a contract that lured Djorkaeff to the capital and now they had a forward who they felt was capable of filling some of the gaps left by Ginola and Weah. Julio Dely Valdés also joined from Cagliari, yet if you listen to what Luis Fernández had to say, his version of the 1995 transfer window is vastly different to what actually happened.

Fernández claimed that in the window he had lined up five targets who he had been in contact with and was ready to bring in to build a new team around. The first on his list was Laurent Blanc from Saint-Étienne. At this point in Blanc's career, he was fighting relegation with Les Verts and wasn't the player who would eventually win the World Cup a few years later, but Fernández saw something in him that he felt would have improved his side. Blanc didn't sign, instead being purchased by Guy Roux's Auxerre and becoming a pivotal part in the club winning the league and cup double the following season. Second on the list was Sonny Anderson of Monaco who had already shown his talent in France at that point, so while it was a no-brainer to want someone of his quality, it was highly likely that Monaco weren't keen on selling another attacker to their Parisian counterparts. The next few names that Fernández identified in his interview in 2020 was where things got interesting but also – potentially – lost in the timeline.

Fernández said that he wanted Roberto Carlos from Brazilian club Palmeiras, an 18-year-old David Trezeguet, and Samuel Eto'o, who was 15 at the time of this particular transfer window. The reason Roberto Carlos never signed, according to Fernández, was because the PSG board felt that they already had better options than the Brazilian full-back. Regarding Eto'o, it is safe to assume that there was a possibility Fernández mis-remembered exactly what happened. As the story goes, Eto'o had travelled to France with hopes of being picked by a pro club and had a working visa. He made his way to Paris to try out at the Canal Football Club program but was turned away at the entrance as his documents weren't in order. Saint-Étienne and Cannes did likewise, meaning Eto'o had to find his way into football elsewhere. Fernández may have wanted Eto'o during his second stint as manager a few years later when the striker was with Mallorca, but he didn't discover the Cameroonian as he claimed. As an aside, when Fernández was the Cannes boss, he claimed to have stumbled across a youngster called Ronaldo Luís Nazário de Lima, also known as Ronaldo. Ronaldo was still relatively unknown in 1994 and Cannes' board didn't want to pay the 2m francs for him. With Trezeguet, the striker himself laid blame to the Canal+ board as to why he never arrived in Paris, saying, 'I wanted the club to provide an apartment for my family and I, but Denisot and Moutier [PSG board members] did not want to. Fernández, on the other hand, was hot.'

In hindsight, these are huge misses yet understandable ones. Blanc was 29 and wasn't getting any younger and the perception was that his best days were behind him, while Roberto Carlos was unheralded at the time. Sonny Anderson may have been a player who Fernández had wanted but there was no way PSG were going to sign him and Djorkaeff in the same summer. The Eto'o and Trezeguet deals were similar to the mistakes you hear every major club make. Arsenal would have a Harlem Globetrotter-esque side if the rumours of players they nearly signed were true, but such is the life of football clubs. PSG missed out on two great strikers but they wouldn't have made an impact on the first team that season, especially when they brought in the top scorer from the previous campaign, Patrice Loko.

With Loko and Djorkaeff being brought in to the fray (26 goals between the two in the previous season), in theory PSG should have added more goals to their game. Julio Dely Valdés wasn't a bad option to call on for goals either, but Loko and Djorkaeff were the two high-profile signings who had the expectation to score goals placed upon their shoulders. Bruno N'Gotty also joined from Lyon while the fourth-choice striker at the time was a young Parisian from Le Chesnay called Nicolas Anelka, who had found his way through the PSG youth system to play a handful of games in 1995/96. Coming from the famous Clairefontaine academy and being snapped up by PSG to play in their youth sides at weekends while continuing his training at the academy, it appeared that the striker was destined for big things. On one hand, Anelka's story should be one of incredible hard work and he should be one of the poster boys for young Parisians who make their way into professional football. On the other hand, Anelka's time at PSG tells the story of how the club was with young local prospects and, even though Anelka made his debut in the mid-1990s, the issues that both he and PSG faced at the time were still prevalent almost a quarter of the way into the 21st century.

Anelka was 16 when he reached the first-team set-up at PSG and was by far and away the best young player at the academy. He had electric pace but the coolness and finishing prowess of a pure goalscorer, the kind of talent that one is born with rather than taught. Anelka made his debut for PSG in 1995/96, albeit only two appearances that totalled up to 11 minutes, in defeats to Monaco and Montpellier, but there was a feeling that he was special. A criticism that had been launched at PSG was that while Paris – more precisely the suburbs of the city – was a hub of exciting young talent, the club never seemed to produce any for themselves. Bear in mind that, at the end of 1995/96, Thierry Henry was named French Young Player of the Season for Monaco after coming through their academy despite being born and raised in the Paris suburb of Les Ulis. Henry had slipped through PSG's hands without the club even realising he was there. With Anelka, they felt determined not to let the same thing happen.

But while Loko, Djorkaeff and Dely Valdés were playing and starting the season well with a nine-game unbeaten run in all competitions, Anelka was nowhere near the first-team squad to start off with. Djorkaeff was running the show in both Division 1 and in the Cup Winners' Cup and PSG were top of the table prior to an October blip in form that saw them drop to fourth. Djorkaeff and Loko were the new additions to an already strong team that still had the likes of Lama, Fournier, Roche, Guérin, Bravo and Raï. There would be games where Loko wouldn't start and Dely Valdés would, such as in the 2-1 victory away at champions Nantes in the second game of the season. PSG's was a title-winning squad with top-quality players, explaining why Anelka – despite his status as being a prodigious and highly talented striker – didn't get a look-in during the early part of the season.

The league form was up and down for large parts, dropping to fourth and then back to the summit up until very late on in the season. The Cup Winners' Cup gave the team the chance to shine on a European stage, defeating Ole Gunnar Solskjaer and Molde in the first round, before a Djorkaeff masterclass in Glasgow against Celtic which resulted in the home fans giving the PSG players a standing ovation when they left the pitch at full time. Paris Saint-Germain were just too much for Celtic and everything good that happened to PSG that night had Djorkaeff at the heart of it. His assist for Nouma's goal – the third for PSG on the night – was wonderful but the touch when he brought Lama's long ball down was just special. The more you saw of him in that game and the way PSG played, the more you understood why Celtic's fans applauded them off.

Into the quarter-finals they went and they were paired up against Parma, led by Gianfranco Zola and Hristo Stoichkov with Dino Baggio, Fabio Cannavaro and a young Gianluigi Buffon on the bench. Parma were the favourites for the tournament given their star players, but PSG weren't afraid of them after their own European exploits in years gone by. If they could knock out Real Madrid and Barcelona, they could beat Parma. They could take inspiration from previous European nights but their domestic form heading into the tie was a nightmare, a borderline crisis if it wasn't already one. They were knocked out of the Coupe de la Ligue by Guingamp, which wasn't ideal, but at that point they had only lost twice in the league and were still top. But by the time the Parma game arrived, things had deteriorated. Losses to Monaco, Montpellier and Strasbourg in February meant that PSG's grip on top spot was loosening, and their Coupe de France loss to a vastly improving Auxerre side didn't make the situation any easier. The team was clearly lacking confidence and Lama even labelled the team 'ridiculous' after the Auxerre defeat. Out of both domestic cup competitions, being hunted down by the side that knocked you out of the Coupe de France and a vice grip-like hold of the top of Division 1 weakening was not what they needed heading into the quarter-final of a UEFA competition.

Wins against Lens and Rennes put PSG back on track and restored some confidence heading into their trip to Italy. Many were saying that Parma vs PSG was a final before the final and that these were the two up and coming clubs to keep an eye out for in the future, but the present was all that was on the minds of the two teams. PSG's target was to restrict Parma to as few as possible and steal an away goal, but Stoichkov managed to eventually get a shot past an incredible Lama to give Parma a 1-0 advantage heading to Paris. Fernández said after the game that he was happy with the performance and wasn't too downbeat by the result. Perhaps he knew that a night under the lights at le Parc would be enough to intimidate any opponent.

Just like any big game at the Parc des Princes, the crowd was lively and so were the 11 on the pitch in Parisian red and blue. It was Raí's turn to be the match-winner and orchestrator, scoring a penalty after nine minutes and eventually adding another later on to send PSG through 3-2 on aggregate; Loko also scoring in a 3-1 win on the night. Top of the league and into the semi-finals of the Cup Winners' Cup. It had the makings of an incredible season despite the hiccups in the domestic competitions.

After that Parma game, however, it was an all-out disaster in the league. A handful of days after their European triumph, PSG travelled to face Auxerre in a clash that was all about the title race. If PSG won then it would be highly likely that the championship would return to Paris, but if Auxerre won then the race would be reignited and the pressure would be back on to PSG. 'We did our best, but Auxerre were stronger than us. It's difficult to play three days after a European game,' said Luis Fernández at full time. PSG didn't just lose to Auxerre, they were embarrassed, going down 3-0. Fernández's side didn't lay a glove on to Guy Roux's charges and if you didn't know any better, you would have been forgiven for thinking that Auxerre were the ones top of the table. Nevertheless, the battle for Division 1 was back on and it felt like Auxerre were in the driving seat despite PSG still being top, albeit not for much longer.

A 3-2 home defeat to Metz cost them their position. Djorkaeff, Loko and Raí were missing, but there was enough on that field to beat Metz, especially for a team that was hanging on to first place for dear life. A youngster by the name of Robert Pires started for Metz that day and scored a brace.

PSG had lost top spot but had the wanted distraction of the Cup Winners' Cup against Deportivo to deal with. A defensive masterclass from an inspired back line plus a last-minute winner from the returning Djorkaeff meant they had one foot in the final. Part one of the job had been done but part two had to wait for a week while PSG travelled south for a must-win game against Nice, who they duly dispatched 2-1 thanks to yet another late winner from Paul Le Guen after being assisted by Djorkaeff, who had initially given them the lead. If it wasn't clear already, Djorkaeff held the key to any kind of success. He played a huge rule in the semi-final second leg against Deportivo too, setting up Loko for the winner on the night and sealing PSG's place in the final of the Cup Winners' Cup, a truly historic achievement.

With a place in the final against Rapid Vienna sorted out, it was back to domestic duty with bottom club Martigues travelling to the capital. A win was expected and PSG would carry on chasing Auxerre and fending off Monaco, but Martigues weren't there to roll over for anyone. Such was the visitors' defensive resoluteness, PSG could have played 90 more minutes and still wouldn't have scored. All that they could manage was a damaging and dull 0-0. Laurent Fournier said at full time, 'We do not deserve to be champions,' while Luis Fernández said, 'I am obviously very disappointed. We didn't have the flame that would allow us to win this match. We tried things, but without much construction. Now we have to quickly forget and refocus on the game against Lille if we still want to foster the hope of being champion. There may still be a turnaround.' He sounded more hopeful than expectant, but Lille were the next to travel to Paris, the

following week. Lille themselves were not having the best
of seasons and needed a win to ensure their safety in the
top flight, while PSG needed a win to avoid losing the
title. However, a terrible 1-0 loss meant their season was
wasted by those two April results and the championship
was gone. 'It's certainly the biggest mess I've had in my
career,' said Alain Roche after the final whistle against
Lille. 'We have been in free fall for a few weeks now,'
explained Le Guen.

Fernández reiterated the fact that PSG had a
European final coming, but couldn't escape the sheer
failure of throwing away a title that was firmly in their
own grasp, 'I don't have much to say. We lost the title
and we have no excuse. We are the main culprits. I don't
know what happened this week. We had no more ideas,
no more games. Now we have to tell ourselves that we
have a unique chance, because in ten days we are playing a
European final. And this match should not be missed.' He
was right, they did have a European final to play. They had
also just crumbled in the most important stretch of games
in the entire season to hand over the championship to an
Auxerre side that was led by a resurgent and revitalised
Laurent Blanc, the man Fernández wanted to sign at the
beginning of the season.

It was incredible for Auxerre and Guy Roux, who won
his first and only Division 1 title alongside his second
Coupe de France, winning the double ahead of PSG, but
for the Parisians it was an embarrassment. Lama later
criticised Fernández for being a 'cup manager', a claim
Fernández would always deny, but when you look back
at how his seasons in charge unfolded, maybe Lama had
a point. PSG excelled in the cup competitions under

Fernández but never got over the line in the league while their title triumph came under Artur Jorge before Fernández was appointed.

Following the disappointment to Lille, PSG had to pick themselves up to try and win the Cup Winners' Cup. Immediately after the Lille debacle, a cup final was probably the best thing for the team as it distracted them from the pressures of domestic football, albeit pressure that they had put themselves under. It was also a historic moment for the club. It was their first European final and, while it wasn't the Champions League, it was still a prestigious competition to win. The Cup Winners' Cup may not exist now, but for a large part of the 20th century UEFA viewed it as their second-most esteemed tournament and it was a trophy that a lot of clubs, players and fans took very seriously. No Manchester United fan who was in Rotterdam for their 1991 triumph over Johan Cruyff's Barcelona will ever forget that night, nor will Arsenal fans in Copenhagen in 1994. It was Arsenal's first European trophy, had been Chelsea's first in 1971, Tottenham Hotspur's victory in 1963 was the first in Europe by any British club, while Rangers' first European win also came in this competition in 1972. The Cup Winners' Cup was the perfect breeding group for European success. It established a lot of clubs on the continental stage and gave them a platform to grow, which they otherwise wouldn't have had in the European Cup/ Champions League or the UEFA Cup. The same goes for PSG. They weren't quite ready to go all the way in the Champions League the season prior, but they were more than capable of pushing aside the clubs they faced in the Cup Winners' Cup.

Their opponents Rapid Vienna were the surprise package of the competition. Led up front by German big man Carsten Jancker, they weren't a fashionable side but were more than capable of upsetting the odds. Sporting Lisbon, Dynamo Moscow and Feyenoord all fell aside to the Austrian club, but PSG's performances also indicated that they would almost certainly have too much quality to be victims of an upset. Despite their performances on home soil, PSG were a different animal on the continent, and throughout the final they showed how good they could be. With Rapid targeting Raí, the Brazilian was forced off after just 12 minutes becauseof an ankle problem and replaced by Dely Valdés who went up front with Loko and Djorkaeff dropping into the attacking midfield position that Raí had been occupying. PSG were on top throughout the first half. Rapid couldn't touch Djorkaeff, who was unlucky to see his shot cannon back off the crossbar, but there was a sense that a goal was always on the horizon for PSG and they wouldn't have to wait too long for it, despite the fact it came from an unusual source.

Bruno N'Gotty wasn't a regular scorer, posting just two prior to the Cup Winners' Cup Final. Seeing him score would be described by a cliché-addicted commentator as a 'collector's item' such was the infrequency of his strikes, but as PSG won a free kick around 30 yards from goal Luis Fernández rose from the bench to scream at the centre-back. He hadn't done anything wrong, but Fernández wanted him to take the free kick. His stride indicated that his shot was going to be a piledriver. It was, and took a slight deflection on the way through, but the pace on the shot meant that deflection or no deflection it was going to end up hitting the back of the net. Staff erupted from the dugout to celebrate, while the players rushed over to mob N'Gotty for his unbelievable effort. As for the fans, it was pandemonium.

As the game went on, PSG's talent and know-how shone through over their opponents, picking them off with intricate passing and killer instinct, although they were rather wasteful in front of goal. Bernard Lama, who had been untroubled, so much so that he could have pulled out a book on his goal line, read a few pages and not even had to worry about saving an effort, eventually did come to the rescue late on. Jancker had a chance to level the match in the dying embers but Lama's cat-like reflexes meant that PSG held on and won a European competition for the first time in their history. 'It's fabulous. The players did exactly what I expected of them,' said Fernández at full time. 'Overall, I think it was deserved. We beat the best teams during this cup.'

Another cup win for Fernández had confirmed his status as PSG's most successful coach at that point in time. But while Fernández was clearly a good coach and knew how to win, perhaps the former France midfielder understood that his time with the club may have been up or was about to expire in the not so distant future. With Ginola and Weah gone as well as – allegedly, according to Fernández himself – missing out on a host of targets, he had delivered European silverware but failed to produce the championship when it looked harder to throw away than not. For some, the cup win may have been enough to some fans to keep him, but it must have felt like the right time to move on. Athletic Bilbao in Spain came calling and off went Fernández, just prior to another summer of upheaval and change at the club, but one transfer in particular needs to be dissected in detail. One, because it's indicative of one of the biggest problems at PSG, but two, because it would end up costing the club a record fee a handful of years later.

Former defender Ricardo Gomes returned to take his first managerial role after retiring the season prior at Benfica. Ricardo was only 31 but many at the club felt he had all the experience and ability to take over from Fernández and deliver the championship. Yet the new boss had to make do without the star man, Youri Djorkaeff, who had been sold to Inter Milan for just over £5m. Weah, having gone to Milan the previous year, and now Djorkaeff to Inter, both for sizeable fees, showed that PSG possessed players who were capable of cutting it at the highest level but they had to leave in order to do so in the best league in the world at the time in Serie A.

Leonardo joined from Kashima Antlers in Japan but the main transfer from this season wasn't Djorkaeff or Leonardo – instead, it was of a teenager who had barely played for the first team. Anelka, who made his first appearance of the season and scored his first PSG goal against Lens in September, was in and out of the squad throughout the first half of the season. He only started one game that season, a Coupe de la Ligue defeat to Lyon, but one could argue that at his age – he was just 17 when 1996/97 started – limited game time was beneficial. He was getting minutes but also not being overexposed in terms of playing too much and affecting his confidence. Anelka, however, had other ideas, as did new Arsenal boss Arsène Wenger.

Anelka was reportedly unhappy at PSG midway through the season due to his lack of playing time, and was getting impatient at his lack of opportunities. With the amount of attacking talent ahead of him, one could have been forgiven for thinking that Anelka was wrong to consider that he should be getting minutes ahead of Loko and the rest, but he was incredibly confident and sure of himself to the point where, even at the age of 17, he felt his talent demanded a starting berth. Luis Fernández spoke to *The Athletic* in April 2020 about Anelka and blamed his entourage for how his attitude changed, saying, 'Sometimes I think of Nicolas in his early days ... He's someone who wanted to play, to succeed. He had enormous potential. When he started out, a certain entourage of bad advisors drew him to the dark side ... Nicolas badly negotiated the different turns of his career, at least the first. He wanted to go too fast.'

Anelka and his advisors felt that a move to Arsenal was the best move for his career. His brothers, Claude and Didier, were representing the young striker and felt that the best way to get a move to Arsenal was to force PSG into selling him immediately. Because Anelka was still a youth player, rules in France at the time meant that PSG could either sell him for whatever price they could get or keep him until the end of the season and lose him for absolutely nothing. After the winter break, Anelka failed to return to PSG training, making it abundantly clear that he wanted out. In February 1997 Wenger and Arsenal tabled a bid of £500,000 for Anelka, and PSG, not wanting to run the risk of losing him for nothing six months later, accepted it and sold him to the north London club.

Anelka was gone, PSG had lost a star for the future and by the time he left the French capital, the club were embroiled in a title race against Monaco. Led by Jean Tigana, Monaco were looking like a force to be reckoned with. Sonny Anderson led the way up front and would eventually finish third in the Division 1 golden boot table that season with 19 goals, while the likes of Thierry Henry and David Trezeguet were able to pitch in when they could. Emmanuel Petit and Enzo Scifo, as well as the excellent Ali Benarbia, made up an exciting-looking midfield, and having Fabien Barthez in goal was never a bad thing. Monaco would eventually go on to win the title by 12 points, amassing 79 points and scoring 69 goals, a joint-record points tally in French top-flight history at the time, only a few years after three points were awarded for a win instead of two. PSG were just outmuscled and beaten by the better team over the course of the season and would eventually end up trophyless despite reaching the Cup Winners' Cup Final again, which they lost 1-0 to Barcelona.

Losing to Lyon in the Coupe de la Ligue and Clermont on penalties in the Coupe de France wasn't what was wanted, but they quickly learnt that they couldn't keep sacking managers every time they didn't win a particular competition. Jorge left after winning the league, Fernández left after finishing second in the league despite his cup wins, so PSG needed a bit of stability or at least some continuity, both on and off the field. Players were leaving for new clubs seemingly every season, even those who weren't starters in the first team at that point, and a strong managerial presence was key for any success. But the problem when you keep selling stars and replacing them every season is that, at some point, the well will dry up.

You can't find a Youri Djorkaeff every season, you can't bank on finding stars every season, and that affects the chemistry and cohesion of your team. They went from Weah and Ginola to Loko and Djorkaeff to Loko and Julio Dely Valdés and then Loko to Marco Simone, who joined from Milan in the summer of 1997 for just under £1m and hit the ground running in impressive style. His 22 goals in 1997/98 were enough to win the Coupe de France and the Coupe de la Ligue, with Simone scoring in both finals. The cup successes were incredibly important anyway because, to any fan or any club, a trophy is a trophy. But as the season went on, both the runs gained in significance because of the poor form in Division 1 and in the Champions League. Champions League hopes were over after failing to qualify from their group ahead of Bayern Munich and Beşiktaş, and the league form was even worse. While at one point after 12 games PSG found themselves top of the standings, consistency was a massive problem. After the turn of the year into 1998, PSG won two games in the league, whereas prior to the winter break they were second and in with a chance of winning the title.

That dreadful form in the second half of the season was embarrassing for everyone involved, none more so than Michel Denisot, who was stepping down as club president in May 1998. For the man who had presided over an era of success that was unlikely to be matched for quite some time, fans felt that the players owed him silverware not only after his tenure in charge but also because they were so poor in the league. The first of the two finals was in the Coupe de la Ligue against Bordeaux, an exciting game against Élie Baup's side containing the likes of Jean-Pierre Papin, Johan Micoud and Sylvain Wiltord. PSG could easily have lost after going 1-0 down in the first half, but Simone and Raí gave them a 2-1 lead before Papin pounced to take the game to penalties. Patrice Loko had the honour of scoring the winning kick, making it six trophies in seven years for Denisot with the chance to make it seven later in the campaign in the Coupe de France. That final, however, gained even more significance.

Captain, talisman and legend Raí announced that he would be leaving to return to Brazil and play for São Paulo, and the Coupe de France Final would be his last game in a PSG shirt. If the departing Denisot wasn't enough incentive to win yet another domestic trophy then the exit of arguably their greatest-ever player had to be. Naturally, there could only be one outcome. PSG were 2-1 victors thanks to a winner from Simone but the scoring was opened by Raí himself, whose header was placed expertly into the corner to set PSG on their way to victory.

At the full-time whistle, the joy on Denisot's face was clear for all to see. He rushed down the steps in the stands and embraced Ricardo and his assistant manager Joël Bats beside the dugout, not letting go and quite literally holding on to this moment for as long as time would allow. Paul Le Guen, who was retiring at the end of the season, spread his arms and screamed with joy up into the Parisian sky. For everyone involved at Paris Saint-Germain at the time, this felt like the end of an era. With the president, captain and experienced leaders and figureheads leaving, a massive turnover was on the agenda. Ricardo and Bats would eventually leave and be replaced by Alain Giresse, while a whole host of players went too. Raí and Le Guen were joined out the door by Vincent Guérin, Laurent Fournier, Bruno N'Gotty and Didier Domi, and it became clear that the end of the Denisot era was staring PSG in the face. Some clubs know when the time is right to reset the clock and PSG took the hint right before France celebrated their first World Cup win in the summer of 1998.

Raí was reduced to tears in his Parc des Princes send-off thanks to a beautiful tribute from the PSG fans. As the teams walked out, led by the attacking midfielder, fans unveiled a banner reading 'Rai, a jamais Parisian', which translated to Rai, forever a Parisian, while waving miniature Brazilian flags, painting the sections of ultras green, yellow and blue. At full time, despite losing 2-1 to Monaco, Raí was the only thing the fans would sing about. The result was secondary compared to the Brazilian, who got down on his knees to bow before those who chanted his name continually. It was raining and PSG had lost yet again, but no one cared. All they wanted was Raí to be given a salute on his exit from the stage.

For someone whose career was probably overshadowed by that of his older brother, fans in Paris still adore Raí. If you go to the Parc des Princes you'll find his face sprayed on to a wall outside the ground alongside other notable PSG players from across the years. While the likes of Weah, Ginola, Djorkaeff and Anelka all departed, Raí was a constant presence and a reminder that PSG still had a special talent in their ranks. Built like a defender but with the grace and guile of a diminutive midfielder, he was the perfect player at the perfect time. In the middle of a golden era of trophies and success, Raí encapsulated what fans loved: flair, skill, agility, ability, enjoyment and winning. No one loved entertaining more than Raí but also, no one loved winning more. He was a part of those trophy-winning teams and was someone who the fans fell in love with once he settled in.

The adaptation was difficult and his issues at the 1994 World Cup did knock his confidence, but he came back stronger and better than he had been before. It was no wonder that the PSG fans voted Raí their player of the century. But Raí's departure indicated that things were changing and that the years of success were about to stop abruptly. Jay-Jay Okocha was signed for £14m, making him the most expensive African player of all time at that point, while German defender Christian Wörns joined from Bayer Leverkusen although he returned back to the Bundesliga just one season later to join Dortmund after failing to adapt to life in Paris. Okocha was the replacement for Raí, but the lack of replacements for other key players resulted in a drop-off in fortunes for several years. But with PSG it was always clear that no matter the situation they found themselves in, they were always happy to spend a bit of money to make things a bit easier to deal with, even if it meant breaking their transfer record for a player who stormed out of the club due to a lack of playing time some years previously for a mere £500,000.

13

Ronaldinho and samba à Paris –
Ronaldinho and samba in Paris

AT THE turn of the millennium, Paris Saint-Germain were facing a crossroads of sorts. Under Canal+ they had reached the heights of league titles, European glory and glamour Champions League ties against AC Milan and Bayern Munich. The memories of George Weah, David Ginola et al were still fresh in the minds of a lot of fans, even if it had been more than half a decade since the club last lifted the championship.

After finishing second in the 1999/2000 season under the stewardship of Philippe Bergeroo, a former goalkeeping coach for the French national team who had been brought in to steer the club away from any potential relegation danger in 1998/99 when the return of Artur Jorge didn't go the way that many had hoped or expected, the board at PSG felt that it was the right time to spend big and try to take the team to another level. Second place was great but the Champions League offered footballing bait to anyone who was interested in signing. The Parisian lifestyle and Champions League football would be a tempting devilish duo, especially with big money involved. Stéphane Dalmat joined for just over €10m from Marseille, with Frédéric Déhu, Bernard Mendy and later Didier Domi forming the majority of a new-look defence costing €14m after Domi returned from three years at Newcastle. Sylvain Distin returned on a free transfer after leaving PSG's youth team at a young age, while Mauricio Pochettino joined from Espanyol and a young Mikel Arteta arrived on loan for the season from Barcelona.

The recruitment drive pointed towards a mix of young talent who were ready to develop quickly at the club alongside more experienced heads like Pochettino and Déhu. Adding those into a squad that already contained Jay-Jay Okocha and Laurent Robert and it had the makings of a team that could challenge now and be exciting for the future. But there was one thing missing from the perspective of the board: they wanted a marquee signing. And by the end of the window, they thought they had made the perfect transfer.

Midway through the summer of 2000, Real Madrid were in the midst of a presidential election. Florentino Pérez was going up against Lorenzo Sanz with Pérez using the financial issues under Sanz's stewardship as a stick to beat him with publicly (Real Madrid were £75m in debt at the time) while simultaneously promising that, if he was elected, he would sign Luís Figo from Barcelona. However, aside from all the posturing about star players arriving, both candidates had to find ways to remove the debt from the shoulders of Los Blancos. Sanz had assumed that the Champions League wins in 1998 and 2000 would be enough to see him re-elected, but Pérez's tactics of highlighting the financial problems proved key. The pair had to find money from somewhere and they both seemed to have the same strategy in mind: sell Nicolas Anelka.

After leaving PSG a few years prior, Anelka's form for Arsenal had been electric, eventually earning himself a move to Real Madrid after helping the north London club with the Premier League and FA Cup double in 1998. After being nicknamed 'Le Sulk' by the English press and professing that by signing for Real Madrid he was joining 'the biggest club in Europe', Anelka looked like he was at a club of the stature that he – and his brothers – felt he deserved. He wasn't played enough at PSG, and Arsenal, apparently, wasn't a big enough club for him, so getting plenty of game time at Real Madrid would surely give Anelka everything he needed. Well, not exactly. Real spent £23.5m on the striker, but he only lasted in Spain for 12 months. Vicente del Bosque struggled with Anelka, saying, 'I think he is confused and that he lives in a world of his own,' yet Anelka's torrid time in Madrid escalated in March 2000 when he publicly apologised after refusing to appear at training for three days when he was told to train alone following his criticism of team tactics, something that led to the club giving him a 45-day suspension. It also didn't help Anelka's cause that many of the Spanish players in the Madrid squad reportedly disliked his arrival as they felt it was a slight to Fernando Morientes.

The only thing to do was to sell him to the highest bidder, Paris Saint-Germain, who felt a returning Anelka was the perfect player to lead their new-look, young and suburb-driven team. Paris was – and still is – a city bursting with talent in every area and for Anelka to be signed as the figurehead of the PSG squad but also, symbolically, as the star of Parisian suburbs meant a lot of pressure would be placed upon his shoulders. At Arsenal he had the pressure of replacing Ian Wright in the team. At Real Madrid he faced the almost unbearable pressure of being a big-money signing at an elite club but at PSG it was different. He wasn't replacing a legend like he was at Highbury nor was he facing the same level of scrutiny he did in Spain. There was expectancy, of course, but perhaps for the first time in his career Anelka was the star of a team.

The entire PSG project was centred around Anelka. They kept his favourite shirt number, nine, free for his arrival, and they broke the French top-flight record for highest transfer fee paid for a player at €32m. They even gave him a seven-year deal just to prove that he was the figurehead of the new-look PSG, built around players like Anelka who grew up in the shadow of the Parc des Princes and had the club and city sewn into their hearts. The Canal+ board financed the transfer while Nike would help pay his wages.

It's easy to forget, given his nomadic career and the anecdotes about his attitude, demeanour and the 2010 World Cup debacle, but Anelka was still deemed a 'wonderkid' in 2000, and for PSG to bring him back to the club was astronomical. Real Madrid fell over themselves to sign him from Arsenal but now he belonged to Paris and PSG. Yet, while his signing and introduction at the Parc des Princes were cause to celebrate for fans, his performances – and those of the team in general – weren't. Anelka made his debut away at Rennes in a 1-1 draw, coming on for Ali Benarbia just before the hour, but had to wait a few more weeks to get on to the scoresheet, scoring twice in a 3-1 home win against Bastia. He followed that up with a goal and an assist in a defeat to Troyes before again scoring a brace in a 5-1 thrashing of Saint-Étienne. Despite the five goals in his first six appearances, Anelka would only score three times after that in the league and only one came after the winter break. Five goals in the Champions League helped his cause but it became obvious that the team around Anelka at that point wasn't up to scratch compared to previous PSG offerings.

Despite going top of the table in late October, the form dropped off massively after a win at Toulouse. Six straight losses in Division 1 meant Philippe Bergeroo was destined for the door and was quickly sacked, replaced by former boss Luis Fernández. Unfortunately for the returning Fernández, there wasn't that much of an upturn in fortunes after his arrival. PSG were knocked out of the Champions League after the second group stage and had to settle for finishing ninth just like in 1998/99. A gap to the top of 24 points wasn't good enough and Fernández was looking to bolster the squad around Anelka in order to bring the best out of the striker and to get the best PSG side possible. Instead, all Fernández did was eventually alienate Anelka and push him to the side. Peter Luccin, Pierre Ducrocq, Édouard Cissé, Didier Domi and Stéphane Dalmat, all of whom Anelka was friends with in the squad, were either sold or loaned out and replaced by Aloísio and Alex Dias from Saint-Étienne, while Gabriel Heinze was brought in from Real Valladolid for just over €3m along with 21-year-old Atlético Madrid star Hugo Leal, a player who was viewed as an investment for the future. However, one signing that summer arguably took more shine away from Anelka than anyone had anticipated. Anelka, the big-money Parisian, was about to be upstaged and overshadowed in the excitement stakes by a 21-year-old Brazilian from Grêmio who would turn down advances from Europe's elite to join Paris Saint-Germain and eventually become one of the best players of an entire generation.

There are very few players who make football fun. Not in the 'my-team-is-winning-therefore-football-is-fun' kind of fun, but the kind where you go out of your way to watch them play, sporting an ear-to-ear smile for the whole 90 minutes. In Brazil there seems to be a prodigy produced every week but, in Grêmio, one youngster stood out from the rest. Ronaldo de Assis Moreira, known across the globe at Ronaldinho, was starting his career in 1998 and made his debut in the Copa Libertadores but it wouldn't be until 1999 that he really started to break out. Inspired by the likes of Diego Maradona, Romário and Ronaldo, Ronaldinho combined Brazilian futsal technique with pace, quickness of mind and the unique ability to manipulate the ball in whatever way he pleased. He gained even more fame when he embarrassed 1994 World Cup-winning captain Dunga with a display of tricks and flicks that made the latter seem like the inexperienced youngster, with the performance making those who hadn't been aware of Ronaldinho's talent firmly aware of what they were witnessing.

Ronaldinho had the world at his feet and he had clubs calling him from the moment they realised just how good he could be. He nearly joined Arsenal at the turn of the century but due to work permit rules the deal was called off. Real Madrid, Barcelona, Inter Milan and Leeds United were all interested, but Ronaldinho had a plan for his future. In Brazil it's accepted that the moment you get a young superstar, European clubs will pick them off for big fees. Ronaldinho, however, knew exactly what path he wanted to take. He planned to establish his name in Brazil, join a European club that would give him substantial playing time in a top league, and then make the jump to an elite-level club.

In December 2000, Ronaldinho signed a pre-contract agreement with Paris Saint-Germain, a move that was surprising to many but a strategic one from his own standpoint. He would play plenty in Paris while having the opportunity to play for Brazil in the 2002 World Cup and be close enough to other major leagues to grab their attention. His brother even got a move to Montpellier out of it too. Except there was one problem: Grêmio didn't know a thing about it until PSG announced it on their website. 'I've just read the news on PSG's website. We are in the middle of negotiations to renew Ronaldinho's contract and PSG have never contacted us,' said a shocked and angry Grêmio president Jose Guerreiro. What Ronaldinho had done was take advantage of the Brazilian equivalent of the Bosman ruling to sign for PSG in the summer for no fee, despite Grêmio trying to negotiate a new contract which would allow him to still move on in the summer but give the club a hefty fee for their star player.

Grêmio took Ronaldinho and PSG to court and FIFA ruled that the player couldn't play until the situation was resolved. He soon moved to Paris, in April, but hadn't even kicked a ball in months and, with the ban still in place for the foreseeable future, he had no idea when he would make his debut for the Parisians. It even got to a stage where his agent was trying to loan him out to St

Mirren just to get him game time, but a myriad of reasons have been given over the years as to why the infamous loan never came to fruition.

St Mirren boss Tom Hendrie claimed that the Brazilian FA 'shut down' to watch a Brazil international which meant no one from the FA was around to clear the necessary papers needed for the loan move to be completed, while Stephen McGowan of ESPN said in 2001 that Ronaldinho was 'embroiled in a fake passport scandal in his native land, making it impossible for St Mirren to obtain international clearance for the player prior to the signing deadline'. But whether that was the reason or FIFA upholding their ban, PSG eventually got their man for a fee believed to be around €5m and the punishment was lifted in mid-August, just in time for Ronaldinho to play a part in the second game of the season away at Auxerre.

Ronaldinho arrived with superstar status in the eyes of the PSG fans, thrilled that this new superstar of Brazilian football had chosen them over more established elite clubs in Europe. Gabriel Heinze linked up in defence with fellow Argentine international Mauricio Pochettino, while Anelka was now being supplied by both Ronaldinho and Jay-Jay Okocha, with the Nigerian taking the Brazilian under his wing and influencing him in his style of play. Ronaldinho would try to imitate Okocha's skills and flair, at least according to the mentor in an interview with Egyptian TV in 2021, but the two seemed to be a good fit for each other on paper.

However, as the season progressed in the early months, PSG still didn't look like a team that had gelled. Replacing Laurent Robert, who had been sold to Newcastle in the summer, was never going to be an easy job for a young Ronaldinho especially after the rigmarole surrounding his transfer, but being reduced to cameos off the bench and looking extremely lightweight for the harsh European leagues, he almost tried too hard when he was on the pitch. He was over-elaborate in attack, going for the flamboyant option rather than the simple one, making people in the stands and in the media question his transfer even so early on in his time in Paris.

As the team struggled to gain a head of steam, the forward line faced intense scrutiny. Ronaldinho, Okocha and Anelka should have been good enough to create and score goals no matter the situation, but it wasn't clicking. Anelka was facing criticism for literally anything while Okocha was showing his talent in flashes rather than sustained spells and Ronaldinho was being benched with even his cameos disappearing. Nothing was going right. Against Bordeaux, PSG were trailing 1-0 and needed a goal late on but instead of bringing on Ronaldinho, they introduced Alex Dias instead. It felt like a new low for Ronaldinho, but if sitting on the bench away at Bordeaux was rock bottom, the only way was up. It may have meant him taking every opportunity that was given to him, but he had to do it the hard way.

Thankfully for Ronaldinho, his first chance came the very next week against Lyon. Lyon were top of the league and were in the infant stages of their incredible dynastic run of seven Division 1 titles in a row when they travelled to the Parc des Princes looking to make a statement. With the visitors leading 2-1 in the second half, Ronaldinho entered the fray. After threading a pass into Bartholomew Ogbeche, who managed to make the most out of the contact from the onrushing Lyon defender, Ronaldinho stepped up to take a penalty that was huge in the context of his season and PSG's. Score and it was possible that both he and the team could have kick-started a good run of form, but miss and the criticism would have only become louder for both parties. He stepped up to the plate and slotted it into the bottom-left corner, sending Grégory Coupet in the Lyon goal the wrong way. 'This goal will give me a little more confidence. I will now play more liberated. I've been waiting for this goal for a while,' said Ronaldinho in his post-match interview.

A few days later in the UEFA Cup against Rapid Vienna, he scored a brace, but the moment that stood out most wasn't his two goals – rather it was a piece of individual skill. With 64 minutes on the clock he collected a long ball out wide, hugging the touchline. Controlling the ball out of the sky with his left knee, Ronaldinho fronted up his man and dangled the ball out in front of him, urging the defender to make the first move. The defender blinked first and tried to adjust his position but Ronaldinho pulled out the 'Elastico' move that he would become synonymous with. This piece of trickery was so key because for the first time since moving to Paris, Ronaldinho was having fun on the pitch. His smile was on show for all to see and when Ronaldinho had the confidence to pull something out of his box of tricks, you knew he was going to hit top gear very soon. He changed the game against champions Nantes the following week as well, coming on at half-time and scoring the winner. Ronaldinho had arrived. His performances were fantastic but an injury soon after cut his superb form off until the winter break. And in Christmas 2001, a lot changed at

PSG that aided Ronaldinho's cause but was also indicative of the entire situation the club was in. Naturally, Nicolas Anelka was front and centre of everything.

On Saturday, 22 December PSG had just beaten Sochaux 2-0 away from home to remain fifth in the table. Meanwhile, 741 miles north, Anelka was away signing for Gérard Houllier and Liverpool, sealing a return to the Premier League. Former PSG title-winner Houllier was the one who set the deal up while he recovered from heart surgery and his time working with Anelka in the youth set-ups of French football helped too.

Eighteen months previously, PSG had rolled out the red carpet to welcome Anelka 'home' but were now happy to see their record signing leave on loan. At the beginning of December, PSG were knocked out of the UEFA Cup by Rangers in a thrilling tie which ended 4-3 on aggregate, but Anelka was the one who was booed at the final whistle. He had a chance to win the tie but failed to convert, earning him the floods of jeers that came his way. Clearly, whatever bond Anelka had with the fans – if he had one at all – was broken. He wasn't even a regular starter and was rarely completing 90 minutes. Anelka claimed that his relationship with manager Luis Fernández deteriorating due to his lack of playing time was the main reason as to why he moved, but his own form didn't help matters, nor did the situation he was placed in. PSG had purchased a plethora of players for hefty fees since Anelka's arrival in a bid to give Paris a team that the ownership felt represented Parisians. In theory, they had created a close-knit, tight group of young Parisians who would be ideal for the fanbase but, in reality, it was a disaster. There was no planning or structure and with Anelka placed right in the middle of matters as the face of the project, the benefit of hindsight allows us to realise that, due to the expectation placed on his shoulders and the supporting cast around him, failure was always going to be how people viewed Anelka at PSG unless he delivered every trophy possible. Whatever he did, for some it was never going to be enough.

Reading reports of the situation at PSG in late 2001, you see that Anelka was blamed for a lot of what was going on at the club. The general consensus in France and in reporting in the UK was that Anelka was falling back into the 'Le Sulk' persona that many had given him during his time at Arsenal. He was demanding more game time but his record of two league goals suggested that Fernández was right to drop him and, with there being no outcry from the PSG fans, Anelka and his pleas fell on deaf ears. Perhaps his final straw wasn't even on the pitch but in the training centre where a journalist from *L'Equipe* lodged a complaint with the police claiming that Anelka had assaulted him. The journalist said 'Bonjour' to Anelka, but the forward said nothing. 'I said, bonjour,' he tried again, but still Anelka said nothing. A few insults were traded and Anelka slapped the writer. The whole ordeal was caught on camera and Anelka was eventually urged to apologise, although many failed to see the apology as genuine.

So when Liverpool and Houllier came calling, a move away from Paris suited everyone involved. Anelka got game time ahead of the 2002 World Cup, PSG got a wantaway player out, and the star of the new Canal+ project had failed and departed. With Anelka gone and Okocha leaving for the Africa Cup of Nations for six weeks, PSG's star-studded forward line had been dismantled for all but one of its pieces: Ronaldinho. The Brazilian returned from his injury to find Anelka being ushered out of the door and Okocha at an international tournament leaving him as the new star of PSG, albeit for a few weeks.

When Ronaldinho next appeared on the pitch, against Monaco, everything seemed to click in to gear at the perfect time for him. The Monaco game showed that the injury hadn't slowed him down and his performance was lively enough to win PSG a penalty, but not the three points, as Monaco trotted out winners. It wasn't until the next match, against Guingamp in the Coupe de la Ligue, where Ronaldinho stepped out of his shell for perhaps the first time in a PSG shirt.

Coming on as a half-time sub with PSG level 1-1, Ronaldinho was the match-winner and difference-maker rolled into one. He scored a brace including a 50-yard sprint to slot underneath the goalkeeper before celebrating in front of the ultras behind the goal. For the first time, it looked like Ronaldinho was ready to be PSG's star and the fans were ready to embrace him as the driving force of the team, at least in the absence of Okocha and Anelka. Up until this point, Ronaldinho was the 'nearly man' of the team, only producing fleeting moments of brilliance and offering glimpses of the ability he had shown in Brazil, but after the Christmas break the perceptions of him had flipped on their heads. He controlled proceedings in a 5-0 demolition of Lorient and scored two outrageously good goals in a win against Troyes.

Ronaldinho had become the main focal point of the team. Whenever something good happened, there was an incredibly high possibility that Ronaldinho was the cause.

He was playing with a smile on his face for the first time in Europe and had gone from bench-warmer to PSG's star man. He was their best and most important player, which was evident in him finishing as their top scorer that season and earning a place in the team of the year too, helping PSG to finish fourth in the table and just one point from Champions League qualification. Not bad for someone who wasn't getting a game just seven months prior.

If anything showed how good his season ended up being, it was Luiz Felipe Scolari picking him for Brazil's 2002 World Cup squad, where Ronaldinho started to go to the next level. He joined PSG as a promising young talent behind the likes of Okocha and Anelka in the pecking order and by the end of his debut season he was top scorer and about to play a massive role in winning the World Cup. Surely he would come back from the tournament as the new superstar of Paris, ready to put the team on his back and take another step forward to being considered as one of football's great players of the time? Not exactly. Okocha was sold to Bolton while Anelka never even returned from his loan at Liverpool as he was shipped out immediately to Manchester City, leaving Ronaldinho with the entire weight of attacking pressure.

There was a feeling among some at PSG that Ronaldinho had changed after the World Cup. Most of the concern came from his manager, Luis Fernández, who wasn't happy with Ronaldinho because of his party lifestyle. 'He is a boy who had no father, like me. He had his mother, his brother and his sister who were there. But they left the second year. They left him alone, with a driver,' said Fernández to RMC radio in 2020. Fernández also recalled being told 'every morning' by security at the club about Ronaldinho's escapades and admitted in the same interview that he 'tried everything' to manage Ronaldinho in a way that he felt was appropriate. 'When Nicolas Anelka arrived late at Real Madrid, he was suspended because there is an institution, a club, a regulation. Here in Paris, there was nothing,' Fernández said in another interview. 'He starts to party, all the possible bullshit. He should have been our leader, leading us to the top, winning the title and the European Cup. He brings girls to his room during a greening [away trip]. We were in the hotel lobby with the staff. We see four girls arrive. I asked my assistant Eric Blondel to follow them and they went to Ronnie's room.' The manager didn't want to lose his star man but felt the club needed to punish him in some way, if only to ensure their own optics of being a club that wouldn't take, as Fernández so eloquently put it, bullshit from anyone no matter who they were. Ronaldinho was still the best player at PSG but Fernández felt that he had started to pick and choose matches, an accusation not too dissimilar to that which George Weah faced and which Fernández batted away in the 1990s.

What Ronaldinho was doing is a problem that still plagues Paris Saint-Germain to this day. He would eye up the games that would be watched by a larger audience to really showcase his talents. In an era before every goal and highlight was seen by millions instantly, the big games on television were how you stood out from the rest. In a 3-0 win at home to Marseille in October 2002, Ronaldinho scored twice. They were only his second and third goals in wins for PSG in Ligue 1 (Division 1 rebranded this season to what it's now more commonly known as).

His other amazing performance that season also came against Marseille in what was probably his defining game in a PSG shirt, and for good reason. Marseille were fighting for the title while PSG, who hadn't won at the Stade Vélodrome for 14 years at this point, were nothing more than mid-table dwellers. Their fans were electric, sensing that this could be the perfect opportunity to both go closer to Lyon in the Ligue 1 title race and also embarrass their arch-rivals. When Gabriel Heinze collided with Fernando and forced him off the pitch through injury, the Marseille fans constantly booed the Argentine every time he touched the ball. In the 27th minute PSG went ahead when Jérôme Leroy curled in an effort that silenced 55,000 people simultaneously. No one in the Vélodrome had expected it, but what came next was simply magical. Unfortunately for Marseille, this was one of the games Ronaldinho decided to become simply unstoppable in. Tricks, flicks, extravagant passes; Ronaldinho was going through every page of his genius playbook to show Marseille who was boss on this occasion. His goal arrived through intelligent reading of the game, incredible speed and a finish that looked like it was harder to pull off than anything else.

Frank Leboeuf was about ten yards inside his own half when he shaped to spray a pass to the right-hand side of the pitch to try and build an attack. Ronaldinho, however, was lurking on the halfway line. He knew that if Leboeuf's pass was even a fraction off, he could step in and grab the ball, which was exactly what he did. His first touch stole the ball in mid-air and set him up perfectly to sprint away from any defenders around him. Touch after touch, he drove towards the goal and just when you felt it was one touch too many, he just managed to get his right foot under the ball to lift it over the onrushing goalkeeper Vedran Runje, who was left helpless. Simply remarkable. The third and final PSG goal wasn't too dissimilar either. Ronaldinho was given a pass that allowed him to burn past Brahim Hemdani before going around Runje as he got to the edge of the box. But he didn't round Runje the traditional way; instead he checked back inside and forced Runje and Hemdani's momentum to take them out of the equation before rolling the ball goalwards. Leroy actually tapped the ball home on the line, so officially the goal was his, but to everyone it belonged to Ronaldinho. He made it and, in some eyes, he scored it. That was his genius. He could decide massive games whenever he wanted to, but that was also the problem. When he wanted to.

A piece in *The Guardian* in February 2003 didn't hold back when discussing Ronaldinho during the 2002/03 season, labelling him a 'spoilt brat' and claiming that Fernández 'hated his guts' even if the Canal+ ownership loved him 'not for what he does on the pitch, which these days is very little, but for the riches he represents'. The piece was rather cynical but gave a glimpse into how Ronaldinho's 2002/03 season was going up until that point. It even drew upon comments from Fernández that he made just a few weeks into the season, saying, 'Ronaldinho has a problem. He does not perhaps have the hygiène de vie [lifestyle] of a top-level sportsman. But while I can control what goes on inside our training camp I cannot control what goes on outside it.'

Clearly all was not well in Paris, but it hadn't been well for the entire season. Ronaldinho had publicly called out Fernández for playing him out of position, he had questioned the manager's tactics, and even went as far as to say that he would leave PSG if Fernández wasn't sacked by Christmas. In the ultimate act of confidence towards a manager, PSG chief Laurent Perpère said, 'Losing the services of Fernández would be less damaging than letting Ronaldinho go.'

PSG didn't sack Fernández at that time, but Ronaldinho decided to return five days late from the winter break, citing that he stayed behind in Porto Allegre to take advice on possible dental surgery. PSG weren't impressed by the excuse and even released a statement saying Ronaldinho benefited from 'regular, quality dental care'. For the club, the situation was fast developing into a farce so the expectation was that they would come down hard on the Brazilian. In the end they fined him €2,000 before Xavier Couture, the chairman of Canal+ and PSG, went on to say, 'It's a storm in a glass of water. Besides, the weather's nice in Brazil right now. It's summer. I can understand Ronaldinho wanting to spend a few more days down there.'

While PSG were trying their hardest to keep Ronaldinho happy and at the club for as long as possible, it became abundantly clear that the Brazilian would be leaving in that summer. Many felt that he was playing as if PSG were underneath him, like being a World Cup winner was enough to elevate him to the next level of football club. A divorce felt inevitable, but it would be one that actually suited all parties involved.

By the end of a forgettable season, changes were afoot in Paris. Vahid Halilhodžić was in as Fernández's replacement, having been rumoured to be taking over since Christmas. Various board members refuted claims that they had spoken to him at the time. Ronaldinho, meanwhile, was set to be the transfer sage of the summer of 2003, with three clubs in particular eyeing his signature. Real Madrid, Manchester United and Barcelona all wanted the Brazilian superstar and had different reasons as to why they sought after the man who caused such commotion in Paris for two seasons.

Real Madrid and Florentino Pérez were searching the market for their next Galáctico, with Ronaldinho's name quite high up on their list. However, an associate of Florentino Pérez told Spanish newspaper *El Pais* that there simply was no point signing the Brazilian because he was 'so ugly that he would sink the club as a brand'. Real Madrid turned their noses up at Ronaldinho because of his looks and not because of his ability, which also simultaneously caused massive headaches for both Manchester United and Barcelona. Madrid and Pérez were determined to get their Galáctico and, instead of Ronaldinho, they opted for David Beckham who was, at the time, perhaps the most famous athlete on the planet. Beckham was a more profitable and marketable player, which appealed to Madrid more.

However, the signing of Beckham was exactly what Barcelona president Joan Laporta had based his entire election campaign on which now meant that he had to find a superstar signing from somewhere to appease the club or else his reign would be getting off to a disastrous start. As for Manchester United, they now needed a replacement for Beckham and also wanted to bring in Ronaldinho, who even said he had a preference to play for the club. United had tried to sign Harry Kewell from

Leeds but he chose to go to Liverpool, while Damien Duff opted for Chelsea over United that summer also, leaving Old Trafford with just one target. Barcelona eventually bid around £29m for Ronaldinho, an amount that Manchester United apparently weren't comfortable with, and thus brought the Brazilian to the Camp Nou and began the legacy of one of football's icons.

But for PSG, it ended up being a profitable situation. They pocketed a huge sum for a player who had one very good half season and a second season full of glimpses of quality more than anything else and they were prepared to use that money wisely. Yet the question remains about whether Ronaldinho is a PSG legend. Considering the amount they received for him after only paying a few million for the Brazilian, some may be very grateful for those two seasons which turned out very beneficial to the finances of the club, but to call him a legend seems like a stretch. He had memorable moments and perhaps his career after PSG clouds the reality of his time in Paris but while he had all the talent in the world, he never quite showed his full potential at le Parc.

Outside of the Parc des Princes there are graffiti artworks of former PSG players who could rightly make the claim to be legends at the club. Ronaldinho is one of them. It's entirely possible and perhaps very likely that the aura around Ronaldinho is why PSG consider him to be one of their icons but the reality is that his time there wasn't that successful. He had outstanding performances and made Marseille his own at the Vélodrome but he left trophyless after a second and final season filled with ultimatums, tantrums against managers, teeth advice in Brazil and parties, parties and more parties.

The question of Ronaldinho's legendary status at PSG is something that can be debated by fans from morning until night, but one player who was brought into the club using the money spent by Ronaldinho's sale has undoubtedly earned that recognition. For many years, he was the greatest and most prolific striker to step foot on to the Parc des Princes turf. He cost less than €9m and his face is featured on that very same mural of legends that Ronaldinho, George Weah, David Ginola and Bernard Lama – to name a few – are featured on. Signing from Bordeaux, PSG had found a goal machine. They had found Pauleta.

14

La légende du Portugal est arrivée –
The legend from Portugal has arrived

AS RONALDINHO was approaching his eventual departure, PSG were already searching for who they would spend a large portion of the incoming money on. Would they improve the entire starting 11 or would they buy a star name to create a buzz around them ahead of the 2003/04 season? Meanwhile, Lyon had just lost Sonny Anderson to Villarreal in Spain so were also on the hunt for a new star forward to help them add to their ever-growing list of trophies.

Lyon and PSG both had their eyes set on the prolific and experienced Bordeaux and Portugal striker Pauleta, but PSG had the lead in the race. Francis Graille, the new president of PSG, was determined to get the deal done. Since May, PSG had been searching for his signature, and with Pauleta and his wife clearly impressed and taken aback by how much they wanted him, it became quite clear that if the clubs could reach a deal then the Ligue 1 Player of the Year would be making the move. Yet there were still concerns and criticism. Pauleta's age played a factor, with many asking how PSG could justify spending €12m on a 30-year-old. Many felt that it would have been better to use the money to sign a younger striker like Djibril Cissé from Auxerre or Didier Drogba from Guingamp. Drogba signed for Marseille instead before making the move to Chelsea a year later while Cissé stayed in France for one more season before moving to Liverpool, so hindsight gives PSG the benefit of the doubt in the sense that Pauleta stayed put in Paris while both Cissé and Drogba moved on fairly quickly from Ligue 1. How did PSG battle off criticism about their new acquisition's age? Vahid Halilhodžić simply pointed to the fact that when he was 34, he was still able to score 28 goals. Age, as it always will be, is simply just a number in football.

While Pauleta wasn't the star name that Ronaldinho was, signing a player of his calibre was probably the next best thing PSG could have done. Adding to players such as Frédéric Déhu, Fabrice Fiorèse, Gabriel Heinze, Bernard Mendy, Lorik Cana and Juan Pablo Sorín with one of Ligue 1's deadliest marksmen was arguably a better fit at that moment in time than Ronaldinho was. Pauleta was pure goals, which was exactly what PSG needed. The season prior to Pauleta's arrival they had scored 47 times, the fifth best in Ligue 1, but the goals were spread out quite evenly. Ronaldinho scored the most with 12 but he was the only player to hit double figures. With the Brazilian out of the door, goals became the question surrounding the team heading in to the 2003/04 season, and in the first handful of games it became evident that the lack of goals could be a serious issue. The Parisians drew blanks in their opening two matches, against Bastia and Lille, but defeated Metz 1-0 to arrest the poor start, before the fourth fixture at home to Monaco proved to simultaneously be one of the most entertaining and important games for PSG that season. Pauleta got himself off the mark by giving PSG the lead, tapping in from a Fabrice Fiorèse cross, before Ludovic Giuly and Emmanuel Adebayor put Didier Deschamps's side ahead at the break. PSG would eventually go on to lose 4-2 but Pauleta's proved to be the main takeaway from the game. 'Little by little, the team got to know me better and vice versa,' said the Portuguese forward at full time. 'It's true that I needed to score, that gives me confidence and I saw that the coach and my team-mates were also very happy with this goal. I felt good and did everything to register a second. But we are a group and I cannot do everything alone.'

Settling into life at PSG took some time for Pauleta, but he sparked into action after the Monaco game. Scoring in four consecutive matches, against Guingamp, Auxerre, Sochaux and Le Mans, helped pushed PSG up into third, which was where they stood at the winter break. Nine goals in the first half of the season was certainly not a bad return, but once action resumed, Pauleta was ready to assume his role as PSG's star man.

The first game back was the Coupe de France first round against Troyes, in which Pauleta scored the winner. The first Ligue 1 game back was against Montpellier, the Portuguese scoring a brace in a 6-1 demolition. Pauleta had fully arrived and he was determined to bring at least one piece of silverware to the Parc des Princes in 2003/04. The championship was a three-horse race with Lyon looking for their third consecutive title, PSG chasing their first in a decade and Monaco eyeing up a potential Ligue

1 and Champions League double. Lyon and Monaco were both in the quarter-finals of the Champions League in March and were first and second in Ligue 1, while PSG were preparing for the semi-finals of the Coupe de France at the same time, with Pauleta having scored in every round up until that point. All three kept close to each other throughout their title run-in fixtures and, with Lyon being knocked out of the Champions League by José Mourinho's Porto, they had the upper hand in one sense. Monaco were still in the Champions League awaiting their semi-final against Chelsea and PSG were preparing for their Coupe de France Final against minnows Châteauroux, so Lyon had a clear run at the title. No distractions, just focusing on their domestic games and doing what needed to be done in order to win another championship. Monaco's form dropped off with draws against the likes of Bastia, Toulouse, Ajaccio and Lens while PSG only lost twice after December, against Lens and Bordeaux, yet the signature moment of their domestic campaign came in match 33 at the Parc des Princes in the biggest game of the season: Le Classique.

The sheer size of the game was enough to give PSG an extra ten per cent but Monaco slipping up at home to Nantes would have had them seriously eyeing up second spot. Any game against Marseille has always been big but this one felt bigger. It also delivered what was arguably Pauleta's signature moment in a PSG shirt. Juan Pablo Sorín picked the ball up on the half turn just as the clock ticked into the 11th minute, then looked up and saw Pauleta making a run in behind the Marseille defence. Sorín dinked the ball between the right-back and centre-back, reaching Pauleta who was greeted by an onrushing

Barthez, closing any angle down. Barthez forced Pauleta outside of the area, on the edge of the touchline, before the striker turned back to face the goal. As he did so he looked up to see Barthez well off of his line and no one covering for him, so in one swift motion he swivelled and lifted the ball high over the head of the goalkeeper. It dipped just under the crossbar at the perfect time and an iconic moment was born. It was a sublime finish and it set PSG up for a vital win, giving Pauleta the victory against fellow marksman Didier Drogba in a duel that was hyped up pre-game as the battle between two top-tier strikers in Ligue 1. It is one of those goals that no matter how many years pass, you will always ask yourself, 'How did he manage to get it in from there?' Every time, you will always fail to fully understand it, but that was the genius of Pauleta. In the blink of an eye he changed the game in PSG's favour.

With PSG in the Coupe de France Final and picking up wins at a key point in the season, they were overtaking Monaco in the race for second and catching up on Lyon. They reached second after the win against Marseille but a draw against Strasbourg saw them slip back down to third. With wins over Rennes, Lyon and then on the final day against Bastia, PSG would eventually finish second in Ligue 1, just three points behind Lyon. The major disappointments, in hindsight, were the draw against Strasbourg and the 3-0 loss away at mid-table Bordeaux, two results that if they had gone in PSG's favour would have seen them lift the title.

But while Ligue 1 disappointment lingered briefly, the club prepared for a Coupe de France Final that they were more than heavy favourites to win. Ligue 2 side

Châteauroux, now run by former PSG president Michel Denisot, were more than capable of pulling off a shock and knew how to play in their role as the underdog. With Pauleta preparing to star at Euro 2004 with Portugal, he was determined to cap off his excellent season with a trophy, but it wouldn't go all their own way and certainly not in the way that perhaps many had expected. Châteauroux were happy to frustrate and disrupt how PSG played, forcing them and almost daring them to break their defence down. Eventually the pressure was just too much for Châteauroux. The breakthrough came in the 66th minute courtesy of Pauleta and PSG took home their sixth Coupe de France title, a first since 1998.

The post-match interviews gave an insight into how the players viewed their future as a team, expecting to build something successful and special, with president Francis Graille saying, 'The evening was extraordinary. PSG will be ambitious next season, that our supporters can rest assured,' while manager Vahid Halilhodžić said, 'Paris deserves its victory. This trophy marks the return of PSG to the front of the stage. Next year, we want to build an even more competitive team, but above all we will keep this spirit that allowed us to get there, and against all odds.' There was a massive feeling that this wasn't the peak of what this PSG side could do, but that it was only the beginning. A few more pieces to the puzzle were needed but the general expectation was, if they could bring in the right players, they would be the perfect foil for an imperious and near-impenetrable Lyon side.

What followed was not a sustained period of success or challenging for Ligue 1 honours; rather an unexpected downfall and perhaps the darkest era in PSG's history.

There was success in domestic competitions but it's an era that is remembered for all the wrong reasons where everything on the pitch seemed to go wrong. The summer of 2004 should have been one where Pauleta was joined by players who could go up against Lyon's mighty side containing the likes of Grégory Coupet, Michael Essien, Nilmar, Juninho Pernambucano, Sidney Govou, Sylvain Wiltord and Florent Malouda, but instead the summer signings struggled to produce the kind of performances expected from them. Gabriel Heinze left to join Manchester United while PSG spent €27m to bring in Sylvain Armand from Nantes, his colleague and Colombian centre-back Mario Yepes, and Jérôme Rothen from Monaco. Rothen came with high expectation mainly due to his performances for Monaco that saw them reach the Champions League semi-final under Didier Deschamps the previous season, but also because he admitted that moving to PSG was a dream move as a Parisian himself. It was supposed to be a homecoming of sorts but it didn't quite work out how Rothen and PSG had planned.

Rothen managed to agree personal terms before PSG agreed a fee with Monaco and spoke of his desire to move to Paris, 'I am interested by PSG, the team which is on its way up.' In theory, they were on the up and adding Rothen was meant to be another piece of their puzzle. A left-winger who had fantastic ability, he could dribble and shoot, cross the ball accurately and had pace to beat his marker, generally a great attacking asset to have. Forming a partnership down the left flank at Monaco with Patrice Evra, he showed enough quality to warrant PSG paying a big fee for him. He was meant to be the main supply

line to Pauleta and, if all went to plan, could easily serve
him goals on a plate with his crossing and dead-ball skill,
but injuries struck almost immediately. He managed
to get four Ligue 1 games under his belt before being
forced off with a groin injury in the Champions League
defeat at home to Chelsea which kept him out for three
weeks. He only lasted for two more Ligue 1 matches and
a Champions League victory over Porto in October before
being sidelined yet again with a fractured ankle. That kept
him out of action until the end of February and by the
time he returned to face Bastia, PSG were languishing
in mid-table, only winning six times in the first half of
the Ligue 1 season. In the second half of the season they
managed the same amount, meaning they had gone from
runners-up the season previously to residing cautiously in
ninth, not even reaching the quarter-finals of either of the
domestic cup competitions and being dumped out of the
Champions League at the group stage (they weren't even
good enough to drop into the UEFA Cup).

While Rothen isn't to blame for the poor season, he
is perhaps indicative and a good metaphorical example
of how things went for PSG. There was optimism at
the start, with big-money signings breeding hope and
expectation, but as the season progressed, various
obstacles prevented them from reaching where they
wanted to be. Manager Vahid Halilhodžić was replaced
in February by former player Laurent Fournier, a member
of Artur Jorge's league-winning team, who had stepped
up from the reserves to oversee proceedings until the end
of the campaign but, by the time Fournier took over, the
season was all but finished for PSG. They crashed out of
the Champions League and only managed two wins from

12 games between mid-November and mid-February, as well as being knocked out of the Coupe de la Ligue by Montpellier. At the start of March, Guy Roux's Auxerre booted them out of the Coupe de France. The worst part about the latter defeat was PSG were 2-0 up within 25 minutes yet still managed to lose. PSG managed to pick up their form towards the end of the campaign, reaching as high as seventh before a few losses and draws saw them settle in ninth, capping off a thoroughly disappointing and miserable season for all involved at the Parc des Princes.

Off the pitch, there was upheaval and change in the form of the presidency. Francis Graille was dismissed and replaced by former Rennes president Pierre Blayau, tasked with improving matters outside of the team and ensuring that Paris Saint-Germain were in a healthy state financially too. This extract from an article in *Le Monde* details exactly why Graille was removed, at least from an off-field perspective, 'Justice is investigating questionable transfers to PSG between 1998 and 2003, before the presidency of Francis Graille. The latter had to dismiss his right-hand man, Rodolphe Albert, suspected of having embezzled several hundred thousand euros for his benefit. In addition, the economic situation of the club in the capital is not very bright either. An audit commissioned by Canal+ points to poor management. At the end of 2004, PSG posted 31 million euros of net losses and the 2005 balance sheet should again reach a negative balance of ten million euros.'

To put it bluntly, PSG weren't in a position to spend big like they had done in previous seasons. In the summer of 2005 they spent €18m and only made €12m from player

sales, still operating at a loss in the transfer market despite
the profit margins being healthy in the close season.
Bonaventure Kalou arrived from Auxerre while Vikash
Dhorasoo joined from AC Milan, with the latter adding
Ligue 1 championship experience to the mix after his two
wins with Lyon. Dhorasoo was a silky playmaker who had
bundles of ability but also had the tendency to fall out with
authority figures around him, something that happened
at Lyon with Jacques Santini, who sent Dhorasoo out
on loan to Bordeaux in 2001 where he formed a great
partnership with Pauleta. Returning to Lyon following
the loan spell saw success fall Dhorasoo's way in the form
of two Ligue 1 titles where he was the focal point for a
lot of Lyon's attacking output. Now managed by former
PSG man Paul Le Guen, Dhorasoo was like a man reborn
alongside the likes of Juninho. His form for Lyon was so
impressive that he earned a move to AC Milan and earned
a recall to the French national team five years after his
first cap. Things started to look like they were on the up
for Dhorasoo, but his move to Milan didn't quite go to
plan. He didn't start as often as he would have liked, so
a return to France beckoned. However, it would be the
capital where he would now call home.

On paper, PSG looked like they could challenge
for honours. Dhorasoo and Rothen supplying the likes
of Pauleta and Kalou had some fans salivating at what
delights they could be witnessing in the Parc des Princes,
but instead of unbridled entertainment it was a campaign
riddled with inconsistencies and a clear split in home and
away form. The home supporters clearly drove PSG on
but on their travels, it was a completely different story.
Towards the end of November, having just defeated

Bordeaux 2-0 courtesy of goals from Yepes and Pauleta, PSG found themselves in second place. One win in their next four games saw them drop to sixth but they rose to third the following week, looking set to be one of the teams who could challenge a formidable Lyon side but at the very least they appeared as certainties to gain a Champions League spot.

Of course, that didn't pan out the way they had hoped. From January until the end of the campaign, PSG won just four games in the league. They won just twice away from home all season in Ligue 1, both of which came in the first half. It was, to be frank, abysmal. Yet, despite their form in Ligue 1, PSG found themselves on yet another run in the Coupe de France. While their league form was in tatters they seemed to reserve their best performances – or certainly their most important performances – for the Coupe de France. After beating Auxerre 1-0 in the last 32, CFA side Lyon La Duchère 3-0 in the last 16, Lille 2-1 in the quarter-final and Nantes by the same scoreline in the semi-final, they set up a historic occasion as, for the first time, Paris Saint-Germain and Marseille would face off in the Coupe de France Final. The game on its own was a massive occasion in France but to meet in the final was extraordinary, and the rivalry had gone up a few notches in recent years. Since that famous game at the Stade Vélodrome where Ronaldinho ran riot, the rivalry had become France's premier match.

In the mid-2000s, Le Classique had become a speciality for PSG, almost assuring them of at least one victory over their rivals every season. Between October 2002 and October 2005, they went nine games unbeaten against Marseille, matching the then record set by their opponents in the mid-1990s. While trophies may have escaped them during this period, PSG were on top in the rivalry and that was something the fans reminded Marseille of at every opportunity. There was Pauleta's magical display at the Parc des Princes where he lobbed Fabien Barthez, but the following game that same year in November was dangerously tense, with projectiles raining down on to the players and the field of play. Two players, Frédéric Déhu and Fabrice Fiorèse, had made the jump from PSG to Marseille that summer and both drew the fierce wrath of the Paris Saint-Germain ultras.

Déhu was a beloved captain of PSG and, prior to the Coupe de France win in 2004, it was announced that at the end of his contract he would leave and join Marseille for nothing. Throughout the final, Déhu was booed and jeered by his own supporters. You can see on Déhu's face every time the camera focuses on him how emotional he was. He misplaced passes, he mistimed tackles and it became clear that, mentally, Déhu was not focused on the game but rather the noise coming from his own fans. Déhu barely lifted the trophy above his head at the presentation and ran down the tunnel in tears to get away from the boos. 'It's a shame,' said Fiorèse after the game, visibly disgusted. 'We thought we had our audience behind us. The party is ruined.'

Fiorèse, however, soon followed his team-mate to Marseille and quickly became the joint most-hated man in Paris in 2004. 'A sect and a prison' was how Fiorèse described life under Vahid Halilhodžić in the French capital with the two quickly falling out and the player being placed on the transfer list. Rumour has it that Déhu had persuaded Fiorèse to ditch Paris and go south, but when the latter said that Marseille was 'the club of his dreams' the Parisian fans who had fallen in love with his tenacity, aggression and hard work soon fell out of love in the blink of an eye. Fiorèse was the kind of player you would hate if he was playing against you, known for his simulation and tendency to like a booking or five (there was even an incident where he spat at Marseille fans in the Vélodrome), but any goodwill had gone instantly and the duo were set to start for Marseille in their first return to le Parc since their departures. It's safe to say that the Parc des Princes was ready for blood that night and the fans knew exactly who they wanted.

Le Parisien described it as a 'night in hell' for both players, with PSG's ultras unveiling 13 distinct banners just aimed at those two. 'Déhu, Fiorèse, only rats leave the ship' read one, while another – with more than a hint of homophobia attached to it – said 'Fiorèse, if PSG is a prison then return the bar of soap!'. PSG captain Sylvain Armand received a straight red card in the first half for a tackle on Fiorèse, who PSG fans didn't take their eyes off from the first warm-up pre-match. PSG eventually won 2-1 with goals from Pauleta and Édouard Cissé, who would ironically go on to play for Marseille later in his career – but the story of the two former Parisians now plying their trade for their arch-rival took precedent over anything else. PSG had not only beaten Marseille, but they had stuck one in on the two 'traitors'.

Three days later, in the Coupe de la Ligue, the two sides met again. PSG decided to rest the majority of their first-team players and played a reserve team against a full-strength Marseille. The PSG kids won 3-2 and wrapped what PSG fans would call 'Le Grand Huit' (The

Great Eight) to signify the eight consecutive wins over their rivals. Fast forward almost a year and tensions were rising yet again. Lorik Cana, another PSG fan favourite, jumped ship and would score the only goal in Marseille's 1-0 win, their first since April 2002. Two hours before kick-off, PSG players and staff complained of the smell of ammonia in their changing room. Marseille president Pape Diouf responded, 'There was a sewage problem in the dressing room area earlier in the day and we used the same cleaning product we always do. The reason the smell wasn't so strong in our dressing room was because we opened the window a little earlier ... and as for them being told to change in some box under the stands, that's total rubbish.'

Which brings the rivalry up to the 2005/06 Coupe de France Final, a meeting that French football had been anticipating for months. For Marseille it was a chance to win their first trophy since 1993, while for PSG it was the last chance to bring any positivity to what had been an indifferent season. Finishing ninth in Ligue 1 wasn't good enough but domestic cup triumph equalled silverware and a place in the UEFA Cup the following season, as if they needed any more motivation.

Bonaventure Kalou opened the scoring with a thunderous shot within the first five minutes, wheeling away with unreal speed to celebrate with his team-mates and fans. PSG, the perennial cup team of the season, had stormed into the lead with relative ease. Marseille weren't completely ready to let the game slip from their grasp in the first half and held out to keep the scoreline down into the half-time break, which provided time to regroup and change strategy, but PSG had other ideas. Just three minutes after the break Dhorasoo picked up the ball on the halfway line. He kept running into the acres of green space that Marseille's midfield had afforded him, before teeing up a shot from around 25 yards out. Dhorasoo hit it like an arrow and, despite Barthez's attempts to get a strong hand on to the effort, he could only watch as the ball skimmed his fingertips and went in. An incredible goal. Toifilou Maoulida would grab one back for Marseille but it was too little too late as PSG ran out winners in a sensational final, watched at home by 11 million viewers. Pauleta lifted the trophy aloft as Marseille fans drifted out of the Stade de France, but the Parisians partied long into the night. They were ready and prepared, after a long and arduous season, to celebrate. Yet, this coincidentally marked the start of the period at Paris Saint-Germain that is simultaneously unforgettable and disastrous.

The tone for the 2006/07 season was set almost immediately after the World Cup in Germany. France had reached the final but lost on penalties to Italy, with the nation still bemused by Zinedine Zidane's now infamous headbutt on Marco Materazzi. But while the nation was coming to terms with the loss, Vikash Dhorasoo was putting the finishing touches to perhaps the most unique and personal football documentary to date. *Substitute* was a joint project by Dhorasoo and French director Fred Poulet, filming the playmaker's time in the France squad for the finals. Filmed entirely on a handheld 8mm camera, it documented the mood of Dhorasoo throughout the tournament as he dealt with being somewhat of a forgotten member of the squad and how the breakthrough of Franck Ribéry essentially pushed him into the background. There's a sense throughout that Dhorasoo felt cheated by

France boss Raymond Domenech, who picked the PSG man for every qualifier. 'For two years, he [Domenech] trained me to climb a mountain. And the day I could climb it, he took the neighbour's son.'

That 'neighbour's son' could have been either Ribéry or Zidane. Dhorasoo benefited from the retirement of Zidane following Euro 2004 and with Ribéry still not breaking through fully at that point and Robert Pires having an irreparable relationship with Domenech, Dhorasoo was free to flourish. He felt, rightly so, that he deserved a chance to shine at the World Cup given that he had been a driving force in getting France there in the first place, but Zidane returning from retirement put him on the bench yet again. Fans booed Dhorasoo in warm-up games when he replaced Zidane simply because he was replacing Zidane. 'I'm getting fed up here in Germany. I wonder what I came here for, except for a film, because my World Cup went wrong,' said a despondent Dhorasoo into the lens of his camera. If it wasn't clear before, he had made it clear now. What should have been the peak of his career created a different range of emotions and sparked the downfall of his time at Paris Saint-Germain.

Dhorasoo openly criticised manager Guy Lacombe in *L'Equipe*, claiming to be 'completely demoralised', and questioned why both he and Jérôme Rothen were banished to the reserves in the early stages of the new campaign. Lacombe wasn't pleased with their attitudes and dropped them to essentially send a message to the rest of the squad that any ill-discipline would be met with banishment to the reserve team. Lacombe claimed that Dhorasoo had a back injury, but the latter then accused the former of lying about it. The back and forth continued with the manager saying in the press, 'In the business world, he would be dismissed on the spot. Abroad, we can impose fairly strong penalties. In France, it's a bit complicated because of labor law. In absolute terms, he has excluded himself. Now we have to see what is legally possible.'

Soon after, Dhorasoo became the first player since the advent of the Professional Footballers' Charter in 1973 to be sacked by his own club. The official statement from Paris Saint-Germain listed his 'refusal to play for the reserves, his lack of loyalty, also his insubordination, disobedience and his permanent air of provocation' as to why they took the decision.

Perhaps predictably, the PSG season continued on a downward spiral after the very public fallout, winning just four games in Ligue 1 up until February. It had got to a point in January where the possibility of relegation became a real issue and, when Guy Lecombe was sacked after a 2-1 home defeat to ten-man Valenciennes, the club decided to return to their glory days of the 1990s by appointing Paul Le Guen as his replacement.

Le Guen had won three consecutive Ligue 1 titles with Lyon a few seasons prior but was coming off the back of a nightmare spell with Glasgow Rangers where he achieved the incredibly rare distinction of being the club's shortest-serving manager (at the time) and the first to leave without completing a single season. To say Le Guen's stock was low at this point is putting it mildly, but returning to the club where he spent the most successful years of his career was perhaps the best opportunity to rekindle the glory he achieved at Lyon. However, the job in Paris was one that few could turn around. When Le Guen joined, PSG had failed to win their last eight Ligue

1 games and looked like a team gripped with worry. 'We're too tense, we're shackled by fear. Any time our opponents hint at getting the upper hand, we bottle it,' said striker Bonaventure Kalou, and he wasn't wrong. Not only did PSG have to deal with the intense focus from the majority of the media – most of whom were based in Paris anyway – but they had to deal with the even more intense, volatile and occasionally violent fanbase.

PSG's ultras, who by this point had gained a reputation for being violent, demeaning and in some sectors racist, demanding nothing less than 100 per cent from their team. Anything short of that usually resulted in booing, jeering, physical altercations or arriving at the training ground to 'advise' the squad on how to perform better. PSG sitting just three points off the relegation zone only amplified any issues. Bernard Mendy was once targeted by some ultras for his performances and responded by flipping them the middle finger. This only made the relationship between Mendy and the ultras worse, but it was a visual expression of how the full-back – and probably the rest of the PSG team – felt in those moments. But while all this hectic chaos was underway, Le Guen was busy putting his team together. Jérôme Rothen was reintroduced to the fold while players like Pauleta, Mario Yepes and a host of others were brought back onside by Le Guen's man-management. Of Le Guen's first six games in charge, he lost just once and won twice, against Monaco and Nancy, in a run which saw them get up to 15th and seemingly in a good place, until a run of four losses in a row plummeted them into the relegation zone. They were second from bottom in the table with nine games to go. Relegation had gone from a mere silhouette in the distance to a harsh reality within the space of four weeks. Somehow, Paris Saint-Germain pulled a rabbit out of the hat.

Six wins from nine games – as many wins as they had prior to the miraculous turnaround – were enough to save PSG from disaster and to finish nine points clear of relegation. Crisis averted, so now it was time to learn their lessons and build upon their seemingly strong foundations. With experienced players such as goalkeeper Mickaël Landreau, Yepes, Rothen, Mendy and Pauleta mixing it with a fresh group of talented youngsters like David N'Gog, Mamadou Sakho and Youssouf Mulumbu as well as new signings Zoumana Camara from Saint-Étienne and Peguy Luyindula crossing the divide from Marseille into Paris, many felt that PSG had a team capable of challenging for honours. President Alain Cayzac was one of those who was especially optimistic over life under Le Guen, saying, 'I trust Paul Le Guen to find the solution that will make us win. We don't forget that we endured a tough season last year, which left some scars. But we're ambitious and I'm convinced that we'll have a much better season, even if we don't claim that we will win the league. I am confident.'

The club, internally, was optimistic as a whole. A good squad of players working under a manager who had a habit of winning Ligue 1 titles seemed like a promising mix. Yet somehow things got even worse. It took six Ligue 1 games for PSG to get off the mark – 2-0 away to Le Mans – and at the beginning of December they were in the relegation zone. 'Nothing went our way. We had no luck, and plenty of injuries, and we lost confidence. The negative spiral brought us down really quickly. It was almost like we had forgotten how to play football and win matches,' said

Rothen in an interview with *FourFourTwo*, echoing the blips of many struggling teams from the past.

The luck goes against you, you get a few injuries to key players at key moments, a misfiring striker finally scores, only for the goal to be ruled out for offside – they're all common tropes of teams in horrendous form. The problem for PSG was that this wasn't a blip anymore. Taking into account the past two campaigns, this was a pattern. That run of six wins in nine games at the back end of the previous season was looking like the anomaly while the losses, weak performances and fan unrest was becoming more and more common at the Parc des Princes.

Poor tactical decisions from Le Guen and scrutiny of his man-management thrusted him further into the spotlight, with many questioning if he was the right man for PSG in their current situation. There seemed to be a lack of drive or fire from within Le Guen, the polar opposite of what you want from a manager in a relegation battle. The ultras asked for Le Guen to walk several times and called for him to be sacked as well, leading one to believe that both fans and players weren't convinced by the former Rangers boss. Strangely, however, this same team enjoyed good runs in both the Coupe de France and Coupe de la Ligue. While PSG were on their knees in Ligue 1, Le Guen's men recorded a Coupe de la Ligue triumph over Lens courtesy of a stoppage-time Mendy winner, while in the Coupe de France, only an extra-time winner from Lyon's Sidney Govou in the final prevented Paris Saint-Germain from winning a domestic cup double. Clearly, this was a team built for the occasion and one-off match rather than a sustained period of time.

Success could not go without controversy and in that Coupe de la Ligue Final, the PSG ultras unveiled a banner that said 'Paedophiles, unemployed and inbred: welcome to the Ch'tis'. Ch'tis is a negative nickname given to people from the region in northern France where Lens is located, popularised by the hugely successful French film *Bienvenue chez les Ch'tis* or *Welcome to the Sticks* in English. France went into uproar with the mayor of Lens demanding the final be replayed. It wasn't, and PSG kept hold of the trophy, but they were subsequently fined and banned from the competition the following season – albeit the punishment was overturned on appeal. The ultra group the Boulogne Boys disbanded as a result of the incident and PSG fans as a whole were tarnished with the same brush.

It wouldn't be the last time that the ultras affected PSG's results either, taking matters into their own hands midway through the season when they showed up to the training ground to threaten players verbally and physically to perform better. From December they boycotted the first 15 minutes of every home game. They would be in the stands but wouldn't sing or cheer the team. Just silence. Unsurprisingly, the players didn't respond well to threats and silence in the stadium, but in April following a 3-0 defeat at Caen, things took a turn for the worse.

Between 23 January and 20 April, PSG picked up seven points. The crisis had become a harsh and stark reality; they were in a relegation fight. With just four games left, PSG were in the bottom three of Ligue 1 and panic had started to set in among the fans. The ultras painted the sentence 'You go down and we will gun you down' across the walls of the training ground, they destroyed the windshield of Sylvain Armand's car and threatened anyone in sight. The ultras felt like the players didn't care as much as they did and that the only way to motivate them to perform better was to trash the training ground. In an interview with Julien Laurens in *FourFourTwo*, one member of the ultras explained their actions, 'We felt all the players weren't focused and committed enough. It looked like they didn't care – but for us, PSG is everything. It's our life. We felt we had to save the club because it was going down the wrong path. The only thing we could do to get the players to wake up and raise their game was be aggressive and put them under pressure. The best way to do it was those visits to the training ground.'

Did this action from the ultras help? Absolutely not. The players, now frightened for their own safety, felt the extra pressure put on them by both the situation and the fans. Not only did they have to fight relegation, they had to fight their own ultras too. Club president Alain Cayzac was also sacked and replaced by Simon Tahar, who was then replaced by Michel Moulin, a man who knew little about the inner workings of football. Moulin and Le Guen had to steer the club through perhaps the most important four games in their short history; four games to save their Ligue 1 status and maybe even the future of the club.

Up first was Auxerre at home, a chance to show the ultras that they could fight and perform. A double from Amara Diané plus a quick opener from a retiring Pauleta gave the Parisians a huge win and set them up perfectly to get a positive result in their next game, against Toulouse. It finished 1-1 after PSG conceded an 87th-minute equaliser and, while not a disaster of a result, it wasn't a positive one either. PSG remained in the relegation places and had to pick up at least four points in their final two games, at home to Saint-Étienne and away at Sochaux. When they drew against Saint-Étienne and managed to keep their fate in their own hands while jumping out of the relegation zone, the nerviest of nervy finishes was playing on the minds of everyone at the club.

Only 800 PSG fans were able to travel to Sochaux but many estimate that a few thousand could have made the journey. Everyone wanted to be there, whether it was to witness the relief of survival or give the club a piece of their mind. All PSG needed to do was win and they would be safe, a simple task but one PSG had struggled to see out for the majority of the season. Heading into the final ten minutes, the two sides were level at 1-1. Diané had scored the opener and had been the saviour of PSG for the few wins they managed to pick up. Against Sochaux, he was the man for the occasion. As the clock struck 82 minutes, Diané's weak roller of a shot trickled over the line to give PSG a massive, massive lead. The fans, penned into their allocated area behind the corner flag, erupted. They celebrated like they had won the league and, in some ways, this was just as monumental.

When the final whistle went, emotions got the better of everyone. Tears flowed down faces of both fans and players, while Pauleta revealed a shirt saying 'Merci Aux Supporters' as he bid farewell to those who had worshipped him for many years. He and his team-mates had kept the club up when many felt they were simply too big to go down. But the most important part of this survival was not to be realised until a handful of years later. Those on the pitch and in the stands knew it was an important moment but it would be one that changed Paris Saint-Germain, Ligue 1, French football, European and world football too. If they had gone down that night in Sochaux, there's a high chance that a big event in June 2011 would never have happened.

15

Ruée vers l'or du Qatar –
Qatari gold rush

THE YEAR of 2010 may go down as the one when French football changed drastically, both on and off the pitch, and, to understand exactly how, you have to go back to March 2009. That was when Qatar officially registered its bid for the 2022 World Cup, aiming to become the first Arab nation to host the event and wanting to do everything in its power to obtain the tournament. The chairman of the bid committee, Sheikh Mohammed bin Hamad bin Khalifa Al Thani – who was the son of the then Emir of Qatar and also the president of the Qatar Football Association, Hamad bin Khalifa Al Thani – had a close friend in the Qatari tennis scene by the name of Nasser Al-Khelaifi. Al-Khelaifi was a middling tennis player who made less than zero impact in the worldwide tennis game, but had befriended the Emir's son and grew to be one of his most trusted allies.

Qatar had the aim to become one of the world's leading forces in practically every department, or at least partner up and invest in major companies. In 2005, the Qatari

Investment Authority (QIA) was established to develop, invest and manage state reserve funds and other assets, and in 2006 its operations officially began. It started investing into all sorts of areas such as real estate in London. As of 2017 the group owned 879 commercial and residential properties in the city and purchased the Canary Wharf Group (CWG), which owns the building nicknamed the 'Walkie Talkie', among others. QIA also purchased the HSBC Tower in Canary Wharf, as well as Harrods, and has a 95 per cent stake in The Shard, while another unit of the QIA, named Qatar Holding, owns a whole host of London hotels. Essentially, you cannot walk through London without seeing something that Qatar either owns or has invested in.

Yet, despite these rich portfolios of land in London, hotels and dealings with major banks like Barclays, one sector of the world was missing for the Qataris. Sport, more specifically football. They had their eyes on the 2022 World Cup by registering their bid in 2009 and they knew that to secure the hosting rights, they had to make promises to people in high places. One of those influential individuals was none other than UEFA chief and French football legend Michel Platini, whose vote in the World Cup bidding was crucial. On 23 November 2010, at the Elysée Palace, Platini was to have lunch with then French president Nicolas Sarkozy and it wouldn't be hyperbole to say that the following events changed football forever.

As Platini walked in to the Elysée Palace, he quickly realised he wasn't the only person due to sit at the table. Sarkozy was alongside officials from Qatar including crown prince Sheikh Tamim Bin Hamad Al Thani. Platini soon realised what the message was: vote for

Qatar to host the 2022 World Cup. Nine days later, FIFA awarded the 2022 World Cup to Qatar. What followed brought FIFA down and marred the legendary career of arguably France's greatest player.

The decision to award Qatar the World Cup opened up allegations of corruption against FIFA and those involved in the bid, with this lunch meeting being at the forefront of the investigation against Platini. The former Juventus star has maintained his innocence throughout the investigation and denied that Sarkozy urged him to vote for Qatar, but did admit, 'Sarkozy never asked me to vote for Qatar, but I knew what would be good.' Platini later admitted that he may have changed his vote from the USA to Qatar, but still maintains that no wrongdoing occurred in the securing of the World Cup to Qatar. But while Platini voted for Qatar, Qatar ensured France benefited from Platini's 'generosity'.

In 2011, Qatar Airways purchased 50 aeroplanes from Airbus, the French aviation company, while Doha-based network Al Jazeera spent hundreds of millions of euros to broadcast Ligue 1 and the Champions League in Qatar. Yet the biggest beneficiary was yet to come. In 2018, as part of the Football Leaks story, it was alleged that Sarkozy told Hamad bin Khalifa Al Thani that if he launched a brand-new sports channel in France and bought a football club under the Qatari Sports Investments (QSI) name, the president would persuade Platini to vote for Qatar. Platini's son Laurent would soon end up working for QSI, beIN Sports was launched, and Paris Saint-Germain, the club that Sarkozy and his two sons supported, was taken over by QSI (Qatar had previously shown interest in buying PSG back in 2006 but then-owners Canal+ and the City of Paris felt uncomfortable taking money off of a regime that they felt had 'questionable' human rights laws). It was at a time when Sarkozy was under major pressure due to the rise in unemployment and, in some ways, his move actually saved French football – or at the very least prevented a potential collapse.

There were fears that the 2012/13 Ligue 1 campaign would not go ahead due to the pending television rights crisis. Some chairmen were rumoured to believe that clubs could have gone out of business if no one was able to compete and bid against Canal+. In that summer, however, Al Jazeera Sport bought the international TV rights for Ligue 1 for six years at a cost of €192m and its involvement was described as a 'god send' to French football at the time. The director of Al Jazeera then was none other than Nasser Al-Khelaifi, the man who QSI and Sheikh Tamim – the head of QSI – placed as the new Paris Saint-Germain president. The Qatari revolution of PSG and French football was well and truly under way, and it didn't show signs of slowing down. Al Jazeera's involvement in the television rights situation gifted clubs the revenue they needed to survive, while PSG's seemingly unlimited wealth saw them barge into the transfer market with a blank chequebook. Much like Manchester City in 2008, there was a new player in town and they weren't prepared to wait and sit around. PSG wanted to make an immediate splash, but first a structure had to be put in place off the field.

Before delving into what effect and impact this had on football, it's just as important to look at what was happening off the field to prompt this purchase. To put it bluntly, Qatar's human rights record is shocking and appalling. According to the United States Department of State, expatriate workers from nations throughout Asia and parts of Africa are routinely subjected to forced labour and, in some instances, prostitution. They regularly have their rights violated in various ways, mainly beatings, withholding of payment, charging workers for benefits, severe restrictions on freedom of movement (such as the confiscation of passports, travel documents, or exit permits), threats of legal action, and sexual assault. Most of the workers who have been constructing the stadia for the 2022 World Cup have been subjected to these punishments, and it hasn't gone unnoticed. They are tortured, beaten, essentially enslaved and made to work ungodly hours. It's barbaric and is condemned across the world by nations and groups such as Amnesty International. Qatar still has the death penalty with Amnesty reporting that the number of death sentences passed in Qatar increased from at least two in 2019 to at least four in 2020, with a Nepali man being sentenced to death via firing squad in April 2021.

Homosexuality is illegal and in 1998 an American citizen visiting Qatar was sentenced to six months in prison and 90 lashes for homosexual activity. Yet this is a country that FIFA deemed suitable for their largest event. FIFA knew, yet did nothing about it. The awarding of the World Cup to Qatar fits perfectly into their overall plan to use sport as a way to deflect from their own issues and to create an image of Qatar that isn't accurate and isn't exactly how they are presenting it. The World Cup in 2022 will not be the Qatar that everyday citizens see, the same way Russia in 2018 wasn't. The World Cup and the purchase of Paris Saint-Germain are all sports-washing tactics – the practice of a controversial company or country using sports sponsorship to improve its reputation – by Qatar.

It's why buying PSG was all part of the plan of Qatar and QSI. By purchasing Sarkozy's favourite club, they got their feet under the table in France. It also presented QSI with an opportunity to build a brand of their own, a centrepiece of their entire portfolio. In theory, QSI would build a team full of superstars that would eventually win the Champions League, thus making them heroes in Paris. At least, that was the theory. All sports-washing projects rely on the fanbases of the clubs to worship the ground they walk on. Manchester City fans loved Sheikh Mansour for giving them billions to spend on title-winning teams and they thank him for the success he's given them. If Newcastle United have the same success as City then their fans will do the same with their Saudi ownership. It's sports-washing 101. The big challenge for QSI in Paris was convincing the notoriously opinionated and violent ultras that Qatar was the way forward. Would they tackle it head on or would they focus more on a wider audience of younger Parisians and those across the world? The first move of the QSI appeared to point in one direction, however: when in doubt, splash record amounts of money.

With Nasser Al-Khelaifi as president, a sporting director/general manager was needed to oversee the incomings and outgoings. Former Milan and Inter manager Leonardo returned to the club as general manager in the hope that his contacts in Italy and Brazil could find talent from overseas to add to the pre-Qatari signings of Nicolas Douchez from Rennes and highly rated young Lorient striker Kevin Gameiro. A young Belgian winger at Lille called Eden Hazard was linked with a move to Paris but the French champions were reluctant to sell to a domestic rival, no matter the price, while the central attacking midfield area was identified as a key position almost immediately.

The remit was to spend big on a young, exciting and dynamic playmaker who could be the lynchpin of the attack and be the creative hub of the team. Leonardo eyed up Santos youngster Ganso, someone he had identified from his time working as Milan manager. Ganso and fellow Brazilian forward Neymar had propelled Santos to glory in the years prior, but the club's high estimation of the midfielder meant PSG, even with their new-found riches, walked away from a deal. Hatem Ben Arfa, who was at Newcastle by this time, was also considered by Leonardo's links to Serie A and Italy came up gold for who they ultimately decided to settle on.

By spending €43m on Javier Pastore from Palermo, PSG did a few things. They not only set a club and national transfer record – beating the previous high when they signed Nicolas Anelka from Real Madrid in 2000 – but they made a statement. They essentially said that while they were prepared to spend big, they wanted to do so on younger players rather than go for star names immediately. Was that due to their relatively small reputation at the time akin to what Manchester City went through in 2008 or was it a mission statement and a well-thought-out strategy? Either way, Pastore represented PSG's transfer strategy perfectly. He was young, exciting, extremely talented and straight out of Serie A – a Leonardo special, as you'll find out with some of the signings going forward – but he was the ideal first major signing. Pastore joined alongside Jérémy Ménez from Roma, Blaise Matuidi from Saint-Étienne, Mohamed Sissoko from Juventus, Salvatore Sirigu from Palermo and the centre-back pairing of Milan Bisevac from Valenciennes and Diego Lugano from Fenerbahçe. That was the summer window out of the way, with Pastore being the headline act, but questions remained over the managerial position. Would QSI and the new regime want their own man in charge?

Antoine Kombouaré had been in charge of PSG since 2009 and had been performing well in the two years prior to the Qatari takeover. His debut season saw the team finish in mid-table but take home the Coupe de France while his sophomore campaign saw PSG finish fourth and maintain their Europa League status. So far, Kombouaré had achieved what he had beenasked. The hierarchy at PSG wanted to regain their status as a club that regularly played European football, and under him, they had done just that. So, with a line-up including the likes of Nenê, Pastore, Guillaume Hoarau, Matuidi, Mamadou Sakho and many more, hopes were high for PSG heading into the 2011/12 season.

Pastore and Gameiro appeared to have formed a formidable partnership with one another, yet PSG weren't sailing away from any potential challengers just yet. A slight dip in form in November opened the door for the chasing pack to close in, but PSG rectified that by going unbeaten in their four remaining Ligue 1 fixtures of 2011. Sat top of the table with the January transfer window approaching and the winter break allowing valuable rest time for the squad, it would surely be madness for PSG to remove their manager. Wouldn't it?

Well, for any other club it would be ludicrous to replace the manager who got them to the top of Ligue 1, but the powers that be in Paris weren't entirely pleased with Kombouaré. For weeks prior to the winter break, reports kept emerging that Leonardo was talking to out-of-work managers about potentially taking over, including Carlo Ancelotti and Frank Rijkaard. Some within the QSI regime felt Kombouaré's style of football was too conservative and that he wasn't up to the task when it came to managing the potential big-name signings that they aimed to make in the summer (just to be clear – QSI weren't happy with how they thought Kombouaré would deal with signings they hadn't made yet). In other words, Qatar and Leonardo felt that he just wasn't fashionable enough or a big-enough name to lead their modern-day Galácticos – or shall we just call them the Galáctiques?

When Kombouaré was moved on, the rumours of Leonardo liaising with Ancelotti were true and the Italian was appointed just after Christmas in 2011. The remit for Ancelotti was clear: win domestically and guide PSG in the direction of becoming a European giant in the next few years. Europe was all that Qatar really cared about. Ligue 1 and domestic French football, to them, was a mere formality. The mentality among some was that while winning the league was important, they would do so at a canter due to their wealth and array of stars. Ironically, the first season under QSI showed exactly why that mentality is completely wrong and why, if you think like that, you'll always get punished for it.

Montpellier, managed by former Bordeaux player René Girard and owned by the charismatic yet controversial figure of Louis Nicollin, weren't expected to do anything in 2011/12. Mid-table and maybe a good run in the Coupe de France would have been a more than suitable campaign, but they started like a house on fire. Up until mid-December, they had only lost twice and saw themselves battling with PSG at the top of the table but a dip in form heading in to the winter break put Montpellier back into second, probably leaving PSG thinking that their rivals' race was starting to slow down and that, eventually, les Rouge et Bleu would romp to the title. It didn't exactly work out like that. Montpellier returned from the break with five straight wins, then a draw at the Parc des Princes followed by two wins over Bordeaux and Caen and a draw away at Dijon. After beating Caen, Montpellier would only lose two more Ligue 1 games and took PSG to the wire, needing just a point at Auxerre on the final day to clinch a historic title. PSG would come from behind to take the three points at Lorient but it was all in vain. Montpellier had pulled off the unthinkable and clinched the Ligue 1 championship by winning at Auxerre (it took two and a half hours to finish the game due to protests and crowd trouble from the Auxerre fans, but they did it).

The minnows had triumphed over the new evil empire of French football. Girard would go on to say that their title win was 'A shot in the arm for French football. It just goes to show that everyone can beat everyone and that money isn't the be-all and end-all. We're a club of mates, a club that brings young players through and gives them a chance. At the end of the day, it's worked out well for us.'

Very nice words from Girard, but was he right about their success being a shot in the arm for French football? As spectacular and historic as Montpellier's title win was, it effectively ended the underdog in France and in Ligue 1.

To QSI and the new-look Paris Saint-Germain, this was highly embarrassing. With all due respect to Montpellier, the perception at the time was, 'If you're losing Ligue 1 to minnows, how do you expect to compete with Europe's elite?' They weren't wrong. Once the excitement around Montpellier had died down a bit, the focus and attention turned towards Paris. What would the Parisians do to prevent this happening again? They just spent even more money.

Between the 2007/08 and the 2011/12 season, four different teams won Ligue 1. Between 2012/13 and 2015/16, only one won it. PSG reacted to failure by filling up their squad with superstars and world-class talent – spending around €100m on Marco Verratti, Gregory van der Wiel, Ezequiel Lavezzi, Thiago Silva and Zlatan Ibrahimović – further extending the gap between themselves and the rest of French football.

The acquisitions of those elite-level talents saw PSG win their first Ligue 1 title since 1994 and officially ushered in the QSI era. Finishing top by 12 points and with Ibrahimović being crowned top scorer with 30 goals, PSG were dominant and imperious, everything Qatar had wanted from them. A quarter-final exit at the hands of Barcelona in the Champions League wasn't ideal, but it was progress. They had shown that they could go toe to toe with one of Europe's elite and much was expected when Laurent Blanc was appointed as Ancelotti's replacement the following season (Ancelotti went to Real Madrid and, ironically, won the Champions League at the first attempt).

Blanc had carved out a relatively impressive managerial career up until his PSG appointment, winning Ligue 1 with Bordeaux in 2009 and carefully dealing with the post-2010 World Cup fallout of the French national team. With Edinson Cavani and Marquinhos joining from Napoli and Roma respectively and the retirement of David Beckham – who spent the final six months of his career on loan in Paris, a huge coup for the 'brand' of Paris Saint-Germain – as well as Lucas Digne joining from Lille, PSG yet again were formidable domestically. They strolled to a nine-point victory in Ligue 1 over nearest rivals Monaco and a Coupe de la Ligue triumph over Lyon gave Blanc two trophies in his first campaign, but Champions League success eluded him and PSG once again, this time exiting on away goals to José Mourinho's Chelsea.

An unprecedented domestic quadruple followed with the third consecutive Ligue 1 title wrapped up alongside the two cup competitions and the Trophée des Champions. Yet again, however, the Champions League proved to be the stumbling block for Paris. They managed to eliminate Chelsea courtesy of goals from David Luiz and Thiago Silva, but another loss to Barcelona sent them packing in the quarter-finals once more. The first knockout meeting between the two clubs a few years ago looked like the beginning of something transformative in Paris in terms of European football but instead it brought about stagnation and a metaphorical brick wall because no matter who they played, no matter what the circumstances, PSG would always find a way to be eliminated in the quarter-final stage. And that frustration was what changed their managerial approach the following season.

Once again, PSG reigned supreme in France. They were untouchable, losing just twice and collecting 96 points as part of another domestic quadruple, but once again they were knocked out in the quarter-final of the Champions League. On this occasion, the board felt it was such a terrible exit that changes were needed in the dugout. Laurent Blanc decided in the second leg away at Manchester City – when chasing a goal due to having drawn 2-2 at home and thus losing any advantage – to start with a 5-3-2 formation, something they hadn't done all season and knocking the line-up out of its stride. A 4-2-3-1 system was the tried and tested method, but the deviation in tactics almost meant that PSG were put on the back foot immediately by their own formation. QSI and the board were not pleased. Not only was this another failure in Europe, but it was a failure against Abu Dhabi and Manchester City, the one team they didn't want to lose to.

Blanc was out despite his haul of trophies, with PSG essentially directing their entire focus on Europe. The project had pretty much become Champions League or bust for Qatar and every decision after Blanc's sacking was made with Europe in mind. The feeling was that Ligue 1 and France had been conquered and dominated, with no one able to create a team able to battle PSG's stars, giving them ample time to focus entirely on Europe. In hindsight, it was a plan that could only end in failure and in the first post-Blanc season, it certainly went that way.

Unai Emery had just guided Sevilla to three consecutive Europa League titles. He had rightly earned his crown as the Europa League King. The powers that be at PSG saw his CV and assumed he would be the right man to lead the club to European glory. The one glaringly obvious issue with that logic was simple: Emery had won the Europa

League, not the Champions League. Before joining PSG he had only progressed from the Champions League group stage once, in his first campaign, with Valencia in 2010/2011. Excluding that, Emery had won just five games in three separate Champions League seasons. It was a bold strategy but it became abundantly clear early on that it was not going to pay off.

The first half of Emery's debut season included four losses, just one more than the previous two campaigns combined. Monaco, who had slowly been putting together an outstanding team across the years under the guidance of sporting director Luis Campos, led the way. Radamel Falcao, Bernardo Silva, Fabinho and a young forward from the Paris suburb of Bondy named Kylian Mbappé were proving to be the main threat to PSG's Ligue 1 crown. The Parisians' air of invincibility had evaporated and while their second half of the Ligue 1 season improved drastically, their year was overshadowed by the Champions League last-16 tie against their European brick wall Barcelona. Essentially, the entire season was dependent on these games. Ligue 1 and Monaco were proving a stiff test but if PSG could finally conquer Europe, domestic matters could be forgotten. When Barcelona were dealt a footballing lesson at the Parc des Princes, losing 4-0 in one of the best and most complete performances in PSG's recent history, many expected that, finally, the capital club had got over their Barcelona hoodoo.

A video was posted on to social media, after the 4-0 first leg, of Thomas Meunier, Marco Verratti, Blaise Matuidi and Julian Draxler having lunch, discussing the unlikely possibility of a Barcelona comeback in the second leg. 'If we lose 5-1, do you think we would be happy?' asked Verratti. 'No, I would be annoyed,' replied Meunier. 'Yes, I would be happy,' said both Draxler and Matuidi. Meunier, clearly perplexed by the opinions of his two team-mates, replied with 'If you lose 5-1, people will mock us. People talk and criticise them for being thrashed by PSG and we know they are a great team, but losing 5-1 to Barcelona? That's not good.' Matuidi and Draxler were happy with the prospect of simply making it out of the tie alive, while Meunier and Verratti admitted that if they were to be thrashed yet still advance, they would be unhappy. What actually transpired was outside the realms of what anyone in football could have imagined.

Barcelona scored within three minutes through Luis Suárez and, almost immediately, the nerves in the Parisian ranks set in. It was a sell-out in the Camp Nou and the atmosphere clearly affected the PSG players. The look of fear and nervousness was apparent, but there was still a long way to go and Barcelona still had to score four more goals and hope PSG didn't score one of their own.

With 40 minutes on the clock, Layvin Kurzawa tried to block a shot from Andrés Iniesta but diverted it into his own net. It was 2-0 on the night but Paris still led 4-2 on aggregate heading in to the half-time interval. Time to clear their heads, rest up, reorganise and see the tie out. That was the initial plan, but that went out of the window within five minutes of the restart. Neymar was brought down by Meunier and Messi dispatched his penalty for 3-0 but, just after the hour, Cavani got an all-important away goal and surely this was it from PSG's perspective. They had the away goal and now had a 5-3 lead on aggregate. In typical PSG fashion, however, they proceeded to throw their lead away and conspire to make their lives as difficult as possible. On 88 minutes Neymar scored a brilliant free kick, although PSG still led 5-4 on aggregate and had that away goal.

One minute into stoppage time, there were only a few more moments for Paris to waste time and seal their win. The referee had other ideas. Suárez was 'tripped' by Marquinhos in what many saw as one of the worst refereeing decisions in Champions League history (match official Deniz Aytekin was eventually removed from UEFA games over the next two seasons). Neymar converted the penalty and now it was 5-1, but still the game wasn't over. Neymar dinked a ball into the box and Sergi Roberto, unmarked at the back post, got his toe on it, diverting it into the back of the net. Barcelona 6 Paris Saint-Germain 1. The 'Remontada' had been completed. Paris Saint-Germain had just become victims of the most incredible comeback, perhaps in the modern history of football. Everyone connected with the club was shellshocked. Unai Emery paced the touchline, eagerly awaiting a giant hole to open up beneath him and swallow him. Players slumped to the ground as Barcelona staff and players paraded the pitch. PSG complained following the game, about the quality of the refereeing but the damage was done. Yes, the referee made multiple questionable decisions that went in favour of Barcelona, but PSG still threw away a four-goal first-leg advantage.

Yet the impact of this game changed everything. PSG and QSI, enraged by this travesty of a defeat, seemingly waged war on Barcelona. Verratti was supposedly keen on a move to Barcelona that summer, according to his former agent Donato Di Campli, before being 'persuaded' to stay, by Nasser Al-Khelaifi. Part of the 'persuading' from Al-Khelaifi was a simple message that signified a huge moment in the history of the club. 'We are going to sign Neymar, we are going to extend your contract, but you have to change your agent,' Di Campli said to *L'Équipe* of what he said he had been told. Paris Saint-Germain had laid the foundations down for the biggest, most lucrative transfer in football history. They were going to swoop in and snatch one of Barcelona's biggest stars and the orchestrator of the Remontada. Neymar was going to be a Parisian. And it all started with a phone call.

PSG had actually tried to sign Neymar the previous summer but the Brazilian stayed put in Spain. Neymar signed a new deal with Barcelona and his release clause – which was mandatory in all Spanish football contracts – was raised from €190m to €222m. But after the 2016/17 season, Nasser Al-Khelaifi received a phone call from Neymar's entourage. Neymar was ready to leave Barcelona so the Parisians kicked into action. They didn't want to fall foul of FIFA's Financial Fair Play Regulations but calculated that with the impact Neymar would have on the club financially, they could pay his release clause without receiving any sanctions from UEFA. Messi, Suárez, Gerard Piqué and even Neymar's own father tried to persuade him to stay in Barcelona, but Neymar wanted something new. He wanted his own team where he was the focal point. While Messi was around, that was never going to be the case. Dani Alves, who left Barcelona in 2016 for Juventus then moved on to PSG after a season, helped convince Neymar to join the Ligue 1 club. Lucas Moura, someone Neymar had known since the age of six, alongside his holiday partner Marquinhos, also helped welcome the Brazilian superstar. Perhaps most crucially was his national team captain Thiago Silva being there to add to the flurry of Brazilians at the club.

Neymar had become the world's most expensive player and had become a PSG player in one fell swoop. This is what QSI had envisioned. They were the ones breaking the transfer records, splashing all the cash on superstar talent to bring them to France. No one ever stepped back to ask if spending €222m on Neymar was the right move from a footballing sense, but no one seemed to care. There were two schools of thought from the Parisian point of view. You were either massively excited about having Neymar in your team or you were salivating at the branding opportunities. I can't imagine any of the fans saw the signing and thought, 'Wow, this is really going to increase our brand awareness in China.'

With Neymar's deal taking centre stage, PSG were also working on bringing in another star forward. Kylian Mbappé had grown up in Paris but moved to join Monaco's youth system at a young age. He was sublime in their title-winning team and captivating in Monaco's run to the Champions League semi-final of 2017, but a call from his hometown club became the next part in the Mbappé story. An initial loan for a season before a permanent transfer the following summer for €155m was all done so PSG didn't break any FFP rules.

Neymar and Mbappé were added and after a summer of unprecedented spending – albeit on two players with one fee not set to be counted until the following year – the message became clear. Don't annoy Paris Saint-Germain because, if you do, they'll just go out and buy the best. If it wasn't clear already, it was now. Money was no object to this club anymore. It was down to those on the pitch and in the dugout to make it all work.

Combined, Neymar and Mbappé scored 49 goals between them as PSG regained their Ligue 1 crown in 2017/18 and continued their domestic dominance, but yet again they failed in Europe against a Spanish giant. Real Madrid dispatched them with ease over two legs in the last 16 and while the big-money signings impressed over the course of their debut season, it was clear that managerially things had to change. The rather unspectacular, unimaginative and uninspiring Unai Emery reign was over, but now it was time for the energetic and frantic era of German Thomas Tuchel.

From the off, however, there were problems. Sporting director Antero Henrique, who was excellent at selling players at a relatively high fee, struggled to find an all-important replacement for the retiring Thiago Motta and the squad went in to the new season under Tuchel with just five recognised midfielders (Leandro Paredes was added in January). To make matters worse, it was rumoured that the managerial choices were split into three camps. Neymar and his entourage wanted Luis Enrique, the owners wanted either Mauricio Pochettino from Tottenham Hotspur or Thomas Tuchel, while Henrique wanted Sérgio Conceição or Monaco boss Leonardo Jardim. Assuming Tuchel understood that Henrique didn't want him as his first choice, the relationship between the two would be more than a bit frosty.

However, on the pitch, Tuchel had PSG back to their formidable ways again. Their first Ligue 1 defeat of the season wouldn't come until February, away at Lyon. Again, the Champions League was the one remaining jewel that PSG wanted and needed, but once more they collapsed in spectacular fashion, to Manchester United. In some ways this was even worse than the Barcelona Remontada because this Manchester United team was not at all good enough to beat a team like PSG, or at least they shouldn't have been. With a 2-0 lead from the first leg at Old Trafford, PSG had away goals in their back pocket and home advantage, yet critical errors defensively from Thilo Kehrer, bought for €30m in the summer from Schalke, and fellow summer signing Gianluigi Buffon gifted United a dramatic win.

It was another embarrassment for PSG and to commit such an atrocity in front of their own fans compounded the misery. Neymar was out for both legs due to injury, yet even he couldn't believe his eyes on the touchline when United were awarded a last-minute penalty for a harsh-looking handball by Presnel Kimpembe. PSG and the Champions League – no matter how they approached the competition, the outcome was always the same. They always found a way to embarrass themselves.

There was some initial pressure on Tuchel but common sense prevailed, as the German kept his job heading in to 2019/20, a season that would become like no other. PSG were once again expected to cruise to the Ligue 1 crown with the likes of Neymar, Thiago Silva, Mbappé and new signings Keylor Navas and Idrissa Gueye – a midfielder who was specifically wanted by Tuchel himself – but the other questions remained the same: how would they cope in Europe? During the group stages they handled themselves well. Big wins at home to Real Madrid and away to Club Brugge showcased their attacking prowess while a 1-0 victory at Galatasaray proved that in heated atmospheres they could pull out a result. Finishing top of their group, they drew Borussia Dortmund in the last 16 and faced the cauldron of the Westfalenstadion plus world football's next big thing in Erling Haaland. It would prove to be a test of what Tuchel's PSG were made of, up against one of his former clubs, but Haaland's brute force in front of goal was too much. Neymar got an important away goal but a brace from Dortmund's Norwegian superstar sealed a 2-1 win. That match proved to be PSG's last away fixture in front of any fans for the season.

On 10 March 2020, *The Guardian* reported that, as of that very day, Ligue 1 clubs would be playing behind closed doors until 15 April. The very next day, PSG hosted Dortmund in the second leg of that Champions League tie in front of no fans. COVID-19 had struck and the world had been thrust into a pandemic. No one knew it at the time, but PSG and their fellow Ligue 1 clubs had just played their final league games of the season. On 28 April it was announced that Ligue 1 and Ligue 2 campaigns would not resume, after the country banned all sporting events until September. A few days later, the LFP officially ended the season, and PSG won the 2019/20 championship on a points-per-game basis. They wouldn't resume the Champions League until August when UEFA sent the remaining eight teams to Portugal in bubbles to finish off the competition with one-legged affairs. For once, it seemed like luck was on PSG's side in Europe.

The one-legged ties aided them more due to the fact they could just play and be themselves without having to worry about big comebacks or away goals. They left it late against Atalanta in their quarter-final and strolled past RB Leipzig in the semi-final, teeing up Bayern Munich in the final. An evenly matched game between two very well-coached and highly talented teams was settled by a Parisian – for the Germans, as Kingsley Coman, formerly of PSG but allowed to leave on a free transfer to Juventus in 2014, nodded a winner in for Bayern Munich to give them their sixth Champions League triumph.

That was almost definitely PSG's best chance to win the Champions League and they couldn't quite get over the line. Mbappé had an excellent opportunity to open the scoring but couldn't muster enough power on his shot to beat Manuel Neuer. Neymar had essentially dragged the side past Atalanta and produced a masterclass against Leipzig, but the final was a step too far for all involved. The shot of Neymar in tears on the bench, watching the Bayern players lift the trophy, is one many PSG fans won't forget – or perhaps would rather forget in general. The theory was that after getting so close to glory, after all these years, that the following season they would be able to learn and grow from this experience. Naturally, it didn't pan out like that.

Fast forward to the end of the 2020/2021 season and Lille won Ligue 1, with Christophe Galtier's side incredibly securing the title as PSG finished second, one point behind. Chelsea, managed by Thomas Tuchel and led at the back by Thiago Silva, won the Champions League. Tuchel had been sacked by PSG just before Christmas of 2020 and Silva had been smartly snapped up by the London giants after leaving on a free transfer after the Champions League Final defeat.

Mauricio Pochettino was now the man in charge at the Parc des Princes. Pochettino was chosen by the ownership to replace Tuchel, with the German failing to see eye to eye with returning sporting director Leonardo and the two trading blows in the media over ambition, among other issues. It must be stressed, however, that, at the time, the sacking of Tuchel didn't seem to be the end of the world. PSG were third in Ligue 1 and hadn't looked convincing at any point during the season, but Tuchel's achievements at Chelsea have made that decision look even worse than it actually was.

Pochettino couldn't guide PSG to the top of Ligue 1 and, despite advancing past Barcelona and Bayern Munich in the Champions League, they failed to beat Manchester City in the semi-final and the contrast between the two 'projects' was laid out for all to see. Manchester City's was a superstar system complemented by world-class talent whereas PSG was a team of superstars mixed in with mediocre and dependable players. As both Pochettino and Tuchel have found out, that's an incredibly difficult mix to balance perfectly. By March 2022, over a year after he took the job, Pochettino's Paris Saint-Germain still looked lost and were yet again embarrassed in Europe, this time by Real Madrid, after blowing another lead over two legs. The summer of a lifetime couldn't save the club from capitulating when it mattered most.

Prior to the 2021/22 season, PSG had one of the best transfer windows on record, at least on paper. Sergio Ramos, Gini Wijnaldum, Achraf Hakimi, Nuno Mendes, Gianluigi Donnarumma and, arguably the greatest player of all time, Lionel Messi, joined the club in a bid to create a new edition of the Galácticos. In theory, and initially, it made sense – teaming Messi up with Neymar and Mbappé with Premier League and Champions League winner Wijnaldum bolstering up a midfielder that needed reinforcements; Donnarumma and Keylor Navas wasn't a bad choice of goalkeepers to have; Hakimi and Mendes were the wing-backs the club had been demanding for years; and if you're wanting to win the Champions League, there's perhaps no one better to call on than Sergio Ramos. But all turned into a dismal failure.

PSG romped to yet another Ligue 1 crown – their eighth under QSI – but things need to change yet again and, this time, they only have themselves to blame. There hasn't been a rebuild under the Qatari ownership but with fans openly booing and jeering Neymar and Messi then it's clear that something may have to be altered. Modern-day PSG have been obsessed with fashion and being fashionable, so it would perhaps serve them well to understand that superstar signings is *so* last season.

16

Quel avenir pour le PSG ? –
What is the future for PSG?

PARIS SAINT-GERMAIN is a club quite like no other.
It shares similarities with the likes of Manchester City
due to its ownership model and regime, but the two clubs
are run in different ways. To be the only top-flight team
in a major capital city is extremely rare too, considering
how many London, Rome, Madrid and Berlin have. The
collapses in Europe have become routine now and, in the
2021/22 season, it happened again against Real Madrid.
Of course it did. It will always happen. Why? Because it's
Paris Saint-Germain. There's no reasonable explanation
as to why; despite all the stars and all the ability on the
pitch, they still find a way to shoot themselves in the foot.

On 13 March 2022, two years after that behind-closed-
doors Champions League tie against Dortmund, the fans
in the stands officially made it clear that they'd had enough
with the current regime. Both Lionel Messi and Neymar
were booed against Bordeaux every time they touched the
ball, with the Brazilian even being jeered when he scored.
Fans held up banners calling for change in the boardroom,

specifically wanting Leonardo booted out of the club. Prior to the game, the main ultra group, Collectif Ultras Paris, wrote a statement, saying that the squad was 'nothing but a bunch of "stars" who barely complement one another'; that Nasser Al-Khelaifi was unfit for his job and that manager Mauricio Pochettino was 'not the true decision-maker'. There's a very high possibility that the majority of PSG fans agree with this statement, but for the Collectif Ultras Paris to release it was damning. PSG and their ultras have had their loggerhead moments in the past, with ultras being banned from attending home games between 2010 and 2014 after some scenes of rare violence around the Parc des Princes which led to the death of two fans in 2006 and 2010. But this occasion was different. The ultras are passionate at the best of times and protesting embarrassing European defeats wasn't a new phenomenon, but booing Messi was a step above criticising Thiago Motta (with all due respect to the great man).

It made the footballing world take notice of the fans' opinions and, while some condemned the booing, many others understood their frustrations. They wanted a team to be proud of, one that could compete and one that wasn't based on marketability. They wanted a team that represented them, not Qatar. They may have been a decade late to realise this, but some may say that it's better late than never. In the ever-changing world of Paris Saint-Germain, who knows what direction the club will take next.

By the time you read this book they may be champions of Europe, but there's an equally high chance that they've done something attention-grabbing for all the wrong reasons. More and more fans are wearing Paris Saint-

Germain products now, which is exactly what QSI want, but those closest to home probably feel as disconnected as they have done to the team and to the club since their relegation battles in the mid to late 2000s. A lot of work needs to be done to improve the relationship between the club and the core fanbase, but only time will tell if the club actually cares about what the supporters who follow the team every week think. It's a problem for Paris Saint-Germain but it's a problem for modern football in general. While PSG stood to the sidelines and watched as the European Super League idea crumbled within the space of 48 hours in the spring of 2021, they had the chance to come out of the situation as one of the few elite clubs in Europe to shun the idea, but instead they have come out of it in worse shape than arguably anyone involved in that plan. Fans of Super League clubs were angry with their owners and many stated that they were at breaking point, not feeling very important and being pushed to one side in order to gain more money from travelling fans and overseas opportunities. Sound familiar?

So for a club that only turned 50 in the early 2010s, a lot has happened. They have technically been formed twice, fought relegation and battled for silverware, been home to some of football's greats while also hosting some of the more mediocre of talents, have been taken over twice, and have essentially been used as a sports-washing tactic for the best part of a decade, all while not winning the Champions League and burning through manager after manager, battling a curse of Remontadas that follows them around in every big moment.

And yet it still feels like there is more to be written in the future. After the 2022 World Cup, will the Qataris even stick around in Paris and try to see through their plan of winning the Champions League or will they up sticks and leave, ushering in yet another new era of unknown ownership?

Either way, regardless of what happens, it's bound to be interesting and bound to be captivating. For a club that is younger than Alan Shearer, there's a hell of a lot of history to be told.